Emerging from Meditation

Tominaga Nakamoto

translated with an introduction by
Michael Pye

UNIVERSITY OF HAWAII PRESS
HONOLULU

Published in the United States by
University of Hawaii Press
2840 Kolowalu Street
Honolulu, Hawaii 96822

Published in the United Kingdom by
Gerald Duckworth & Co. Ltd.
The Old Piano Factory
43 Gloucester Crescent, London NW1

Printed in Great Britain

Library of Congress Cataloging-in-Publication Data

Tominaga, Nakamoto, 1715-1746
[Okina no fumi. English]
Emerging from meditation / Tominaga Nakamoto : translated with an introduction by Michael Pye.
p. cm.
Translation of: Okina no fumi and Shutsujō kōgo.
Includes bibliographical references.
Contents: Writings of an old man — Emerging from meditation.
ISBN 0–8248–1309–X
1. Religion—Controversial literature—Early works to 1800.
2. Buddhism—Controversial literature—Early works to 1800.
I. Pye, Michael. II. Tominaga, Nakamoto, 1715–1746. Shutsujō kōgo. English. 1990. III. Title.
BL 2773.T6913 1990 89-29273
291—dc20 CIP

Contents

Preface

This work presents a translation of two writings by Tominaga Nakamoto (1715–1746) the longer of which, *Emerging from Meditation*, appears for the first time in a western language. Tominaga mounted a sharp critique of the various forms of religious tradition known to him, especially Buddhism. In so doing he displayed presuppositions and methods remarkably similar to those of the thinkers of the European Enlightenment, who were his unwitting contemporaries. Yet Tominaga was entirely Japanese in his intellectual formation, being the son of a soya sauce manufacturer in Osaka who gave him the benefit of an intensive early education in the classics derived from China. With the publication of his remarkably perceptive works on the development of tradition in Buddhism, Confucianism, Taoism and Shinto, the Japanese critique of religion in a modern sense truly began. When the Buddha emerged from his meditation beneath the tree of enlightenment in India it led to the foundation of the Buddhist religion, which others developed in endless variations. *Emerging from Meditation* implies awakening to the historically conditioned nature of this religion, and indeed of all religious authorities. Though not in the last analysis anti-religious, Tominaga's writings carried the argument forward to an entirely new level. The translation of his works has implications not only for the correct appraisal of the development of Japanese thought, but also for the general understanding of the relations between religion and history and between religion and reason.

In one of his own prefaces, conscious through sickness of the fragility of human life, Tominaga writes that he cannot refrain from reporting his findings. How can one now regard the matter differently? It must indeed be conveyed to the 'peoples west of China', even beyond the Central Asian lands which

Tominaga had in mind when he used these words. As to whether 'it helps the people to be illumined by the Way', it is necessary now as then to await the combined efforts of others. One thing is certain. The modern view of religion, whether east or west, may be both positive and eirenic, but it must be critically awakened. Behind this there is no return.

Marburg 1989 M.P.

Acknowledgements

Assistance in the understanding of Tominaga's works was given at various points by the following, to whom I am very grateful: Hubert Durt, Ishida Mizumaro, Kanno Hiroshi, Kawasaki Shinjō, Namikawa Takayoshi, Shimazono Susumu, Sueki Fumihiko, Tamaru Noriyoshi and Wakimoto Tsuneya.* A first draft was prepared in 1979–80 while I was teaching at the Department of Philosophy and History of Thought at the University of Tsukuba, Japan. During the period September-December 1985 I was able to work intensively on the manuscript while attached to the Department of Religious Studies at the University of Tokyo as a Japan Foundation Fellow. It is largely because of these privileges that the work was able to reach its completion. May the inadequacies which remain be outweighed by recognition of the significance of what Tominaga himself had to say.

* 石田瑞麿、菅野博史、川崎信定、並川孝儀、島薗進、末木文美士、田丸徳善、脇本平也

All Japanese names in this work are given in their Japanese order, family name first.

Introduction

Tominaga's critique of religious tradition

The seminal importance of the varied intellectual activity which took place during the Tokugawa Period for the later modernisation of Japan is nowadays increasingly recognised. One of the most important achievements of this quiet yet immensely potent period was the attainment of the habit, among intellectuals of both samurai and merchant origin, of widely ranging critical thought. As a result, when the full force of western influence was finally felt, indeed sought, in the nineteenth century, the intellectuals of Japan in many fields were able to assimilate and respond with tremendous speed and skill. Certain critical modes of thought were available, admittedly not universally practised any more than they are today, or elsewhere, but nevertheless available from within the Japanese intellectual tradition itself.

The critique of religion is not merely a particular case of the above state of affairs; it plays a key role, both sociologically and intellectually. In brief, this is because the critique of religion means the critique of dogma, of miracle and magic, and of religious institutions, and because it leads to an intellectual and indeed potentially a spiritual liberation from these. Precisely because religious systems represent the point of ultimate concern, or provide an over-arching system of meaning, the critique of religion leads to a new kind of rationality which has implications beyond what later comes to be regarded as the sphere of religion alone. Viewed sociologically, it has been held that the demystification and consequent desacralisation of 'traditionalistic religion', in favour of less ramified salvation religions, can speed up social change and be conducive to the rationalisation of behaviour in other fields as well.[1] If this is

[1] Cf. Bellah 1957, 8, writing in Weberian terms on Tokugawa religion.

true for the displacement, implying criticism, of one type of religion by another, it is *a fortiori* true for a critique of all known religious systems from a historicist moralising point of view. The pace of change is hard to measure, as too is the weight of inertia, and not all seminal thinkers are equally influential in the short term. What may be safely asserted however is that with the Japanese critique of religion, as expressed pre-eminently in the works of Tominaga, a new ingredient became irreversibly available in Japanese socio-intellectual interaction. In the case of the critique of religion a major shift in presuppositions is implied which has an effect, except in so far as it is resisted and in an indirect sense even then, on all later thinking about religious and ideological systems.

The strength of Tominaga's contribution lies in the fact that he was only partially interested in the *content* of religious ideas. His shorter extant work, *Writings of an Old Man*, does indeed promote a simple, Confucian-inspired morality (see especially Section 6, pp. 57-8 below), in which personal self-discipline and family loyalty are key values. It may be that Tominaga regarded these values as more or less timeless. However, their promotion is not the main purpose of the work. *Writings of an Old Man* was written in an indirect form precisely because it launches into a scathing criticism of the de facto forms of religion current at the time. The religions influential in Japan, so the argument runs, are presented in a form characteristic of other places or times. As a result their essential value is obscured. Buddhism is weighed down by obscurantist Indianisms, Confucianism by imitations of everything Chinese, and Shintō by the customs of distant generations in Japan. These posturings hinder perception of the true way or the 'way of ways'. The argument of the 'Old Man' is that the 'way of ways', sorely needed in his times, should be laid bare in all its simplicity. If correctly recognised it will be found to be consistent with the real meaning of the religions mentioned.

Tominaga however has another interest which accompanies the above analysis. How does it come about that religions assume and maintain forms which obscure their own real meaning? After all, 'There is plenty to show that it is difficult to reject this way of truth and come up with some other way (Section 8, p. 60 below). The followers of 'the three teachings', here those mentioned above, may certainly be regarded as followers of the true way, he writes, 'but only if they … live in this world with other people without behaving in a wrong, weird and extravagant manner' (p. 61 below). The puzzle lies in the tendency for religious people to do just that. It has already been seen that geographical and chronological relativism is a basic assumption of Tominaga's view of religious diversity. The later sections of *Writings of an Old Man* bring in other considerations. The most far-reaching statement, though put simply enough, is as follows.

> Since ancient times it has generally been the case that those who preach a moral way and establish a law of life have had somebody whom they have held up as an authoritative precursor, while at the same time they have tried to emerge above those who went before. Later generations, however, being unaware of this regular practice, are quite confused by it (Section 9, p. 61 below).

In effect these key sentences amount to a theory of religious tradition. The next three sections of the work spell this out in brief for Buddhism, Confucianism and Shintō respectively. For further details on Tominaga's view of the development of Buddhist tradition in accordance with this theory we are referred to *Emerging from Meditation* (on which see also further here below). As to Confucianism, Tominaga refers us for more details to a work entitled *Setsuhei*, which is no longer extant, but which was presumably related in conception to *Emerging from Meditation*. In addition to this argument the closing sections of *Writings of an Old Man* emphasise the specific propensities of Buddhism, Confucianism and Shintō respectively. Buddhism tends to make use of supernatural powers or magic, much liked in India, says Tominaga, in order to impress people. Confucianism makes a great show of eloquence, because 'China is a country which likes this, so if one is proclaiming a way and guiding people they will not believe and follow unless it is cleverly used' (Section 15, p. 69 below). Shintō makes a virtue of mysteriousness and concealment, on which Tominaga is particularly scathing. He concludes '… we should realise that ways which are kept hidden, difficult to transmit, and passed on for a fixed price, are none of them the true way' (Section 16, p. 70 below). All in all *Writings of an Old Man* is a compact, accessible writing and may be read as Tominaga's own general introduction to his ideas on religion.

Emerging from Meditation is a much more substantial, and in some ways more difficult writing. Readers not versed in the history of Buddhism may find some of the detailed arguments rather confusing, but the leading idea running through the whole work is not difficult to grasp. This is that the astonishing diversity of Buddhist writings does not lend itself to harmonisation on the basis of some selected dogmatic vantage point, but on the contrary is an indication that the many schools and sects which appeared after the Buddha's own day simply produced new writings (sūtras, commentaries and treatises) in order to compete with each other. The explanation for this never-ending extension of the tradition is the wish on the part of one party to supersede another.

> Thus the appearance of divisions among the various teachings came about because they all first arose by superseding others. If it had not been for this relationship of superseding, how would the path of Dharma have been extended? This is natural for a path of Dharma, whether old or new (p. 81 below).

In principle this is the same, simple idea which has already been met with above. However, such a theory of religious tradition finds itself on collision course with the various established Chinese or Japanese accounts of the relations between the innumerable sūtras received from India. Variety within the teachings had been ascribed to developments within the preaching of the Buddha himself, who was thought to have taken account of the abilities of his hearers and unfolded his message accordingly. The concluding phase of teaching was, naturally, that which coincided with the position of the school in question, e.g. the Lotus Sūtra and Nirvāṇa Sūtra in the case of the Tendai School, the Kegon Sūtra (placed at the beginning of the Buddha's preaching activity, but not understood) in the Kegon School, or the Mahāvairocana Sūtra in the Shingon School. None of these views had questioned the Buddha's authorship of the Mahāyāna sūtras. As Tominaga continued, in sharp tones,

> ... the scholars of later generations vainly say that all the teachings came directly from the golden mouth <of the Buddha> and were intimately transmitted by those who heard him frequently (p. 81 below).

Thus it appears that Tominaga was the first writer systematically to question the assumption that the Mahāyāna sūtras, or indeed others, were transmitted directly from the Buddha himself. He did this by the critical, historical method of juxtaposing innumerable variations in the various texts and illustrating how these arose in order for some point to be made over against another school. His basic perception is clearly stated near the beginning of Chapter 2 (Differences in what the sūtras say):

> We can tell that for long after the Buddha's decease there was no fixed exposition among his followers and there were no writings upon which one could depend. Everybody renewed the teachings according to their opinions and passed it on orally (p. 83 below).

The net result is, of course, that the Mahāyāna sutras cannot simply be ascribed verbatim to the Buddha himself with the traditional words 'Thus I have heard', words which Tominaga takes provocatively as the heading of Chapter 3. On the contrary, 'Many of the sūtras were compiled by people five hundred years after the Buddha, so they contain many words from these five hundred years' (p. 86 below).

The subsequent chapters of *Emerging from Meditation* contain innumerable variations on this theme, many of them fascinating for the specialist in Buddhist studies who is familiar with particular themes such as cosmology, supernatural abilities, the question of meat-eating, and so on. In principle Tominaga's method and theory remain consistent, whether he is talking about historically early problems such as the classification of the Tripiṭaka (as in Chapter 5) or later ones such as succession in the Zen schools (as in Chapter 20). All attempts to demonstrate consistency in the teaching while maintaining the superiority of one's own position mask, he argues, the real diversity of schools and the artificiality in the unfolding of new forms of teaching. Thus his historical critique, which certainly had its historical implications vindicated by later research, is accompanied by what might be called a theory of the dynamics of religious tradition.

It remains to draw attention to three subordinate themes in *Emerging from Meditation* which were not fully elaborated. First, when Tominaga deals with the varieties of cosmology in Buddhist writings (in Chapter 4), he concludes with what might be regarded as a projectionist theory of cosmological myth-making, at least in embryo form. The full force can only be appreciated after reading his patient account of, for example, what is said in different Buddhist writings about the depth of the earth, whether it is 68,000 yojanas deep, or 800,000 yojanas, or 600,000, 6,800,000 and so on. After rehearsing this and several related topics with learned detail, Tominaga concludes

> Teachings about the cosmos are in actuality quite vague and do no more than tell us about the inner working of the mind. There is no way of knowing whether they are right or wrong. Hence I say that the cosmos arises on the pattern of people's minds (p. 93 below).

Secondly, attention may be drawn to the ideas expounded in Chapter 11 on the nature of language. Tominaga regarded all language as being conditioned by the chronological period, by the special intention of the person using it, and by the type of expression being used. The details of this analysis, especially as to 'type', five different kinds being differentiated, are perhaps less important than the fundamental recognition of the relativity of language, which Tominaga certainly regarded as underpinning his view of the relativity of religious forms, including the conflicting forms within Buddhist tradition. 'At any rate,' he wrote, 'looking at it in this light, I have not yet found any Way of Dharma in the whole world, or any language, which cannot be approached and interpreted in this way' (p. 123 below).

Thirdly, Tominaga devoted one chapter of *Emerging from Meditation* to the idea, popular in China and elsewhere, of the harmony between 'the three teachings', here meaning Buddhism, Confucianism and Taoism. Broadly speaking, this chapter may be regarded as a counterpart or forerunner (see discussion of dating questions on p. 11 below) to *Writings of an Old Man*, which applies 'three teachings' theory to the Japanese situation, replacing Taoism with Shintō. What is important in Tominaga's argument here (Chapter 24) is that he rejects what he regards as spurious harmonisations of the three religions in favour of a historical awareness of their diversity.

Thus while Tominaga was not uninterested in the content of religion, his concern both with historical perceptions and with systematic theory about religion is more important. In arriving at his view of these matters he displayed himself to be methodologically detached from any one religious view, although this did not imply, in turn, that he scorned potential religious truth. His method of argument is quite uncompromising in that he insisted on seeing every religious form in its chronological and cultural context, and then understanding it in terms of its function within the developing tradition, before asking its value in contributing to 'the good'.

Tominaga's life

Although there is little circumstantial information available about Tominaga's life there are a small number of undisputed and highly significant aspects which may be here further recorded. First, he was the offspring of a successful business family in Ōsaka which contributed to the increasingly independent merchant culture of the time. Secondly, he was trained in a Confucianist school which was open to the influence of competing lines of intellectual tradition. Thirdly, he became extremely familiar with a wide range of Buddhist scriptures without taking on the piety of any particular Buddhist denomination. It was the combination of an independent social position and a detailed knowledge of two complex traditions which enabled Tominaga to write works with such an incisive critical quality. These three aspects will be considered in more detail in the following paragraphs.

In any discussion of Japanese thinkers of the early modern period one runs into the problem of names. Tominaga, as he will be called here, in fact had several names, the details of which are of secondary importance.[2] Over the family name, Tominaga, there need be no dispute. As to his given name, some variation may be observed as to how it is pronounced, for the same characters can be read either as Nakamoto, in

[2] Ishihama Juntarō for example consistantly refers to him as Kensai Sensei (Sensei meaning teacher, as a title of respect), in recognition of a personality from his own locality, as he explained, who was at the same time a national genius (Ishihama 1940, 225-6). He was also known as Chūshi or Shichū, and it is presumably through the combination of this (the character for *chū* can also be read *naka*) with his earlier personal name of Tokumoto that the name Nakamoto arose.

Japanese style, or as Chūki, in so-called Chinese style (though of course this is not really Chinese pronunciation). In Japanese publications the pronunciation is hardly ever indicated, but when it is then Nakamoto seems to be the more usual. This reading was followed by both Tsunoda *et al.* (1958) and Katō (1967) in English publications, and it is also adopted here. It seems better to maintain a common usage in order to avoid confusion.[3] In any case, for the purposes of discussion in western languages there is no strong reason for not using the family name Tominaga.

Tominaga lived between 1715 and 1746 in Ōsaka, being the third son of a soya-sauce manufacturer named Tominaga Yoshimine. His father also bore the name of Dōmyōjiya Kichizaemon, Dōmyōjiya presumably being the name of the business. The fact that Tominaga sprang from a successful business family in the merchant city of Ōsaka is of considerable importance in that it helps to explain the independent intellectual stance which he adopted. He was neither schooled by nor beholden to any governmental Confucianist agency or any Buddhist sect with a limiting dogmatic structure. Thus he was one day able to write: 'I am not a follower of Confucianism, nor of Taoism, nor of Buddhism. I watch their words and deeds from the side and then privately debate them' (*Emerging from Meditation*, Chapter 24). This was possible for someone supported, sheltered and formed in the increasingly independent urban or merchant culture[4] of the early middle Edo Period (or Tokugawa Period). Thus it was not inappropriate for the modern protagonist of Tominaga's work, Ishihama Juntarō, to express considerable local pride on behalf of Ōsaka, beginning

[3] There is a slight tendency to regard the Chinese-style pronounciation as more formal or more fitting for the author of a literary work; however there is little doubt that the weight of usage in Japan favours Nakamoto, and to some at least this seems to be more euphonious. A further problem for western usage is that thinkers of the Tokugawa period are often referred to by their second names (in the Japanese order), that is, their given names rather than their family names. Thus Itō Jinsai is Jinsai while Itō Tōgai is Tōgai (this being a helpful distinction), Motoori Norinaga is Norinaga, etc., rather as if Rousseau were constantly called Jean-Jacques. While recognising that this is a respect-worthy tradition in itself it seems preferable not to import it into the literature in western languages.

[4] Two Japanese terms are relevant here: *chōnin bunka* (townspeople's culture) and *shōnin bunka* (merchants' culture).

his best-known account with the words: 'Tominaga Nakamoto Kensai Sensei is a man of Ōsaka' (Ishihama 1940, 1). However apart from the intrinsic interest of this burgeoning merchant culture there is also considerable significance in it from the point of view of comparative reflection on the social conditions which facilitate particular kinds of intellectual development. Tominaga's social circumstances were such that he held no privileged position and yet at the same time was beholden to nobody. This was a necessary condition of his intellectual contribution.

Tominaga's father was sufficiently successful in business to be able to join with a few others[5] in founding a private school of Confucian studies known as the Kaitokudō, and it was this school which Tominaga himself attended from the age of nine onwards. This was without doubt a formative period of the utmost importance during which he became aware of the competing claims of the Chu Hsi (Japanese: Shushi) school of Neo-Confucianism, those of the Wang Yang-ming (Japanese: Ōyōmei) school, and those of the critics who wished to get back to the early form of Confucius' teaching which was presumed to be original and normative.[6] The recognition of these alternative possibilities of interpretation within the one tradition of learning was surely a major factor in the development of his ideas. Aged only fourteen or fifteen he wrote a critical account of the various schools of the Confucian tradition in their historical sequence, as a result of which he was required to leave the Kaitokudō.[7] This work, entitled *Setsuhei* (*Teachings Determine*) is now lost, but the argument is indicated in outline in *Writings of an Old Man,* especially in Section 11 where Tominaga specifically invites the reader to refer to it for further details. It is not really clear how he spent his time after leaving the school but it appears likely that he did some clerical work and spent his leisure time in various literary pursuits. Contrary to occasional statements there is no poetry extant, but there is evidence, in the form of a manuscript compiled in the Chinese style by various hands

[5] Ishihama 1940, 1.

[6] For an introductory account of these trends with appropriate illustrative extracts see Tsunoda *et al.* 1958.

[7] Ishihama regards this as the main known event in Tominaga's life, followed by his father's death (Ishihama 1940, 32).

and preserved in the public library in Ōsaka, that he had literary friends.[8] He also became interested in Chinese music, upon which subject an extremely obscure work by him has survived.[9] These two works may be regarded as incidental products of the classical training which he received.

There is a tradition that at a later stage in his life Tominaga did proof-reading for the edition of collected Buddhist scriptures of the Ōbaku Zen sect with its headquarters at Manpuku Temple (Manpukuji, near Kyōto). However Mizuta casts doubt on this. According to him Tominaga's acquaintance with Buddhism is adequately explained by the fact that both the Dōmyōjiya Soya Company and the Yasumura family from which his mother came gave massive support to a different temple of the same sect.[10] However this may be, it is quite clear from the internal evidence of *Emerging from Meditation* that Tominaga, at some time between 1730 and 1738, did a great deal of reading in the sutras and treatises of Mahāyāna Buddhism. He was familiar with all the main doctrinal developments in the history of Buddhism and was certainly not biased towards Zen Buddhism as a sectarian organisation. His comments on the Zen tradition make this quite clear, especially when he says for example, twice, 'I regard Daruma (i.e. Bodhidharma) as the man most to be pitied on the whole earth, past and present' (*Emerging from Meditation*, Chapter 25). It might be thought that as he does not deal extensively with the Pure Land Buddhist tradition he had some connections or leanings in that direction and was disposed to be gentle. However although, strangely enough, he does not go into the question of the origins of the Pure Land sūtras dealing with Amitābha (which are a good example of doctrinally important works not stemming directly from the Buddha) his brief comments on the Pure Land (Amitābha's Buddha-Land to which believers are transported after death) are too negative to allow us to presume a strong family interest in favour of that tradition (cf. *Emerging from Meditation*, Chapter 25). Thus the

[8] Entitled *Bunsan*, this work consists of thirty double pages, some of which are heavily annotated in red. Only a small portion of it is by Tominaga himself.

[9] Entitled *Gakuritsukō*, this work was rediscovered in modern times and published photographically by the Kansai University Institute of East-West Studies, in 1950. The original is in the library of Kansai University, Suita, Japan. It appears to stress the historical development of Chinese music.

[10] Mizuta and Arisaka 1973, 647.

precise circumstances of his profound and detailed acquaintance with Buddhist scriptures remain obscure. The proof-reading theory is attractive in that it accounts for knowledge of the whole range of Buddhist scriptures in Chinese without regard to the dogmatic limitations of any one school. Unfortunately the theory seems to be speculative. His knowledge of Shintō, as displayed in *Writings of an Old Man*, and of Taoism, as displayed in *Emerging from Meditation*, was clearly slighter and does not raise biographical questions.

The date of composition of Tominaga's main extant writings is not entirely clear. His own preface to *Writings of an Old Man* is dated Genbun 3, i.e. 1738, and as this preface is presented as an integral part of the text it suggests that this was also the date of composition. In Section 10 of this work there is a reference to *Emerging from Meditation*, which implies the latter's prior existence. The author's preface to *Emerging from Meditation* however is dated Enkyō 1, i.e. 1744. It seems likely therefore that after his experience with his writing on the Confucian tradition Tominaga was not in a hurry, or was unable, to make *Emerging from Meditation* public. *Writings of an Old Man* may have been written quite quickly, but the same can hardly be said for *Emerging from Meditation*. Nothing is known directly about his method of writing. However the final chapter of *Emerging from Meditation* is appropriately entitled 'Miscellaneous' and gives the impression of a series of notes on a variety of topics which were not worked into the preceding chapters on more specific themes. Thus it seems at least possible that parts of the work were assembled slowly. On the other hand his knowledge of Buddhism can only have begun to be acquired from 1730 at the earliest, when he was fifteen. Even then he was not living in a monastery or temple like the famous scholar-monks who thus became learned in Buddhism at an early age. Hence it would seem natural to conclude that he was writing *Emerging from Meditation* between about 1735 and 1737, in other words when he was in his early twenties. The work was not finally published until November 1745. *Writings of an Old Man* appeared in February 1746, six months before the author's death.

The passage of time was of great interest to Tominaga himself, partly because he was struck by the phenomenon of historical development in religion and partly because he was apparently aware of the rapid passing of his own life, hastened by illness. Thus in the Preface to *Emerging from Meditation* he wrote:

> Alas my body is worthless and sick, and I cannot be of any help to anybody. As I am now nearing my end, should this great matter not be passed on? I am now already more than thirty years old, and I cannot refrain from reporting it.

These sentiments have something in common with those of Ogyū Sorai, who wrote:

> I have been ill for a long time without any improvement. Since chance may have it that I will suddenly disappear like the dew in the morning, I took the brush in my better moments and wrote these volumes.[11]

Both writers show a sense not only of individual frailty but also of historic function in the context of intellectual tradition. At the same time subtle differences appear between the two. Ogyū Sorai was successful in his own time, and indeed he was somewhat conceited.[12] It seemed evident to him that a correct and masterly restatement of the original principles of Confucianism (i.e. *kogaku*) must inevitably win acceptance and fame. He ascribed his success to the operation of the will of 'heaven'. Tominaga made no such claim. He was aware that his theory would be upsetting for many readers, though he did not himself regard it as ultimately destructive. His only confidence lay in the basic correctness of his view of the nature of religious development and in the hope that this would later on be vindicated. Thus he concluded the preface to *Emerging from Meditation* as follows:

> I hope that those who take it up will tell it to many, passing it on to Korea and China, to the peoples west of China, and on to the land of the Buddha's divine birth. If it helps the people to be

[11] In a letter to Yamagata Shunan, quoted and translated in Lidin 1973, 103.

[12] The letter continues: 'I slaved and worked without stopping. ... Ah, a thousand years and more after Confucius' death, the Way has come down to our day and is for the first time made clear! How could it have been due to my strength alone? It was Heaven that ordered it. ... When these books are published in the world, my fame will remain alive for untold numbers of years' (Lidin 1973, 103).

illumined by the Way, then my death will not be a mere putrefaction. It may be said on the other hand that this is a bad kind of wisdom, which I would find hard to accept. As to this I will await the combined efforts and supplementary work of later scholars.

It is traditionally held that Tominaga spent much of his time in a lying position because of lung disease and that he read books for much of the night. He died, aged only thirty-one, in August 1746.

The immediate intellectual perspective

The school which Tominaga attended, the Kaitokudō, was a *shijuku* or 'private academy',[13] that is, neither an official school of one of the feudal domains nor a privately run elementary school (*terakoya*). The *terakoya* schools developed rapidly during the eighteenth century, which implies a growing number of teachers willing to work for pay and an increasing pool of parents who assumed the desirability of instruction for their children. The *han* (or 'fief') schools were already flourishing to provide the bureaucratised retainers required for regional administration and for handling the system of 'alternate attendance' of *daimyō* family members at the Shogun's court at Edo (the *sankin kōtai* system).[14]

The private academies arose in part because of the official sponsorship of Neo-Confucianism from 1608 onwards with the appointment of Hayashi Razan (1583-1657) as Confucian tutor to the Shōgun. The school which he ran in Edo was the main source of central administrators, but it was only later that it took on the status of being an official institution. In the meantime other schools giving intermediate and advanced Confucianist education were founded by well-known scholars such as Yamazaki Ansai (1618-1682) who opened a *shijuku* in 1655 in Kyōto.[15] An earlier case, treated in detail by Rubinger, was the school of Nakae Tōju (1608-1648), which though open

[13] The subject of Richard Rubinger's valuable work *Private Academies of Tokugawa Japan* (1982). Unfortunately the Kaitokudō only appears in a footnote.

[14] For a substantial account of education in the Tokugawa period see Dore 1965, and on the *sankin kōtai* system see Tsukahira 1970.

[15] Rubinger 1982, 43.

only for the short period 1636-1648 was an extremely flexible institution.[16] Apart from admitting students of rural provenance Nakae Tōju also introduced the heterodox or, rather, non-dominant Confucianism of Wang Yang-ming (Japanese: Ōyōmei). Another notable example was the school of the thinker Miura Baien (1723-1789) whose interests ran far beyond the range of Confucianism even in its less official forms, ultimately moving, via astronomy, medicine and the natural sciences, into the area later identified as 'Dutch learning' (*rangaku*).[17]

The trend to diversification in the interpretation of the Confucian tradition provided a base for the exploration of fields other than ethics and statecraft. Thus Kaibara Ekken (1630-1714) moved from the dualistic interpretation of the universe in terms of *ri* and *ki* (principle and material energy, i.e. Chu Hsi's *li* and *ch'i*) to a more or less monistic view focused on *ki* as a kind of life-force running through all things. While he wrote popular books to encourage the acceptance of Confucian virtues he also wrote botanical works such as *Catalogue of Vegetables, Catalogue of Flora* and *Medicinal Herbs of Japan*. For Tsunoda this is an example of putting into practice the dictum of *The Great Learning*: 'Investigate things and make your knowledge perfect.'[18] This was but the beginning. The empirical, systematic and pragmatic tenor of independent writing is clearly exemplified in the field of agricultural science, and here 'science' is the only appropriate word. A particularly influential work was *Nōgyō Zensho* (*Complete Works on Agriculture*) by Miyazaki Antei (died 1698), which has been analysed in some detail by Smith (1959). Miyazaki was an experienced farmer who spent some forty years questioning other farmers on their methods, their seeds and their tools. To quote Smith:

> The topics he covered represented the entire range of Japanese agriculture; there was one chapter on each of 19 varieties of grain, 57 vegetables, 11 grasses, 36 trees, 22 herbs – in addition to separate essays on such subjects as planting, tillage, soils, fertilizers, irrigation, and the management of forest land.[19]

[16] Ibid. 44ff.
[17] Ibid. 56ff.
[18] Tsunoda 1958, 375.
[19] Smith 1959, 89.

Confucian studies of an independent kind were promoted through the very well-known school of Itō Jinsai (1625-1705) which opened in Kyōto in 1662 under the names of Dōshikai and Kogidō.[20] Itō Jinsai was a merchant's son, born in Kyōto, who received instruction in the Confucian classics from an uncle described as a doctor. The family was both wealthy and sophisticated and may be regarded as a prime example of how a new self-confidence among Japanese of non-aristocratic and non-samurai descent could lead, if not to social mobility, at least to a high level of intellectual mobility. Jinsai's son, Itō Tōgai, continued his father's approach in seeking to go behind the Neo-Confucian framework bequeathed by Chu Hsi and maintained by the semi-official Hayashi school. Both father and son are representative examples of the *kogaku* mode of Confucian learning which sought to apply the works of Confucius and Mencius to contemporary questions without reference to intervening systems. Itō Tōgai also gave lectures at the Kaitokudō, so that this understanding of the historical depth of the Confucian tradition must have been present in the milieu in which Tominaga's ideas were formed.[21] Itō Jinsai is mentioned explicitly in *Writings of an Old Man*, Section 11.

The same basic presupposition was propagated, though with differing emphasis, by the Edo scholar Ogyū Sorai, who directed a school known as Kenen Juku.[22] While Ogyū Sorai was of samurai descent he himself considered that a period during his youth when his father was exiled for a misdemeanour led to his seeing the world (of Edo) with different, i.e independent eyes. His writings demonstrate that he was able to stand back and regard the theoretically stratified world of feudal lords (*daimyō*) and samurai, of merchants and farmers, of shōgun and servants, as something which *as a whole* required to be reflected upon and managed. Thus although he belonged to it he was not, intellectually, an imprisoned part of it. However we assess his own recollections of his youth, the major stimulus for his reflections was certainly the burgeoning influence of the merchant class and the increasing commercialisation of almost all aspects of life. Hence he sought economic answers to political problems.

[20] Rubinger 1982, 49ff.
[21] Mizuta and Arisaka 1973, 647.
[22] Lidin 1973, 112ff, and Rubinger 1982, 52ff.

The famous schools in Kyōto and Edo were well-known in Ōsaka, and it seems certain that when Tominaga Nakamoto was at an impressionable age the main intellectual thrust of the day, in the Confucian tradition, was that of the *kogaku* scholars. The name is rather unfortunate, as is the usual English translation 'Ancient Learning', for these expressions may seem to convey a strongly conservative standpoint, harking back to the past in the interests of intellectual security. This would be a misunderstanding, however, for the main tendency of the *kogaku* school was an independent-minded attempt to seek new applications for contemporary problems, especially socio-political questions, from what were presumed to be the best original sources for political thought.

This may be illustrated by some words of Ogyū Sorai about his own writings:

> Generally, when it comes to the categories of morality, benevolence, knowledge, rites, righteousness, respect, nature, Heaven's decree, mind, feelings, illustrious virtues, the Mean, and the four forces of life and nature, later generations have lost the meanings of all these characters. Therefore I have written the *Benmei* in one volume. One cannot exhaust the way with one word; the teaching of the Four Classics of later generations is not clear. Therefore, when later Confucianists created their Way, it was not the Way of the Early Kings or Confucius. Therefore I have written the *Bendō* in one volume.[23]

This shows clearly that the thrust of this kind of study was to get back behind the interpretations of the Neo-Confucianists, and in so doing, though this was not in itself the objective, to bring about a relativisation of the 'Way' of these later, intermediate exponents. At the same time the 'Way of the Early Kings or Confucius' remains as a norm against which later generations and interpretations are to be assessed.

In this latter respect Tominaga took a crucial step forward. It is one thing to be able to note that the idea of appraising successive phases of tradition from a present standpoint was widely current. This is implicit in all reformist movements which raise the cry *'ad fontes!'* in order to get the best, pure teaching from the original sources of the tradition. There is a crucial shift however when these presumed fountainheads are

[23] Lidin 1973, 103.

themselves relativised and declared to be *not* the Way of later generations. This shift is clearly demonstrated in the opening sections of *Writings of an Old Man*, where the imitation of past epochs regarded as normative for the present is mercilessly ridiculed. Needless to say, those writers who imaginatively adopted the approach of 'Ancient Learning' would not have considered themselves directly affected by Tominaga's more boisterous criticisms. However what is important is the shift in presupposition.

If Tominaga's thought is something other than the reformism which can be documented in many quarters, so too does it fail to be encapsulated by the principle of polemical apologetics. It is relatively easy to apply critical principles to traditions other than that espoused by oneself. This again may be illustrated by Ogyū Sorai who argued that there was not really any specifically Japanese 'Way' and that what was called Shintō was no more than a construct deriving from the imagination of Urabe no Kanetomo (1435-1511),[24] otherwise known as Yoshida Kanetomo. However he did not go on from there to ask questions about how religious traditions are developed and to apply his answers to all phases of all traditions known to him. It would be fair to say that this was not his field. This is just the step which Tominaga did take, so that although his criticisms of historically known forms of religion were sharp they were not advanced from one established religious or ideological standpoint against another.

The Kaitokudō was a place where the main Confucianist-oriented currents of the time were apparent, and it was no doubt here that Tominaga became familiar with them and advanced his first critique in the form of the lost work *Teachings Determine*. The school was still new when Tominaga

[24] McEwan 1969, 133. The position advanced by Yoshida Kanetomo polemically gave priority to Shintō as opposed to Confucianism and Buddhism, and was known as Yoshida Shintō or Yuiitsu Shintō (commonly translated as 'Primal Shintō'). His position is summarised in the following fictitious ascription to Shōtoku Taishi: 'During the reign of the Empress Suiko, the thirty-fourth sovereign, Prince Shotoku stated in a memorial that Japan was the roots and trunk <of civilization>, China its branches and leaves, and India its flowers and fruit. Similarly, Buddhism is the flowers and the fruit of all laws, Confucianism their branches and leaves, and Shintō their roots and trunk. Thus all foreign doctrines are offshoots of Shintō' (Tsunoda 1958, 271).

attended it, having been founded in 1724 under the patronage of Tominaga's father and four other merchants.[25] While Tominaga departed to pursue a more individual intellectual route, the school itself had an illustrious influence in Ōsaka throughout the eighteenth century. The site is known and marked today by a plaque in the wall of a huge insurance company building, while the name continues as the name of a journal.

The social context

The merchant society in which Tominaga Nakamoto grew up and lived is the key feature in any attempt to locate his thought sociologically. The widespread use of the word 'feudal' to describe Japanese society throughout the Tokugawa Period has caused serious misunderstanding. It obscures the rapid development of large-scale mercantilism and the, for then, massive growth of urban population. By 1731 the capital, Edo, numbered more than half a million inhabitants, and Kyōto and Ōsaka were not much smaller. Hauser reckons nearly one million for Ōsaka, Kyōto and Sakai together.[26] Many other towns, especially castle towns, were turning into significant trading centres with concomitant population growth. It is estimated that between a fifth and a quarter of Japan's population was urban by the middle of the eighteenth century and, as Smith pointed out,

> Enormous quantities of grain, fish, timber and fibres were required to feed, clothe and shelter the growing population of the towns. Most of it came by way of local markets and merchants from Japanese farming and fishing villages, since foreign trade contributed almost nothing.[27]

These goods not only had to be produced but also processed, stored, packaged and traded. Nor was agriculture itself the slow-moving backwater that might be imagined. For one thing there was a steady stream of technical improvements such as seed selection, the intensive use of fertilisers and ever more

25 For this and further details see Mizuta (Mizuta and Arisaka 1973, 645-6).
26 Hauser 1974, 29.
27 Smith 1959, 68.

elaborate terracing and irrigation arrangements. This went hand in hand, in the absence of major mechanical change, with the development of smaller farming units and changes in tenancy and ownership relations. The reliable application of skilled agricultural labour came to be of fundamental importance, and gain for the nuclear family became the main motivation for economic activity on the land.[28] This was but the natural counterpart of the extensive commercial activity which linked town and country through complex chains of entrepreneurs. Regular markets for selling a wide range of tools and products were held all over the country. Specific industries such as cotton spinning, vegetable oil production and of course silk manufacture grew up in what were otherwise agricultural areas to supply the great towns with their basic goods and semi-processed raw materials.[29]

The commercialisation of agriculture was well advanced by the first half of the eighteenth century, as is clear from the dramatic spread in the use of money in the countryside at that time.[30] At the same time the burdens on the peasant class were gradually lightened as the country as a whole enjoyed the prosperity of peace-time conditions and the samurai were slowly but surely turned into bureaucrats.[31] Moreover both peasants and merchants were increasingly influenced by Confucian-derived teachings emphasising diligence, thrift and the like, as has been studied at length by Robert Bellah in *Tokugawa Religion* (1958). Thus the theoretical stratification of samurai, peasants and merchants was increasingly overtaken by a growing consensus as to a small cluster of social values conducive not only to social stability but also to the reliable execution of trade. Almost everybody was agreed on the importance of acquiring and/or spending money.

The importance of these characteristics for the present study lies in the fact that the socio-economic base known as 'urban culture' (*chōnin bunka*) was neither a small nor isolated phenomenon but the sustained and concentrated expression of far-reaching social trends in a complex economy. Indeed it is the real foundation of the culture of the modern Japanese

[28] Ibid. 104-7.
[29] Ibid. 78f.
[30] Ibid. 73.
[31] Cf. Wataru 1977, especially p. 86.

masses. It would be misleading to regard the well-established and sophisticated merchant families of the really big towns as exceptional or untypical. They were the well-buttressed and self-confident representatives of a well extended demographic and economic base. It is not intrinsically surprising that the gifted son of a successful soya-sauce manufacturer in eighteenth-century Ōsaka should come up with independent ideas about things which interested him.

Though not so large as Edo in population terms Ōsaka was in some ways more important in economic terms. Its geographical position made it the main port linking southern Honshū (including the Japan Sea side), Shikoku, the Kinai area itself (which included Kyōto) and Nagoya and Edo to the east. This role was deliberately developed in the 1660s and the 1670s.[32] Secondly Ōsaka became a major rice market in which rice was not only warehoused for numerous *daimyō* but also traded on their behalf. Since all *daimyō* were assessed in terms of measures of rice (the standard measure being the *koku*, which was about five bushels) these dealings were the economic basis of the *sankin kōtai* system linking the *daimyō* to the shogunate.[33] Thirdly Ōsaka was a warehousing and processing centre for a wide range of goods among which vegetable oils and cotton played a significant role. More important than any one product however was the sheer variety of commercial dealings, the overall scale in a town devoted to little else, and the complexity of financial and social organisation which grew up as a result.

Although central government did try to regulate commercial activity in various ways, it seems clear that by the time of the culturally lively Genroku Period (1688-1703) the merchant class and the economic institutions with which it worked had entered on a dynamic course of development which made it independent of (though not in competition with) political institutions. Wealth had created a sense of self-sufficiency and self-esteem. Needless to say this did not, for the great majority,

[32] Hauser 1974, 14.

[33] According to Tsukahira most of the *daimyō* were in debt to the merchants by the end of the seventeenth century and impoverished by the second quarter of the eighteenth century (Tsukahira 1970, 79 and 84). Further details may be found in C.D. Sheldon's *The Rise of the Merchant Class in Tokugawa Japan 1600-1868*, especially ch.4.

hold any intellectual implications, and values seem to have oscillated between a sternly frugal and disciplined commitment to making money and indulgent and flamboyant consumption. In fact it appears that Ōsaka in the early eighteenth century had become a net importer of goods for consumption within the town. Viewed simply this may be taken as evidence for the importance of 'invisibles', a sign of highly developed mercantilism. More important here however is the consequence that the urban population (the *chōnin*) had achieved a position of being able to choose alternative kinds of behaviour. As Hauser puts it:

> *Chōnin* included wealthy merchant property owners, smaller merchants who lived in rented shops or rooms, and itinerant peddlers who purchased goods daily and hawked them on the streets of the city. In addition there were service personnel, entertainers, artisans, employees, and day labourers. Life styles varied dramatically as did the scale of their business ventures.[34]

Telling descriptions of the state of affairs in Edo are found in Ogyū Sorai's *Seidan*, probably dating from 1727, from which a few passages may be quoted in the translation by J.R. McEwan.

> For the period of each alternate year during which the daimyō live in Edo they live as in an inn. Their wives, who remain in Edo all the time, live permanently as in an inn. ...What is more, the number of retainers living in Edo has increased in recent years. ...If the inhabitants of Edo realised that they were 'living in an inn' their expenses might be less, but since they have not the slightest awareness of the fact and regard their 'inn life' as the normal state of affairs the expenditure incurred by the military class is extremely great and the income from their lands is being completely absorbed by the merchants. ...At present it is the practice among the members of the military class ... to retain from their annual rice incomes only the amount required for consumption as food. The remainder is sold and the money received used for the purchase of goods from other localities and in meeting day-to-day expenses. Since they cannot live for one day without buying things, they cannot do without the services of the merchants. ...As a result of it, profits made by the merchants in the last hundred years are

[34] Hauser 1974, 22-3.

> unprecedented in Chinese and Japanese history. ...The reason for the financial embarrassment of the daimyō is that they must spend every second year in Edo and, since they feel that they must maintain the style proper to their station while they are in the city, they sell all their rice income and waste the money they receive for it during their stay there. ...Because of their fear of the Bakufu (i.e. the government) they borrowed money from the merchants of Kyōto and Ōsaka, regardless of the poverty which might overtake them. They were unable to repay the money and in many cases the merchants refused to lend them any more. ...If he has but sufficient money, the basest of the common people can imitate a daimyō with impunity. How sad it is to see that in these times a man is considered of no account if he does not have much money and how, because of this, even men of high degree and great qualities must debase themselves and suffer contemptuous treatment.[35]

Ogyū Sorai complains further about the consummate skill of the merchants in maximising their profit, the buying and selling of futures, the degeneration through commercialisation of the building trade and of paper manufacture, the replacement of hereditary servants by hired servants, the mixing of manners as between the classes and even the mixing of classes through concubinage and marriage. The general tone of the merchant culture in Edo and Ōsaka alike has been succinctly characterised by Charles Dunn:

> On the one hand, the governments, central and local, were continually issuing edicts to restrict the freedom of the populace, yet, on the other hand, the inhabitants often seemed to do more or less as they liked. Countrymen were not allowed to leave their land, yet they constantly migrated to the towns; in the great towns attempts were made to control dress and almost every other aspect of daily life, but the mere fact that such directives were issued again and again illustrates their ineffectiveness. One thing that seems clear is that money talked. ...Ōsaka was also a large town where life was freer than elsewhere, because the *samurai* were few. And, after all, it was beneath the dignity of the *samurai* to concern himself overmuch with the antics of townsmen as long as they offered no threat to their superiors. So the motivation of the townsmen lay in their own moral values, and in their human search for pleasures. It was a struggle between a puritanical and obsessive desire to

[35] McEwan 1969, 36ff. On the context and date of this work see McEwan 1969, 4 and 145.

> earn money and increase the fortune of the family by thrift, which brought into being a complex mercantile society, and an almost equally strong demand for enjoyment, which brought into being a vast entertainment industry. It is the combination of restraint and abandon which makes the Japanese of the Tokugawa period so fascinating.[36]

By the beginning of the eighteenth century the constantly accumulating prosperity of the merchants had swept all before it to create an entirely new base for an urban culture at once popular and in varying degree sophisticated. This may be summed up in the one word Genroku: the Genroku Period being identified with a flamboyant culture of costume and theatre, widely read literature and ephemeral art, and pleasure and entertainment of all kinds. No doubt there were differences of style and mood between the major towns, but in principle there had come into being a non-authoritarian and largely non-didactic culture. This context provided the opportunity for independent intellectual pursuits, whether these were directed towards economic advantage or simply carried on because the subject was there to explore. Admittedly the Confucian-derived values of obedience and filial piety, along with Buddhist sentiments, provided an ideological framework of a most general kind and, as in the plays of Chikamatsu (1653-1724), reference points for the dramatisation of hopeless romances and the like. Nevertheless the Shogunate in Edo, for all its edicts exhorting thrift and diligence, which only go to show that these commodities at least were often in short supply, was as powerless to control the many-faceted culture of the urban centres as it was to regulate the price of rice (which fluctuated wildly in the first three decades of the eighteenth century). The samurai class, though theoretically dominant, seems to have been bemused and fascinated by the new world in which money talked, usually at any rate, more than the sword.

The dominance of the merchant culture in the main urban centres, and especially in Ōsaka, which lacked the aristocratic or the political flavour of Kyōto or Edo respectively, was an

[36] Dunn 1969, 190. Cf. also the whole of ch. 5. An extremely entertaining picture of merchant life dating from 1866 is found in the *Nihon Eitaigura* of Ihara Saikaku (1642-1693), English translation in Sargent 1959.

important social presupposition for the emergence of critical lines of thought. Tominaga Nakamoto was born late enough to be an inheritor of this townsman's independence. There is no reflection whatever in his works of psychological subservience to ideological authorities of any kind. We find simply, from this new vantage point, an intellectual interest in the emergence of religious systems and their competition with each other.

The distant west

It would not be necessary to devote attention to the lack of western influence on Tominaga were it not that westerners confronted with his ideas so frequently ask about the possibility of it. The question has apparently never been dealt with by a Japanese writer, no doubt for the excellent reason that the need to presume it would not normally occur to one closely familiar with the history of Japanese ideas and culture. At the same time the absence of western influence is an important presupposition both for meaningful comparison with relevant strands of European thought and for a consideration of Tominaga's wider significance in the history of ideas. Were it to be shown that his method and theory came by devious routes from the western world, then they would only, or in important respects, be of interest as an extension of the thought of that world. In fact, his thought is an entirely Asian development. Since his ideas will be of interest to many readers precisely because they represent an autonomous counterpart to certain western ideas current at about the same time, the situation as regards possible influence from the western world will be briefly presented.[37]

First, there is not a shred of evidence that Tominaga personally had any contact whatever with any of the very few foreigners who entered Japan during this time. He shows no interest in astronomy or clocks, nor in medicine or military theory, subjects which later developed in the context of 'Dutch studies' (*rangaku*). He also shows no interest in Chinese translations of Jesuit works, some of which were available in Japan. The European world is mentioned only once in his writings and then fleetingly, as an example of different

[37] Cf. also Pye 1973, drawing largely on Keene 1952 and Goodman 1967.

countries having different marriage customs. He had heard that in those distant lands the women were in charge of things![38]

Conversely it may be regarded as beyond dispute that ideas representative of the European Enlightenment were not transmitted from either Spain or Portugal to sixteenth-century Japan. It is amply evident from the extensive researches of C.R. Boxer in this field that neither missionaries from those lands nor sailors could have been familiar with the relevant modes of thinking.[39] As a Jesuit spokesman wrote of the Jesuit College at Macao in 1650, shortly after the Jesuit missions in Japan had come to a violent end:

> From this royal fortress went out and go out nearly every year the preachers of the Gospel in order to make war on all the surrounding heathendom, hoisting the regal standard of the Holy Cross on the highest and strongest bastions of idolatry, preaching Christ crucified, and subduing to the sweet yoke of His most holy law the proudest and most isolationist kingdoms and empires.[40]

This approach clearly was not conducive to rationalist or historicist enquiry. Nor need it be supposed that in this respect Dominicans or Franciscans were any different. As to secular traders from Spain or Portugal, it appears that they, and their Japanese counterparts, were largely dependent on Jesuit interpreters when it came to concluding deals 'since the padres alone had sufficient command of both languages to carry through any complicated negotiations'.[41] Hence even if Iberian traders could be shown to have carried ideas which diverged significantly, in a critical spirit, from Counter-Reformation theology, these could scarcely have been transmitted.

This leaves the Dutch. A few nationals of other protestant lands may be regarded as honorary Dutchmen in this respect.

[38] *Emerging from Meditation*, Chapter 15 (Marriage), p. 136 below.

[39] See especially his standard work *The Christian Century in Japan 1549-1650*, 1951, but also later writings such as that quoted immediately below.

[40] Quoted in translation by Boxer in *Portuguese India in the Mid-Seventeenth Century*, 1980, 15 from Antonio Francisco Cardim, S.J., *Batalhas da Companhia de Jesus na sua gloriosa Provincia do Japão*, ed. Luciano Cordeiro, Lisboa 1894, 19.

[41] Boxer 1951, 243-4.

The Dutch presence in Japan, which took over the role of intermediary with the outside world after the brutal suppression of Catholic Christianity, was almost entirely restricted to the tiny artificial island of Dejima (often referred to as Deshima in western literature) at the port of Nagasaki.[42] It is at first glance conceivable that this tiny community could have been a vehicle for the transfer into Japan of ideas relevant to the present discussion. However it seems to be abundantly clear that this was not so.

Kristof Glamann's substantial work *Dutch-Asiatic Trade 1620-1740*, for example, is able to tell us a very great deal about the fluctuations of Dutch trade in bullion, pepper, spices, raw silk, piece-goods, sugar, copper (exported in quantity from Japan), coffee and tea. The main Dutch motive for being in Japan at all, if residing on Dejima can be described as being in Japan, was to acquire precious metals and camphor.[43] Glamann leaves us with the overwhelming impression that the trade with Japan was merely of some slight extra advantage to an overall Dutch trading operation which had its centre of gravity elsewhere, and that what interest the Dutch did have was entirely commercial. In later writings Glamann continues to give a picture of limited economic interaction with no hint of any intellectual accompaniment.[44] Nor has anything been added in this direction by the publication of extensive archives of the Dutch East India Company (Verenigde Oostindische Compagnie) in the fascinatingly circumstantial volumes of *Dutch-Asiatic Shipping in the 17th and 18th Centuries*.[45] The same may be said for a recent account of the Dutch-Japan trade by M.E. van Opstall entitled *Handeldrijven op Japan 1609 tot 1880*. As archivist at the Algemeen Rijksarchief at The Hague van Opstall enjoyed access to the principal existing collection of relevant records and artefacts and would surely have noticed significantly divergent trends. Recent European interest in Japan and in Euro-Japanese relations has led to exhibitions and publications which naturally seek to display

[42] The precise terms of the documents governing their residence have been presented and explained by Fiorella Leemhuis (Leemhuis 1975).

[43] Glamann 1958, 168.

[44] Glamann 1974 and 1977.

[45] Bruijn *et al.* 1979, 1981. More generally, see also Boxer 1965 and Rothermund 1978.

materials of as much antiquity and interest as possible. Thus in 1983/4 an exhibition was staged in Leiden and in Breda, the Netherlands, on the theme of four centuries of artistic, scientific, linguistic and commercial contacts. Although presented entirely in terms of the positive existence and interest of such contacts only one conclusion can be drawn relevant to the present discussion from the exhibits shown and the associated publication.[46] Japanese interest in what the west had to offer was limited to matters of commercial, practical and scientific importance. It must be admitted that interest in and knowledge of western medicine grew rapidly under the influence of the doctors resident on Dejima, who also joined the official delegations to Edo. However, much was transmitted through demonstrations, pictures and eventually (first in 1771) dismemberment of corpses. Linguistically the breakthrough did not come until 1774 with the translation of a Dutch version of a German text on anatomy.[47] The first doctor on Dejima, Willem Ten Rhijne (1647-1700) was interested in Chinese medicine (*kanpō*) and wrote a book about acupuncture.[48] The second was Engelbert Kaempfer (1651-1716), well known for his extremely informative writing on Japan. His indications of the nature of the Dutch presence at Dejima however, notably in Volume II of *The History of Japan*, give no suggestion at all that there could have been any particularly influential, specific, intellectual influence emanating from that quarter. The doings and writings of the scientifically highly enterprising doctors Carl Pieter Thunberg (Swedish) and Philipp von Siebold (German) are chronologically irrelevant for the present discussion. The appearance of the work *Rangaku Kotohajime*, also after Tominaga's time, is interesting because the title implies how relatively impenetrable the Dutch language must have been for the Japanese until quite late on, and hence how unlikely to have been a vehicle for the transmission of subtle ideas in the early eighteenth century.[49]

[46] Van Opstall *et al*. 1983. See especially the contributions by Margot E. van Opstall ('Japans-Nederlands betrekkingen 1609-1865') and Frits Vos ('Het dagelijks leven der Nederlanders op Deshima').

[47] Bowers 1980, 6-8.

[48] Ibid. 7.

[49] Cf. Orsi 1974.

The very hesitant reception of foreign ideas and the limitation of receptivity to particular subjects such as anatomy, astronomy, navigation and military affairs is clearly seen in two works particularly relevant to questions of intellectual interaction, namely D. Keene's *The Japanese Discovery of Europe* (1952) and G.K. Goodman's *The Dutch Impact on Japan (1640-1853)* (1967). Nor is this picture drawn differently in principle in later articles by F. Leemhuis (1967, 1971) or in a discussion of 'the international component' in Tokugawa Japan by A. Tamburello (1975). The slow start to 'western learning' or 'Dutch learning' – slow, that is, in relation to the question about possible intellectual influence in the early eighteenth century – is also evident from R.P. Dore's detailed study of education in the Tokugawa period (Dore 1965).[50] This picture has been reinforced more recently by Rubinger (1982), especially in his chapters on the teaching of Dutch Studies in Edo, Nagasaki and Ōsaka. It was only in the second half of the eighteenth century that dictionaries were compiled and the ability to read books in Dutch more or less freely was attained and transmitted.[51]

Returning to the time before and during which Tominaga lived, mention should be made of Arai Hakuseki (1657-1725) who, because of his position as 'lecturer' to the Shōgun Ienobu, was able to investigate western matters with a view to assessing their possible political and economic importance. One of his main sources was the unfortunate missionary Sidoty, whom Arai Hakuseki interviewed in 1708, but who was certainly not an apostle of the Enlightenment. Hakuseki concluded, without undue mental stress, that Christian thought was no more than a pale reflection of Buddhism, and he concentrated for preference on obtaining geographical and political information.[52] Documentable exchanges on religious questions outside the disastrous encounter with Catholic Christianity were slight indeed during the Tokugawa Period. In 1717 the broad-minded Shōgun Yoshimune addressed a

[50] See especially pp. 160ff.

[51] See Frits Vos' contribution 'De Nederlandse taal in Japan', in van Opstall *et al.* 1983.

[52] Cf. Kuiper 1921, 240-4. The summary judgment of Joyce Ackroyd, translator of his long autobiography (Ackroyd 1979) is, 'From his contact with westerners, he gained a rudimentary knowledge of the sciences of physics, astronomy and medicine' (p. 9).

series of seventeen questions to the Dutch traders, mainly about legal and political matters, but ending with a question about the care of ancestors and last of all 'How do we know there is a God?' The director of the trading station (the *opperhoofd*) answered, no doubt truthfully as well as expediently, that he was not a theologian and was only there for the trade ('alleen voor de negotie').[53] This response must have been even less stimulating than the safely vague admission by Will Adams a century before that he believed in 'the creator of Heaven and Earth'.[54]

That highly sophisticated and otherwise well-informed thinkers in Tokugawa Japan could long remain untouched by any possible intellectual influence from the Dutch may be seen from the following statement by Ogyū Sorai:

> In the case of other countries, like Holland, they have Heaven-given natures which are totally different, and therefore, of course, they must have languages which are difficult to understand ... like the chirping of birds and the screaming of beasts. They are inhuman in their not being close to human sentiments.[55]

We see here how self-sufficient was the East Asian cultural tradition. Europe was just so much twittering of birds on a distant horizon. The present-day European or American reader may have to make a strong imaginative effort to become adequately aware of this. Yet only so is it comprehensible that a man like Tominaga, who was deeply interested in the diversity of cultures, could mention lands to the west of India once only.

There is indeed a crucial difference in the manner in which Ogyū Sorai and Tominaga Nakamoto moved within the East Asian cultural context. The former went on to comment: 'However, in the case of China and our own country, the sentiments and the proprieties are the same.'[56] In other words, while disregarding India, the home of Buddhism, he drew a closed circle round China and Japan and sought meaning in their cultural unity. Tominaga, by contrast, with the wider perspective given by the addition of India and the complexities of the Buddhist tradition, regarded none of the three as

[53] Kuiper 1921, 240.
[54] Sadler 1937, 190.
[55] Lidin 1973, 130.
[56] Ibid. 130.

identical with another. This amounted to a more radical cultural relativism. Nevertheless this relativism and the other related ideas did not arise out of shock or curiosity produced by encounter with the western world, and still less as a result of intellectual influence from that world. On the contrary, they are an autonomous development which can be satisfactorily understood in the context of Asian intellectual history.

Asian perspectives

Tominaga's immediate intellectual and social context in Tokugawa Japan was discussed above, and it was seen that his work can be understood as belonging in a general way to his environment. It has also been seen that there is no question of western influence, either in terms of circumstantial stimulation or in terms of the transmission of major intellectual presuppositions. Nevertheless there remains a third area of enquiry which is relevant to an understanding of how Tominaga's critical position vis-à-vis religious tradition came to be what it was. This area, unfortunately, is no less than the whole of Asian religious and intellectual history from ancient India onwards and eastwards. Such a vast potentially relevant scenario cannot be surveyed chronologically here, and no doubt many features within it would be interpreted diversely by specialists with different interests. Nevertheless it is essential to ask what features of Asian thought may be regarded as facilitatory or even essential conditions for the emergence of Tominaga's ideas. Moreover it does seem possible to identify several features which together provide a cumulative preparation for the emergence of an Asian modernity in thought about religion. Some are intimately connected with religion itself, while others are broader in their reference, linking up with the beginnings of historical writing and, perhaps unexpectedly, with bibliographical analysis.

First, fundamental to the whole development is the very idea of a critique of the natural existence of man. This first found documentable expression in Asia in the world-renouncing systems of Jainism and Buddhism. These systems, in the sixth century BC, moved into a position of some tension with Brahmanism, the prevailing primal religion which provided an integrative social and cosmological perspective. The world-renouncing systems entailed at least an implicit or potential critique of society, dramatised by the simple fact that people left it in order to seek a different fulfilment in the context of an alternative community. For the Jains this involved a rejection of all possessions, including clothing, and with advancing age the renunciation of food leading eventually to death, or putting it positively, to release (*mokṣa*).[57] It is known that, in the case of Buddhism at least, a negative reaction was aroused on the part of the society which was being relinquished. Thus *Mahāvagga* 24 graphically relates the complaints of the people of Magadha over losing sons and husbands who followed the Buddha in search of nirvāṇa.[58] The important feature of these world-renouncing systems for the present argument is that they lead to independent lines in the transmission of ideas which take on dynamics of their own.

Secondly, as the corporate memory of these independent lines of tradition became extended diachronically, it became possible to reflect on their true import while setting a question mark over the intermediate forms of expression. In a word, this engenders the principle of reform. It bears within it an important seed of critical thinking and relativises at least those authorities which fall between the normative origins and the new present. This by no means amounts to a fully modern critique of religion, for major, normative foci of the tradition may remain in the first instance undisturbed. Nevertheless it is an important constituent factor in the developing complexity of tradition because in the wake of a far-reaching reform movement the shape of a tradition (its *Gestalt*) can never be the same again, though some of its exponents commonly try to make it so. In this sense the emergence of Mahāyāna Buddhism may be regarded as a reform movement, attempting by means of the concept of emptiness to restate the true meaning of dependent origination and the middle way. It must be admitted that in many respects the formative period of Mahāyāna Buddhism was only remotely similar to the European Reformation within Christianity and in some respects quite contrary to it. However the unifying characteristic of reform movements in a general sense is that they seek to

[57]For this and related aspects of Jainism, see Schubring 1927 and Jaini 1979. The oldest documentation of Jainism is in Buddhist texts.

[58] Horner 1951, 57.

re-identify essential qualities of the received tradition and by so doing set a critical question mark against intervening presentations. This entails a relocation of authority and a change of consciousness with respect to the total range of available authoritative foci. Thanks to the Mahāyāna, Buddhism had already reached this level of complexity by the time it entered the East Asian cultural area.

Thirdly, both through reformist innovation and as a result of other pressures, the sheer passage of time saw the appearance in Indian and Chinese Buddhism of a bewildering procession of different religious authorities: scriptures (sūtras), saviour figures (bodhisattvas), and meditation teachers, each more authentic or more effective than the next. While accepted uncritically at the level of popular religiosity the teaching transmitters of the tradition themselves were more or less aware that the projection of such authorities took place at the level of provisional truth. The availability of diverse forms of religious presentation means, to those who, like intelligent and mobile monks, enjoy an overview, that each relativises the other. A preference may remain and be expressed with conviction. One teaches seated meditation while another makes use of a maṇḍala. Thus Buddhism in East Asia has been beset by a proliferation of schools and sects, and questions of authority have been settled, or compromised over, by a combination of social pressure and popular appeal. As a result it is possible, and eventually unavoidable, to regard each expression of the tradition as being in principle a construct. When this is understood the individual is free to decide for himself in any one case whether to recognise the authority of the tradition in that form, or not. The many debatable questions which arose as a result of this diversity in effect form the material for *Emerging from Meditation*, and their appearance is therefore a prerequisite for the development of Tominaga's method for dealing with them.

Fourthly, attention may be drawn to the idea that religious teaching needs to be related to the present time. This arose early in Buddhism, probably having its roots in the way in which the teaching activity of the Buddha himself was remembered. There was always a place and an occasion for his utterances, a particular set of hearers and circumstances to which his teaching was addressed. The point is not that this was so, which might seem obvious enough, but that it was remembered systematically as being so in the opening lines of all the sūtras. In China the idea took a further turn as attempts were made to classify the vast number of sūtras intelligibly. Thus the sūtras were classified in accordance with presumed phases of the Buddha's teaching, the best-known example (but by no means the only one) being the T'ien T'ai scheme which begins with the *Kegon Sūtra* and ends with the *Lotus* and *Nirvāṇa Sūtras*. The idea developed in another way in those forms of Buddhism which appealed to the arrival of the age of 'Latter Dharma' (Japanese: *mappō*),[59] in which the original teaching of the Buddha could no longer be clearly heard or received. This was a justification for selectivity and simplification. Thus it was argued (especially in Pure Land Buddhism) that the people of today could never achieve the sanctity possible in earlier times, nearer to the lifetime of the Buddha himself; or alternatively it was claimed (especially in Nichirenite Buddhism) that the predictions for later times found in the sūtras were now coming to pass. In themselves these are religious teachings, the details and value of which need not be discussed here. They amounted, however, in a lengthening chronological perspective, to an increasingly widespread assumption that forms of faith had to be related to the times in which people were in fact living. This is a strong theme (though without Buddhist piety) in Tominaga's *Writings of an Old Man*. Indeed the idea of 'latter times' specifically occurs in Section 16. The fact that this section is mainly concerned with Shintō shows that by then the idea that mankind was living in a late stage in the arrangement of things was generally available and no longer limited to Buddhist contexts.

A fifth important feature, nowadays taken for granted but certainly not always present everywhere, is awareness of the relation between the claims of diverse religious teachings and groups. For this we may reach back again to the traditions of early Buddhism, where rivalry with Jainism is quite apparent. Subsequent history saw many variations: debate

[59] For this concept see especially Fischer 1976.

and apologetics, rivalry over political patronage, syncretistic symbiosis and harmonisation attempts. All of these are modes of religious interaction which lead to critical reflection on the very existence of religious alternatives or, to use the phrase current nowadays, religious pluralism. In particular the arrival of Buddhism in China led to the recognition in that country that rival claims had to be deliberately considered, and this took place eventually in official debates at court. No doubt popular practice failed to sort out the Buddhist, Taoist and ancestral pantheons into clear groups, just as in Chinese religion today. Nevertheless at intellectual level there were many attempts at both demarcation and synthesis. The earlier positions adopted were apologetic in a more or less confrontational manner, as when Taoists argued that Lao Tzŭ appeared as the Buddha in India, thus playing down Buddhism as an independent system; or when the Buddhists for their part argued that Lao Tzŭ had gone to India to learn from the Buddha, thus subordinating Taoism. From the fifth century AD onwards there were attempts to identify common principles such as quietness and immovability (by Chang Yung), a primordial unity (by Meng Ching-i) or moral order and justice in karma (by Yen Chih-t'ui).[60] The Sung period (960-1279) saw an intensification of such efforts, particularly in the 'inner alchemy' school which emphasised ascetic discipline and meditation along with the teaching that all three major teachings in China shared a common goal, namely the inner transformation of the individual.[61] Of particular interest is the work of the first Ming Emperor himself (reigned from 1368), which bore the title *Treatise on the Three Teachings* (*San chiao lun*). As interpreted by Berling this work regarded 'the Way' as being an aspect of normal life which each of the three teachings served in its own manner, Confucianism tending more towards the external, clear principle of *yin*, and Buddhism and Taoism tending more towards the concealed but virtuous principle of *yang*. Thus without denying the identity of any one of the three teachings (*san chiao*) a place was found for each, which was no doubt politically desirable.[62] Important in the present context however is the reflective recognition of

[60] Cf. Forke 1964, II, 230-2, 237-8, and 238 respectively.
[61] Cf. Berling 1980, 39-46.
[62] Cf. ibid. 48ff.

religious pluralism which, given a separate vantage point (in this case political power), leads on to a new interpretation which relativises each tradition without destroying it. There are many examples of this form of reflection in both China and Japan. It appears clearly in *Writings of an Old Man* and in Chapter 24 of *Emerging from Meditation*, which is also entitled *san chiao* (pronounced in Japanese as *sankyō*). Tominaga also had a separate vantage point, namely political irrelevance, but he came to different conclusions (assessed in Pye 1983).

As a sixth feature may be adduced the perception that there is significant culture, especially religious culture, beyond the borders of one's own country. The extent to which this was recognised in ancient India is uncertain. For China the point was illustrated by the incursion of Buddhism, Manichaeism, Christianity and Islam, while the foreignness of these was variously veiled by Chinese clothing, Chinese versions of texts and so on. The strength of the pressure to sinicise is itself an indication of the gulf perceived from the Chinese side. Thus the Taoist Ku Huan (430-493), who regarded Buddhism and Taoism as identical, wrote: 'Buddhism is not the system of the Chinese in the east and Taoism is not the teaching of the barbarians in the west, just as fish and birds have their diverse ponds and marshes and do not disturb each other.'[63] The sheer scale of the Middle Kingdom itself seems to have dampened the intellectual challenge which might have arisen from the recognition of cultural diversity beyond ethnically perceived borders. In the case of Japan this was different. It was always clear to the Japanese, in historical times, that China lay beyond Japan as a major political and cultural model. Moreover the Indian origins of Buddhism became increasingly clear with the reception of tantric Buddhism in the Tendai and Shingon schools, and thereafter it was evident that Japan was at the end of a chain of major cultural entities. Thus the existence of a pluralism of diverse cultural areas, each with its styles and language, was widely presupposed among literate Japanese well before Tominaga's time.

Increasing sophistication in chronological perspective was, of course, not limited to religious contexts. Of great importance

[63] Forke 1964, II, 235.

therefore, seventhly, is the very idea of history writing. This began, as far as East Asia is concerned, in China. The nature of the historical presentation of events is very difficult to assess precisely. It is a commonplace that much early history writing is little more than dynastic chronicling or moralising from tales of the past, mainly serving political purposes.[64] Nevertheless there are many glimmerings, from antiquity onwards, of principles important in modern history writing, notably a critical care over sources and an interest in motivation. The famous early Chinese historian Ssu-ma Ch'ien (floruit 100 BC) may have written 'in order to bring harmony between heaven and man and to link the events of the time', but in spite of the reference to 'heaven' he was mainly concerned on a this-worldly basis with the relations between politics, morals and events.[65] The first Chinese work which really reflected on history, according to Pulleyblank (Beasley and Pulleyblank 1961) was the *Generalities on History (Shih t'ung)* of Liu Chih-chi, written in 710.[66] For him the following aspects were important: doubt, argument, independence, selection and judgment.[67] The essential point here is that a single fixed model for dealing with the past had been dispensed with in the East Asian context long before Tominaga's time. Admittedly Tominaga himself was not really trying to be a historian as such. It will be evident from his works that they are arranged thematically. Moreover, rather than showing a general interest in the past, he concentrated his attentions on the critical appraisal of religion in diachronic perspective. At the same time, the critical juxtaposition of sources is of crucial importance in *Emerging from Meditation*, and the question of the motivation of historical figures (though not in a detailed complex of events) lay at the root of his theory of tradition. Accounts of the European Enlightenment diverge in the emphasis placed on history, some stressing the timeless quality of reason. A similar ambivalence may be felt when attempting to pin down the character of Tominaga's work.

As important as the appearance of historical writing, eighthly, was the growth of bibliographical skill in the Chinese

[64] Cf. Rosthorn 1920, 7.
[65] Ibid. 17.
[66] Cf. Beasley and Pulleyblank 1961.
[67] Cf. Han 1955, 163.

cultural tradition. Details of this have been presented in Kang Woo's *Histoire de la Bibliographie Chinoise* (Paris 1938), but its significance, as yet scarcely recognised, lies in that it amounted to a systematic, synchronic analysis of knowledge. The key question here, though not posed in the above-mentioned work, is why, given the nature of their contents, there ever came to be a systematic listing of the so-called canonical works of Confucianism. Their contents are not presumed to be revealed, nor was their author or leading instigator, Confucius, identified after death with a cosmic principle. Deification was late and ordinary, hardly one step above beatification in western terms. The clue surely lies in the position which 'the five classics' assumed in early bibliographical arrangements. A clear, early example is the classification of all the works in the imperial library, amounting to the impressive number of 13269 scrolls, carried through in the fourth decade BC and entitled 'The Seven Summaries'. The seven categories applied here were: general works, the six arts, works of the master, poetic works, military works, technical and mathematical works, medicinal and health works. The five classics came into the second section. Thus just as Confucius had sorted the tradition available to him and regarded certain aspects within it as normative for the whole, so the works identified with him came to be regarded as key works for the whole system of knowledge which accrued later.

A later classification, stemming from the third century AD, was a fourfold division into classics, history, philosophical and technical knowledge, literature. At the beginning of the T'ang Dynasty categories for Taoist and Buddhist works were appended. These classifications have been influential down to the present day. A system which Woo, unconscious of the import, referred to as 'the modern system' is nothing other than a reworking of these very same schemes carried out in 1875 and provided with two additional categories: 'various' and 'additional'![68] Thus the idea of an extended store of more or less coherent knowledge in written form, which it was necessary to sort, was basic to the Chinese way of dealing with their ever-expanding libraries. Indeed the Chinese Buddhist systems for classifying the sūtras, which were mentioned

[68] Woo 1938, 39ff, 62,63.

above, are in fact a compromise between the diachronic idea of the Buddha teaching different things at different times and an analysis of the nature of the writings according to their type. Bibliographical arrangements may therefore be regarded as a highly generalised form of 'the investigation of things'. The cumulative effect was that the literate classes became used to taking a broad perspective over a wide range of writings and to reflecting on their nature.

These eight features of thinking may all seem extremely obvious, even platitudinous, to the present-day reader. Nevertheless they have not been available at all places and in all times. For them all to be available at one and the same time presupposes an extended and complex cultural development. This pattern of assumptions had come together at latest by the early eighteenth century in Japan. It may be that this had not happened with the same clarity and force elsewhere in East Asia.

Needless to say, it is not assumed here that ideas arise automatically out of other ideas in a simple unfolding process. Two other factors are also necessary in explanation of the emergence of ideas. The first is the social basis. In this case, as was seen earlier, it was the independent position of a self-confident merchant class which made critical reflection on the nature of all religious authorities existentially feasible. The second is the appearance of an individual whose creative ability can respond to the situation of the times and develop a new idea on the basis of available assumptions. Tominaga had this creative ability. At the same time it should be evident from the above, however brief the sketch of ideas, that a crucial cluster of assumptions was available within the East Asian intellectual tradition known to him.

Tominaga's influence and significance

It is curious that a thinker of world stature should not be more widely fêted in Japan itself. Tominaga has no public monuments and only a very ordinary tomb-stone, set among those of some of his relatives with the family name of Tominaga. These stand in a little-known temple cemetery in Ōsaka,[69]

[69] The name of the temple is Saishōji.

still the commercial centre which it was in Tominaga's time, though of course on an even grander scale today. When I once visited this cemetery, with mixed feelings of sentimentality and curiosity, a caretaker said, 'Tominaga Nakamoto's tombstone is in a corner over there; but he was against Buddhism.'

The direct influence of Tominaga's thought in Japan has been extremely fitful. While provoking interest in Ōsaka he did not become nationally famous in his lifetime. Even today it has not yet become indispensable, apparently, to mention his name in more popular accounts of Japanese thought, and it does not appear in those high-school textbooks which provide the information which grown-up Japanese are supposed to have at their disposal. Yet he was certainly not without influence, difficult though it may be to chart.

Strangely enough both *Writings of an Old Man* and *Emerging from Meditation* led a twilight existence for some time, without getting lost for ever. *Writings of an Old Man* first appeared in 1746, the year in which Tominaga died. Thirty-three years later, in 1779, the work was mysteriously reissued under a different title, namely *Okinamichi no shiori* (i.e. 'Guide to the Old Man's Way'). Some trouble was taken to obscure the relationship to the original edition (for details see Note on editions used, pp. 184-7), but the actual contents are completely unchanged. One can only speculate as to why this should have been done. It is possible that the writing was disapproved of in certain quarters and that this was an inconspicuous method of making it available again. Less dramatically, it is possible that the publisher was no longer aware (or failed to notice, as he might have done from Section 10) that the author was the same Tominaga who had written *Emerging from Meditation*. Did he simply regard it as a useful moral tract and take the understatement of Tominaga's introductory paragraph at its face value? It remains unclear in Japanese, which is without definite and indefinite articles, whether the new title is meant to refer to the Way of *an* Old Man, or whether it implies rather that there was a 'Way of the Old Man' which readers in the Ōsaka area might be expected to have heard of. All we know is that the new publisher (Fushimiya) felt free, more than a generation later, to republish Tominaga's writing with a different title and that he thought it was worth doing so. While the work apparently disappeared from public discussion thereafter for more than a hundred years, this does not mean that it was entirely lost during that time nor that it was entirely without influence.

Emerging from Meditation remained better known, as may be seen from the fact its name was included in the title of another work, *Hishutsujō*, which was intended to refute it from a Buddhist point of view. It was also alluded to in the title of Hirata Atsutane's *Shutsujō shōgo* (*shōgo* means laughing and talking at the same time). On the other hand a concealed, or pirate, edition was issued under a different name in 1805, which may seem to suggest that its true authorship had been forgotten. (Cf. Wakimoto 1967, frontispiece.)

The most notable feature of Tominaga's influence in the Tokugawa Period was undoubtedly the commendation he received from Motoori Norinaga (1730-1801), who wrote:

> Recently in Ōsaka there lived a person called Tominaga Nakamoto, who published during the Enkyō era a book on Buddhism, titled *Shutsujō kōgo*, supporting his detailed arguments by a wide reference to the sūtras and Buddhist treatises. This book opened my eyes to many things. Judging by his style of *kanbun*, I think this man must have studied extensively the Confucian classics. Although he was not a monk, his command of the Buddhist texts seems to have been superior to most of the monks known as scholars of the various Buddhist sects. This is an admirable achievement, indeed. Later a monk called Musō published a book called *Hi-shutsujō*, and tried to refute *Shutsujō kōgo* because he could not bear the idea that Buddhism could be dealt with in such simple terms. But what he did was only to shout all kinds of abuses, without really disproving even a single passage of the book in question. It is obvious that this monk, renowned for his knowledge on phonology, did not know much about Buddhist texts. I feel, however, that this book could not be easily disproved even by a monk who has thoroughly studied Buddhism.[70]

It appears however that Motoori was only aware of *Emerging from Meditation*, and thus remained undisturbed by the criticism of the Shintō tradition found in *Writings of an Old Man*. To Motoori, who was not concerned with defending any dogmatic position on behalf of a Buddhist school, Tominaga's

[70] Thus quoted in English translation in Katō 1967, 16.

arguments seemed entirely plausible. This in itself shows that in principle these arguments were not simply an isolated and incomprehensible phenomenon in the context of Tokugawa thought. Moreover Motoori's understanding of his own preferred Shintō tradition is in some ways quite modern. It was his achievement to provide a legitimation for the Shintō tradition through detailed scholarly activity which at the same time led him to be regarded later as a significant precursor of modern Japanese philological and folkloristic studies. The very name *kokugaku* used for the school associated with him, implies not only an emphasis on the choice of national (*koku-*) materials for study but also (*-gaku*) on the philological and reflective nature of their interest. Indeed the combination of these two factors requires a distancing from naive religious self-expression, and a recognition that since time has intervened between the mythical past and the present, an interpretative effort is necessary. Motoori did not apply the same abrasively radical criticism to Shintō which Tominaga had applied to the Buddhist tradition. Yet consciousness had shifted.

Even the sketchy indications which are available to us are sufficient to show that it would be mistaken to regard Tominaga's works as a flash-in-the-pan which disappeared entirely not long after his death. Naturally the Buddhist world closed ranks to refute or ignore what he had pointed out. No one group or school would be motivated to take up his ideas for themselves and against themselves, only against others, and for that *Emerging from Meditation* is too comprehensive! However once expressed clearly, disturbing ideas do not go away and are not easily forgotten by all. They can be influential without being positively promoted or celebrated.

During the stress and excitement of increasing interaction with the western world it did not occur to any particular body of opinion in Japan to reconsider Tominaga's work directly and, as a result, some features of critical enquiry in the humanities were adopted from the western world which in principle could probably have been developed from within Japan itself. Thus the nineteenth century saw a new growth of historically critical Buddhist studies in Japan, under the strong stimulation of scholars such as Nanjō Bunyū and Takakusu Junjirō who were exposed to the influence of Max

Müller. At the same time, while it is not possible at present to demonstrate that Tominaga's works were known to these persons, it must have already filtered through to most thoughtful Buddhist scholars in Japan by that time that the historical development of Buddhism was not identical with the simplified dogmatic pictures inherited from China. In spite of the great stimulus provided by the encounter with western scholarship, which at that time had still only just got round to a first reading of some of the essential texts, it is not inapposite to regard Tominaga's early critical reflections as the starting point of modern critical Buddhist studies in Japan. This has been increasingly recognised recently, especially by such writers as Nakamura Hajime and Wakimoto Tsuneya, both Buddhist specialists of Tokyo University.[71] Interestingly enough, a critical study of Buddhist origins published in 1899 by Anesaki Masaharu (also professor of religion at Tokyo University until 1949), was dedicated jointly to the German critical theologian Ferdinand Christian Baur and to Tominaga Nakamoto, hinting at parallelism.[72]

However Tominaga is not only important for Buddhist studies. Buddhism just happens to be the prime example in his main extant work. In the twentieth century his more general significance was noticed and explored above all by two men, Naitō Konan and Ishihama Juntarō. They both regarded Tominaga as a genius and did much to make known his contribution to the way in which past traditions came to be studied in modern times.

A link between interest in the critique of Buddhist history and more general considerations in the history of thought probably found their best early expression in the work of Nakamura Hajime who set out the main features of Tominaga's method in the second part of his work *Kinseinihon no hinhanteki seishin* (Nakamura 1965). In his conclusion he stressed two points. First, Tominaga represented a new ideal for scholarship (*gakumon*) in that he did not presume that his own standpoint was absolutely right while others were wrong.

[71] E.g. Nakamura 1965, Wakimoto 1967.

[72] The work, *Bukkyō seiten shiron*, appeared early in Anesaki's career, for he graduated at Tokyo three years earlier in 1866. It is noteworthy that the first critical journal in the field of Buddhist studies was *Bukkyō Shirin*, started in 1894, cf. Wakimoto 1967, 47.

Secondly, though living in the seclusion of Japan he had sufficient recognition of the universality of such scholarship.[73] This point is reinforced by quotation of Tominaga's aspiration, as stated in the preface to *Emerging from Meditation*, that his way of regarding Buddhist tradition might be communicated back to the countries from which Buddhism had come to Japan.

Since it was not until the 1960s and 1970s that Tominaga's works became really widely available in Japan as a result of their inclusion in influential publishers' series, it is perhaps not surprising that they should have been overlooked by well-known writers on the history of Japanese thought. *Writings of an Old Man* had in fact been ensconced in a standard collection of neo-Confucian writings entitled *Nihon Jurin Sōsho* for some time, but it may be that some scholars passed it over with a cursory glance, not noticing that there was more to it than the neo-Confucian morality which it does in fact contain. The introductory paragraph by Tominaga is so modest that it would not necessarily lead one to expect something quite different. Moreover the full force of *Writings of an Old Man* is only really felt when it is read in conjunction with *Emerging from Meditation*, and neither the history of the texts and their reception nor the form of their publication had really encouraged this very much. Be that as it may, it certainly appears that not all Japanese writers on the history of ideas have been equally aware of their importance. Maruyama Masao's major work, *Studies in the Intellectual History of Tokugawa Japan*, contains not one reference to Tominaga. It might be replied that Maruyama's interest is in society and politics; however Tominaga's thorough deflation of all three major ideological traditions current in the period can scarcely be thought of as completely devoid of social and political significance, especially if the context of merchant culture is borne in mind.

There are very few references at all to Tominaga Nakamoto in

[73] Nakamura 1965, 240. Nakamura's own work is so wide-ranging that it deserves a considered appraisal in its own right, both with regard to its influence in Japan and as an example of the way in which Japanese thought may be projected and contextualised in world terms. His contributions may perhaps be regarded as not yet fully integrated in that the high appraisal made of Tominaga's methodological approach in his Japanese writing does not find more than passing attention in his foreign language publications. This applies even to *Parallel Developments, A Comparative History of Ideas*, 1975 and *Ansätze modernen Denkens in den Religionen Japans*, 1982.

English or other European languages. Interestingly enough the oldest presentation appeared as early as 1958, in the *Sources of Japanese Tradition* compiled by Tsunoda, de Bary and Keene. This extremely valuable but non-controversial anthology did not presume to discuss the question of the significance of Tominaga's work in wider terms. The most important contribution lies in the presentation of several paragraphs of *Writings of an Old Man* which are translated from the *Nihon Jurin Sōsho* edition.[74] The introductory text also gives a brief account of *Emerging from Meditation*, drawing for this on Ishihama's *Tominaga Nakamoto*. Particular stress is laid on the theory of language, but it is arguable that this theory does not represent the main thrust of Tominaga's work. In a departure from the original an English title for the work is given as *Historical Survey of Buddhism*, and in this respect it should be pointed out that the work itself is not really a survey, but rather a historical critique of misleading presentations of Buddhism. However it is extremely commendable that space was made for Tominaga here at a time when modern editions of his works were still in preparation. It made possible an attempt by the present writer to compare Tominaga's approach with that of Lessing, thus identifying the phenomenon of enlightenment, in the sense of *Aufklärung*, in Japan and in Europe in the same period (Pye 1973). In this respect the headings used by Tsunoda *et al.*, 'Eighteenth-century rationalism', 'The enlightened Confucianism of Arai Hakuseki' and 'The historical relativism of Tominaga Nakamoto' were extremely stimulating. The only other discussion by a non-Japanese appears to be in a paper by J.-N. Robert, which concentrates on *Writings of an Old Man* and stresses the neo-Confucianist strand in Tominaga's ideas (Robert 1980-81).

In the meantime a complete translation of *Writings of an Old Man* into English had been published by Katō Shūichi, accompanied by an introduction of several pages (Katō 1967).[75] Katō was certainly aware that Tominaga remains underestimated,

[74] Although the translation of extracts from the text by Tsunoda *et al.* speaks of 'the Way of Truth' for *makoto no michi* the introductory text unaccountably translates this phrase as 'the religion of true fact', which is hardly justified.

[75] Inexcusably the present writer's comparison with Lessing was written in complete ignorance of this contribution.

yet his comments remain largely confined to the Japanese context. There is a sentence near the beginning of his introductory remarks which reads:

> It is astonishing that in the Tokugawa Confucian world, Tominaga Nakamoto, probably without any contact with western ideas, could manage to anticipate the possibility of, and even to develop to some degree, a new science which no one else had ever envisaged until our very recent times: a strictly empirical science to explain the succession of different ideas in the past as a historical development along a number of general lines which are in turn considered as defined by immanent laws in the development of ideas, historical evolution of language and environmental features of the culture in question.[76]

Katō was writing for a western readership, in *Monumenta Nipponica*, yet it should be noted that his phrase 'our very recent times' must refer to Japan.[77] Thus Katō, like the rediscoverers Naitō and Ishihama, is fascinated by Tominaga's position in terms of the development of *Japanese* thought.

In fact Katō does then offer western parallels, Andō Shōeki being linked to Montesquieu, and Tominaga himself, because of his rationalism, to Voltaire. However, while Katō is quite clear about the importance of Tominaga's thought in itself, he does not seem to have noticed the *universal* significance of the very existence of such general parallels with French writers. Though perhaps true enough, the following remarks are oddly inconsequential:

> Nakamoto might have become another Voltaire had he lived much longer and had eighteenth-century Japan not been isolated from the outside world and on the eve of its revolution. In fact he died too young even to bring his ideas to fruition; he lived in a too isolated, and perhaps too stable, society to be engaged like his French contemporary in personal feuds, attacking old values, defending new ideas, if necessary, writing his own 'Philosophical Letters' in exile.[78]

[76] Katō 1967, 2.

[77] This is clear from the previous phrase 'probably without any contact with western parallels' which implies that parallel ideas had existed in the west but not in Japan.

[78] Katō 1967, 3.

But in reality Tominaga's importance for the *general* history of ideas is linked precisely with this isolation, which may be regarded positively as the independence of east and west from each other. Vis-à-vis the history of ideas in Europe Tominaga's work is entirely autonomous; while at the same time it is organically related to Asian intellectual traditions. This means that the evident parallels take on a wider significance which does not become apparent in a discussion centred on the Japanese developments by themselves. This significance is not merely internal to the history of Japanese thought but lies in the interrelationship between different elements in the history of ideas in general, of which the history of ideas in Japan is a part.[79] Moreover, by the very nature of the case, this kind of significance could not have been apparent in Tominaga's own time.

The major implication is as follows. It is no longer possible to argue that the main characteristics of the modern European rationality presumed to have surfaced during the period of the Enlightenment are themselves so culture-bound that they are of limited application only. For Tominaga most of the cultural variables were thoroughly different from European counterparts. Nobody in Europe manufactured soya-sauce, all tools were different, the language was entirely unrelated, the writing system was based in large part on quite different principles, traditional modes of argument were different (more different than Greek and Indian ones from each other), and moral systems were unrelated. Yet he arrived at an intellectual attitude with respect to the language and culture of the past, and above all to the ideologically powerful religious authorities, which is markedly parallel in its main principles to that of the European Enlightenment. Naturally, this attitude finds a different mode of expression. The theory of superseding (*kajō*), for example, is not precisely paralleled by any European idea. Nor were the European thinkers of the time familiar with it, cut off as they were from much of what humans had hitherto thought. Diversity at this level of formulation and theory-building is a further proof, if any were needed, of the relative independence, or autonomy of these two intellectual worlds.

[79] On the same lines, cf. a recent article by Allen G. Grapard, seeking Asian parallels to Voltaire (Grapard 1985).

What matters, given this autonomy, is that we may observe the same freely ranging critique of received traditions, the same searching historical investigation of their origins, the same attempt to perceive general laws of religious development.

There is much to be said for recognising, and seeking to understand, the divergent features of the major cultural areas of the world. Nevertheless it is of great interest to observe that in one important respect, namely in the emergence of a rational, historical critique of religion, a parallel development can be documented in two major cultures. We owe this awareness to the works of Tominaga Nakamoto.

Writings of an Old Man

Preface 1

Some time ago there was an old man living in the vicinity of Ikasuri Shrine.[1] I do not know his name. According to some people he was a genius, and very discreet, always liking to work at night. Even when the bell for going to sleep sounded he stayed at his desk, not noticing the advancing night until he heard the voice of the wild goose at daybreak. Since he made learning his friend he hardly even knew his neighbours. It is said, 'A man of virtue surely has something to pass on ...'[2] A certain Tominaga, of Tomo descent, called in when there were no visitors about other than the late autumn showers, heard his message and wrote it down under the title 'Writings of an Old Man'. Since his home is not far from mine he asked me to have a look at it. Being the writing of an old man of the Watanabe district the old story of Tōren came to mind,[3] so I examined it without delay. It is true that the purport of this writing can only be set forth by one who sees pure Chinese clothing in the Miwa river;[4] understanding the Indian <Buddhist> teaching about the fire which has exhausted its

[1] A shrine in Ōsaka, otherwise bearing the name of Zama Jinja.

[2] *Analects* XIV, 5. The statement continues, 'But a man who has something to say is not necessarily a man of virtue'. Cf. Legge 1893, 276.

[3] Tōren was a singing monk of the Heian Period who also took instruction from a 'sage of Watanabe'. The Ikasuri Shrine mentioned above is in the Watanabe district of Ōsaka.

[4] This reference to the Miwa river near Nara, known for its clear waters, contains an allusion to *Kokinshū* 5 (cf. Nakamura 1971, 138n.10). Red maple leaves falling here and there on the waters give a vermilion sheen suggestive of a certain kind of Chinese clothing (*karagoromo*). Thus the Chinese clothing stands indirectly for the (pure) waters of the river and the commingled image suggests that knowledge of Chinese and Japanese matters alike is necessary for the Old Man's argument to arise. This allusion demonstrates that cultural pluralism is one of the assumptions behind Tominaga's writing.

firewood, while rejecting the finger which fails to attain the moon;[5] knowing the way of the sage <Confucius> to be rooted in hierarchical nurture,[6] while disliking the bookishness of China; revering the divinities of our own country, while rejecting the misinterpretations of later generations. Although it is a remarkable work, as it is written in *kana* script[7] it might unfortunately be overlooked by people's carelessness, and so I, though a tedious old man with a worn-out brush, have added these clumsy words.

Sometime in the twelfth month of the first year of Enkyō (1744).
<Hayashi>.[8]

Preface 2

What kind of way is taught by the three teachings?[9] What kind of way is the way of truth?[10] Why is the Old Man explaining these things and getting us into difficulties? Why has the

[5] Fire exhausting its firewood is a standard metaphor for Nirvāṇa. The finger pointing to the moon stands for attempts to indicate the meaning of Buddhism, which all prove inadequate to the task.

[6] The implication of this Confucian term is that when high and low reside in their appointed places everything grows up satisfactorily.

[7] Although *kana* refers strictly speaking to phonetic script the text was originally printed in *kanamajiri*, the mixture of phonetic script and Chinese characters still used normally in Japan. The meaning is that as the text does not have the impressive scholarly appearance of a work written in the style of classical Chinese (*kanbun*), which would be solely in Chinese characters, people might not take it seriously.

[8] Little is known of this Hayashi, except that his 'village name' (*aza*) was Nakaura and that he was a friend of Tominaga's father. Cf. *Emerging from Meditation* Chapter 20, and Nakamura 1971, 139n.11.

[9] The standard Chinese formula of 'three teachings' refers in this case to Confucianism, Buddhism and Shintō (see opening lines of main text below) whereas in *Emerging from Meditation* Chapter 24 the three referred to under the same heading are Confucianism, Buddhism and Taoism, which are the three traditionally referred to in China. Tominaga's attitude to the intellectual problem posed by the existence of three teachings is however consistent, whichever three are referred to (cf. Pye 1983).

[10] The way of truth (*makoto no michi*) is the expression used also by Tominaga in *Writings of an Old Man* for the real way, the real meaning of any teaching, and that which theoretically might unite them. Cf. notes to the text below for variations in the terminology. The Chinese character used for *michi* is the same as that used in Butsudō (the way of the Buddha), Shintō or Shindō (the way of the gods), and for the Tao (Japanese: *dō*) of Taoism. The temptation to print it with a capital letter has usually been resisted.

meaning of the way been unclear for a thousand or even a hundred years, one may well ask. Whether it is clear or not may be of little or no importance. However two or three friends of mine never stop praising this Old Man. What need is there to add superfluities? As I myself do not know the Old Man's name, and have not seen his face, I do not know what there is about him that should be praised. However I recognise that my friend Nakamoto has attended to this hitherto untransmitted yet exquisite way out of sheer kindness for others. In that case we may ask whether Nakamoto and the Old Man think in the same way or not. If not, then why would he express agreement with the Old Man and seek to make it the teaching of his household?[11] Yet if they think the same, is this not contrary to Nakamoto's own thinking?[12] People may come to their own view on the matter. If they chew on the sweet yellow root of the knotweed[13] they will understand Nakamoto's purpose well enough. This may be described as a farewell address to Nakamoto or as a farewell address to the Old Man. If you wish to know the exquisite way then seek it from the moon in the zenith.[14]

The fifteenth of the tenth month of the first year of Enkyō (1744)
written at Naniwa by Layman Zenki.[15]
Tachibana Yō (Shiwa).[16]

[11] I.e. as Tominaga wrote at the end of his own preface to the text (see below).

[12] The point is probably that the mild ethical content in Section 6 of *Writings of an Old Man*, suitable as a family code, is not advanced in *Emerging from Meditation* which was presented as directly authored and not indirectly like *Writings of an Old Man*. It is likely that it was also not present in the presumedly provocative but lost work on Confucianism, which may very well have been known to the writer of this preface. Hence the question arose in his mind, we may fairly surmise, as to the consistency of Tominaga's standpoint. Was the latter himself purely critical in attitude, or did he also advance an ethical standpoint?

[13] A medicinal plant. In other words, the reader should extract the message for his own benefit.

[14] This cryptic instruction is not some kind of nature mysticism, but is probably meant to reinforce the idea that the reader must puzzle out the point of the writing for himself.

[15] The writer of this preface is identified by Mizuta as a medical practitioner named Kawai Ritsuboku (1708-1766) who was interested in meditation (Nakamura 1971, 141).

[16] These names appear in the *yang* and *yin* seals respectively. The *yang* seal is red on white while the *yin* seal (here in brackets) is white on red.

Preface 3

In olden times there were Shintō, Confucianism and Buddhism, each setting out its teaching and leading people out of ignorance and self-indulgence so that they might gain illumination. Though customs change and manners vary the way itself remains strong and pure. Men and women rejoice in it, those who expound it heave sighs of praise over it, the chroniclers[17] preserve it, those of later generations who model themselves on the way also recommend it, dissenting voices are put down, and the intelligent and the incompetent alike all appeal to it. An astute person has now resolved to speak up about it and will bring about a big change for these people. Putting it frankly, this way has come down to us as the best of its kind, surpassing all others, a way which both then and now has but a single pivot. Thus why should there be any difference between the present standpoint and the three teachings? As I have many duties towards my father I did not yet have the leisure to turn this over slowly in my mind. It may be that people will now hear this wise man's way: how though customs change and manners vary, the way itself remains strong and pure, how men and women rejoice in it and those who expound it all heave sighs of praise over it, how the chroniclers all preserve the way while expanding it and increasing it,[18] and whether it is the same as the three teachings or not, and whether it should be accepted or not. In the present-day world those who model themselves on the way are few. However, whether to model oneself on it or not is not a matter of contention. When I consider the wise man's teaching, there will surely be someone on earth who will praise and promote it. If this teaching is once heard and conveyed to the people, they will understand about right and wrong for themselves, and there will be no mistake at the beginning, in the middle or at

[17] Chroniclers: literally 'green historians' (*seishishi*). The term comes from the fresh green bamboo formerly used to make containers for keeping documents.

[18] The idea of 'expanding and increasing' (*chōdai*) picks up one of Tominaga's basic points about the way in which tradition is expanded through being expounded, cf. *Writings of an Old Man* Section 9 and also *Emerging from Meditation* Chapter 11, where the term *chō* is used as part of a more complex discussion of types of language. It will be observed that the idea is slyly introduced here into what is otherwise a repeat of the third sentence of this preface.

the end. This profound statement, shared by myself and others, should be of great assistance on this earth. Yes indeed, the people should know this way. With this way of today[19] there would be no difficulty in changing the manner of people's lives. However only this wise man could practise the way consistently. I do not know whether it was so fine long ago when the three teachings arose. In the spring of the third year,[20] in the third month, people from the neighbourhood who were discussing the wise man's statement, saying that it should be promoted through the world and used as a charter for the people, asked me to write a preface. My words are most pedestrian as I am without talent. Although without talent, shall I now be alone with the wise man in being of one mind with the way?

Written at Kako by Tomo Rei Genkan.
Hakushi (Seika An).[21]

Writings of an Old Man

<Tominaga's Preface>

This writing was lent to me by a friend to look at who said it was composed by an Old Man. Though the world is said to be going downhill, it is notable that an Old Man such as this can still be found. In his teaching he stresses that there is a way of truth apart from the ways of the three teachings. As there could be no possible harm or mistake in following and practising his instructions I found I came into full agreement with this Old Man. Although I asked what the Old Man's name might be, I was told that it was not known, regrettably enough. He must be one of those like there used to be in olden times, living in obscurity but saying what he likes. With a view to

[19] By 'way of today' is meant 'way of truth' (cf. note 10 above), unencumbered by the miscellaneous cultural baggage of other times. Cf. especially *Writings of an Old Man* Section 1.

[20] This could either be the third year of Genbun (1738), in which case it implies that this preface was written in the same year as Tominaga's own (though the latter was as late as the eleventh month); or else it would be the third year of Kanpei (1743); i.e. shortly before Preface 1 (by Hayashi) was written.

[21] Cf. note 16 above. This preface is not dated at the end, but cf. the text and note 20 above.

adopting it as my household teaching, and to passing it on to others, I have copied it down from beginning to end.

Eleventh month of the third year of Genbun (1738).
Nakamoto of the Tomo.

1 In the world today one learns that the three ways of Buddhism, Confucianism and Shintō are the three teachings of India, China and Japan respectively.[22] Some people say that these three coincide, while others dispute about the rights and wrongs of each.[23] However, the way which should be called the way of ways is a special one, and it should be recognised that none of the ways of these three teachings brings the true way[24] to realisation. In any case, Buddhism is the way of India, and Confucianism is the way of China,[25] and because of the difference of country they are not the way of Japan.[26] Shintō is the way of Japan, but because it is of a different age it is not the way of today's world. The way should be the way even if the country is different or the age is different, but the very meaning of the term 'way of ways' lies in that it is to be

[22] Buddhism, Confucianism and Shintō: *shinjubutsu no michi*, that is, Shintō, Judō and Butsudō. The phrase could be translated more literally as 'the ways of the gods, of Confucius and of the Buddha'. However for Tominaga these were clearly terms which referred respectively to each of three systems of teaching and practice.

[23] Buddhism and Confucianism had been loosely conflated into a single state ideology by Prince Shōtoku (573-621), a conflation which has lived on into the twentieth century in the teachings of the *Wa-shū* (Harmony Sect) based on the Shitennō Temple of Ōsaka (building commenced in AD 593). Similarly Shintō had been closely connected with Buddhism in architecture, ritual and doctrine (cf. Section 12 below and notes thereon). However by Tominaga's time the three traditions had also come to be seen as autonomous traditions, as is clear from the frequently adopted independent stance of Shintō and Confucian specialists alike.

[24] *Makoto no michi*: this could also be translated, putting more emphasis on *makoto*, as 'the way of truth'. *Makoto* also strongly conveys the meaning of inward sincerity.

[25] India, China: the names used by Tominaga were Tenjiku and Kara respectively, which to a modern Japanese have the same flavour as, for example, Cathay to a modern English reader. However these names would appear more natural to a reader in Tominaga's own time and hence are translated here with the modern English equivalents.

[26] The three countries correspond to the three religions in question here. However it was common to regard these as the three countries which matter. Recognition of more complexity in East Asian cultural geography is evidenced in Tominaga's preface to *Emerging from Meditation*.

practised, and therefore a way which cannot be practised is not the true way. It must be admitted that none of the three teachings is a way which can be practised in present-day Japan.

2 The Buddhists copy[27] Indian manners to discipline themselves and save others, but nobody can be found who preaches in Sanskrit, nor listeners who understand it. Still less is it conceivable to make everything from household articles to buildings just like in India. The Indians make a polite salutation by pressing the palms of the hands together while one side of the body is uncovered,[28] and it is not thought discourteous to expose the thighs or the knees. Even in a sūtra it says 'ankles and knees bare, genitals stored away like a horse'.[29] Thus even the unclean backside can be openly shown. The Buddhists here should all do this kind of thing too, without any hesitation.

Comment:

The Buddha taught as follows: 'If these instructions of mine are regarded as impure in some other place it will not be wrong not to follow them; if in some other place there are instructions different from mine about what is pure, they should be followed.'[30] The Buddha by no means taught that one should change the customs of one's own country in imitation of India. On the contrary, when Japanese Buddhists do all kinds of things which are not suitable in this country simply to imitate India, they are not following his way. This the Old Man dislikes and ridicules.

3 On the same principle, since meat is an important food in China the Confucianists should raise cattle and sheep for their

[27] *Manabite*: Katō has 'learning', but Mizuta makes a point of saying that the word here means not 'to learn' but 'to imitate' (Nakamura 1971, 147).

[28] This reflects routine accounts in the Buddhist scriptures where monks go forward to the Buddha to ask a question.

[29] This expression is found in Chapter 1 of the *Muryōgi Sūtra*. Similarity to a horse in this respect is one of the thirty-two marks of a 'great being' (*mahāpuruṣa*) or Buddha.

[30] Mizuta could only identify an analogous passage in Buddhist scripture, so perhaps Tominaga was quoting from memory or just paraphrasing to suit his argument. The passage runs: 'If there is something which I decree which in another place is regarded as impure then you should not do it, but if there is something not decreed by me which in another place is regarded as essential to practice then you should do it.' *Gobunritsu* 22, cf. Nakamura 1971, 148.

consumption.[31] Moreover the menu should be composed with reference to the chapter on 'Inner Rules' in the *Book of Rites*. At weddings they should perform the ceremony of Fetching the Bride,[32] and at funerals and so on they should have representatives for their deceased.[33] Similarly for clothes: they should wear Chinese costume and a Confucian hat on their heads. It is not Chinese style to wear our kind of formal dress[34] and to smooth down the hair. Confucianists should read Chinese characters in their Chinese pronunciation.[35] Since there are various kinds of Chinese pronunciation they should copy the pronunciation of the state of Lu in the Chou period.[36] Since there are many styles of Chinese characters they should write with one of the most ancient styles.[37]

Comment:

With sayings like: 'Follow the barbarians when staying with the barbarians', and 'It is good manners to follow the customs', and 'King Yü stripped when he went to the country of naked people',[38] not even the Confucianists say that one should change a country's custom in imitation of China. On the contrary, when Japanese Confucianists do things alien to this country, merely in imitation of China, they are not in accord with the true Confucian way.

[31] Cattle and sheep were not kept by the Japanese at that time, and although some cattle are now kept in twentieth-century Japan this is not the result of Tominaga's ironic advice.

[32] The custom was for the bridegroom to go to meet the bride personally from her parent's house. Cf. Nakamura 1971, 149.

[33] Grandsons were usually expected to perfom this role. Cf. Ienaga *et al.* 1966, 549 and 565.

[34] *Kamishimo*.

[35] Chinese characters or ideographs make up a significant proportion of written Japanese and in principle can either be pronounced as syllables derived from Chinese or as native Japanese words. Tominaga says that the Confucianists should restrict themselves to the former, which would give them a hard time.

[36] I.e. the pronunciation supposedly used by Confucius.

[37] *Kobun, chūbun, kato no bun nado* ... The point of mentioning these three types as examples of what they should use is that they were already out of date by the Han period when the Japanese first took over Chinese writing. Katō (ad loc.) explains the types mentioned at some length.

[38] Mizuta identifies approximate parallels to these apparently abbreviated quotations in the *Chung Yung* (*Book of the Mean*), the *Li chi* (*Book of Rites*) and the *Lü Shih Ch'un Ch'iu*, Nakamura 1971, 150.

4 It is just the same with ancient Japan, for then it was polite to greet people by clapping the hands and bowing four times,[39] food used to be served using oak leaves as dishes,[40] and when mourning people sang and wept after which they performed a purification at the river-side.[41] People learning Shintō should practise each and every one of these exactly as in the old days. The coins used in today's world were not there in the original age of the gods, so Shintoists really ought to give up using them and throw them away. Today's dress too, the Wu style, is modelled on that of the Chinese state of Wu, and so it would be well if Shintoists stopped wearing it.[42] They should also learn up the old words of various things from the age of the gods and call everything differently, for example saying *kazo* for father, *iroha* for mother, *sore* for you, *shiraha* for dress, *haha* for snake and *atsushireru* for sick.[43] They should give themselves different personal names too, such as so-and-so-*hiko-no-mikoto* or so-and-so-*hime-no-mikoto*.[44]

Comment:

It is said that the left should not be changed into the right, nor the right into the left, so even Shintō does not command us to change present-day customs into those of long ago. On the contrary, to model everything on ancient times and only to behave in a queer way as Shintoists do today is not in accordance with the Shintō way. Lord Minister Nonomiya[45] is said to have stated that Shintō today is just a collection of rites and not true Shintō. Indeed the three ways today are nothing

[39] The etiquette of Shintō worship of the *kami* is said to be a survival of an ancient elaborate form of greeting towards superiors. Cf. Nakamura 1971, 151.

[40] As a matter of fact the use of oak leaves as a base for serving certain kinds of traditional cake can still be seen in the twentieth century, but it was clearly quite impractical for ordinary food in Tominaga's day, particularly from the point of view of a soya sauce manufacturer's son.

[41] An ironic challenge to Shintoists to take up pre-Buddhist funeral rites again.

[42] *Gofuku* originally meant clothing in the style of Go (Chinese: Wu), but came to mean clothing generally. Giving it up would be rather like giving up western dress (*yōfuku*) today.

[43] These words are indeed completely different from those used in Tominaga's day.

[44] Archaic endings which frequently occurred in Japanese antiquity.

[45] Nonomiya Sadamoto (1669-1711) wrote various works, including one in response to Arai Hakuseki, but the source of this particular saying is unknown and may just be an oral recollection.

but trifling bagatelles, whether Shintoist, Confucianist or Buddhist, and not the true Shintō, Confucianism and Buddhism. If it had not been for the writings of this Old Man and the words of the Lord Minister I might not have realised this myself.

5 When I speak like this it may sound as though I am twisting and mocking everything, yet when we learn those ways we are told that everything does have to be just like that. But to make it clear, just think how difficult it is to adopt the customs of a place as near as five or ten leagues away, so how much more difficult it is to take over Chinese or Indian ways in Japan. Or again, there are very few people who can remember things even as recent as five or ten years ago, so it is even harder to learn things from the age of the gods for today. Such efforts are both difficult and foolish. Even if things are well learned and starkly set out without any alteration, the people would fail to see any point in them for the world of today. Therefore none of these three teachings is the way of ways which should be practised in present-day Japan. A way which cannot be practised is not the way in which the true way is realised.

6 As to the way of truth, the way which should be practised in present-day Japan, it is simply to perform our evident duty in everything, to give priority to the tasks of the day, to maintain an upright heart and correct conduct, to be restrained in speech and bearing, and, if we have parents, to serve and honour them well.

A note by the Old Man says:

See the <Buddhist> *Rokkōhaikyō*, which emphasises the five relations.[46] The Confucianists also consider them important.

[46] *Rokkōhaikyō*: the Buddhist *Śīgālovāda Sūtra* (Pali: *Singalovāda Sutta*) which is well-known for its instructions to lay believers. In this text the ethical relationships are related to the four quarters of the compass and to heaven and earth. Strictly speaking the 'five relations' are a Confucian formulation, as for example in Mencius: '... between father and son there should be affection; between lord and follower there should be righteousness; between husband and wife there should be distinction of duties, between old and young there should be proper order, and between friends there should be faithfulness.' Cf. Legge 1970, 251-2.

> The <Shintō> *Shinryō* also refers to them.[47] Thus the way of truth is an indispensable feature of the way of the three teachings.

Those who have masters should be devoted to them, those who have children should teach them well, those who have retainers should manage them well. Those who have husbands should obey them well, and those who have wives should lead them well. Those who have elder brothers should respect them, and those who have younger brothers should have sympathy for them. Old people should be treated with affection, and infants should be lovingly cared for. Do not forget to revere your ancestors, and do not treat the intimacy of the home lightly. Be keenly sincere in dealings with others. Do not indulge in wrongful pleasures. Respect outstanding people, but do not despise foolish people. All in all treat others as yourself and do not harm them. Do not be scathing and harsh. Do not be prejudiced and stubborn. Do not be importunate and impatient. If in anger, do not exaggerate it, and if rejoicing, do not lose control of yourself. Do not go so far as lewdness in pleasure or abandonment in grief. Whether things are sufficient or insufficient, consider them all as your good fortune and be satisfied. Do not take even a speck of dust which you should not receive, and if you have to give something up, do not begrudge it, even high state office. Let the quality of your food and clothing be appropriate to status. Do not be extravagant or stingy. Do not steal or lie. Do not be led astray by amorous desire nor confused by drinking. Do not kill people who do not harm others. Take care over your nourishment: do not eat bad things or eat too much.

A note by the Old Man says:

> In the <Buddhist> *Yuga* <Treatise> it says, 'There are nine causes of premature death: firstly, eating too much, secondly, eating at the wrong time, thirdly, eating again before there has been time for digestion' and so on.[48] The <Confucian> *Analects* also say, 'Do not eat when the cut is not right, do not eat when

[47] *Shinryō*, or *Jinryō*, short for *Jingiryō*. The passage adduced by Mizuta does not however match up closely with the Confucian relations. Cf. Nakamura 1971, 156.

[48] *Yugashijiron: Yogācārabhūmi*.

the time is not right, do not eat too much', and so on.[49] Both of these show knowledge of the way of truth.

If you have leisure, learn arts which benefit your person, and strive to become wise.

A note by the Old Man says:

The *Analects* say, 'Energy remaining after the fulfilment of duty should be used in study.'[50] The <Buddhist> *Vinaya* also says, 'Writings may be studied for knowledge of protocol and precedence in assemblies, and new monks are permitted to learn arithmetic.'[51] These also show knowledge of the way of truth.

To write with today's script, use today's language, eat today's food, wear today's clothes, use today's utensils, live in today's buildings, follow today's customs, observe today's regulations, mingle with today's people, to avoid all the bad things and do the good things, – this may be called the way of truth, and it is the way which should be practised in present-day Japan.

Comment:

These things have all been expounded in Buddhist and Confucian works and so do not need to be spelled out again in detail. However the Old Man has declared them afresh, in his own way, discarding what is useless for people and pointing out the way of truth directly. His intention is truly commendable.

7 Now this way of truth did not originally come from India. Nor has it been handed on from China. Nor was it something originating in the age of the gods to be learned in the world of today. It did not come down from heaven, nor rise up from the earth. It only concerns the people of today. If you observe it, people will rejoice, and you yourself will feel cheerful and able to manage things without any difficulties. If you do not observe it, people will be displeased, and you yourself will feel cheerless and meet ever-increasing obstacles in everything you do.

[49] Tominaga abbreviates drastically from *Analects* X 8, cf. Legge 1893, 232.
[50] *Analects* I 6, cf. Legge 1893, 140.
[51] Mizuta gives separate sources for the two halves of this quotation: *Gobunritsu* 26 and *Shibunritsu* 52.

Therefore it will not do not to observe it. It arises from what is natural for people and is not made up as some deliberate, spurious temporary trickery. Thus all those who have been born in the world at the present time, even including those who learn the three teachings, will have difficulty getting through even a single day if they reject this way of truth.

8 There is plenty to show that it is difficult to reject this way of truth and come up with some other way. Śākyamuni[52] taught the five precepts,[53] and he taught the ten virtues.[54] He named greed, anger and stupidity as the three poisons.[55] In one of the three blessings he included 'filial devotion to parents, respectful service to teachers and elders'.[56] He also taught, 'avoid all bad deeds, respect and practise everything good, purify your own mind; this is the teaching of all the Buddhas'.[57] Confucius also taught 'filial piety, brotherliness, loyalty and trust' and 'loyalty, faithfulness, kindness and respect'.[58] He named wisdom, benevolence and courage the three virtues.[59] He also taught 'control anger, close off desire, overcome faults, turn to goodness'.[60] He also taught 'The

[52] Tominaga uses the proper name Śākyamuni in its abbreviated transliteration Shaka. Katō (ad loc.) has 'Buddha', no doubt to help western readers, but obscuring the nuance in favour of the Buddha as a historical figure rather than as the timeless religious principle which he tended to become. To say 'Śākyamuni' is somewhat like referring to 'Jesus' rather than to 'Christ'.

[53] The 'five precepts' are basic moral teaching for house-holders: do not kill, do not steal, do not commit sexual immorality, do not lie, do not take intoxicants. These instructions are more commonly taught in Theravāda Buddhism, and from a Mahāyāna point of view are associated with 'Hīnayāna' Buddhism.

[54] The 'ten virtues' consist in avoiding the 'ten evils': killing, stealing, sexual immorality, lying, two-facedness, slander, fancy talk, greed, anger and heresy. The first four overlap the first four of the five precepts.

[55] The 'three poisons' are also referred to as the 'three fires', the 'three grimes', and the 'three roots of evil'.

[56] The 'three blessings' are worldly morality, observing the monastic precepts and 'the good root of practice and conversion'. Cf. Nakamura 1971, 159.

[57] This phrasing is found in various texts. The fact that Tominaga does not indicate a specific source for any of these Buddhist formulations shows that he presumes them to be very well known to his readers.

[58] The first phrase conflates two separate phrases from the *Analects*, and the second is found in the *Tso Chuan*. Cf. Nakamura 1971, 159.

[59] So named in the *Chung Yung*, cf. Legge 1893, 407.

[60] These have not been identified as a list and probably reflect Tominaga's own conflation of ideas from the *Analects*.

superior man is composed and broad-minded, while the small-minded man is always miserable.'[61] The Shintō people also teach purity, simplicity and honesty. These are all wise sayings in accordance with the way of truth, all approximately the same and with nothing wrong in them. Thus those who learn the three teachings may also be regarded as followers of the way of truth, but only if they understand them in this way and live in this world with other people without behaving in a wrong, weird and extravagant manner.

Comment:

Here the Old Man is expressing his basic attitude. He is by no means arguing that the three teachings should be discarded. He just says that the way of truth should be put into practice.

9 But here this old man would like to make his point. Since ancient times it has generally been the case that those who preach a moral way and establish a law of life[62] have had somebody whom they have held up as an authoritative precursor, while at the same time they have tried to emerge above those who went before.[63] Later generations however, being unaware of this regular practice, are quite confused by it.

10 Śākyamuni[64] regarded six buddhas as his precursors, and of these he recalled Dīpaṇkara[65] when exhorting people to depart birth-and-death;[66] but in so doing he emerged above

[61] *Analects* VII 36, cf. Legge 1893, 207.

[62] 'Moral way' is a slightly expanded translation for *michi*, which literally means 'way', to take account of the complementary relation with 'law of life'; the latter phrase is a similarly expanded translation for *hō*, literally meaning 'law' but having the connotation here of Dharma in a Buddhist sense.

[63] This is a key statement of Tominaga's theory as put into the mouth of the Old Man. Mizuta rightly relates it to the concept of *kajō*, expounded at length in *Emerging from Meditation*. Cf. Nakamura 1971, 160.

[64] Śākyamuni: the historical Buddha, cf. note 52 above.

[65] According to Buddhist mythology the six previous Buddhas all followed identical courses. Note however that it is not these mythical Buddhas which illustrate Tominaga's theory: his point is made through the relation between the historical Buddha and non-Buddhist teachers.

[66] I.e. *saṃsāra*, the succession of karmically determined existences.

those earlier non-Buddhist teachers[67] who saw the devas as their precursors, preaching rebirth in the heavens through disciplined reliance upon them. Each of those earlier non-Buddhists had also emerged above others. Thus Udraka, with his teaching of 'nor non-conception',[68] emerged above Ālāra's 'plane of non-existence'.[69] The teaching of the 'plane of non-existence' emerged above the prior teaching of the 'plane of consciousness'. That teaching of the 'plane of consciousness' also emerged above[70] the ones before it such as the 'plane of emptiness' and the 'self-abiding heaven'.[71] It was in this way that they gradually came out with the exposition of the thirty-two heavens. These were all non-Buddhists, but within the same Buddha-Darma of Śākyamuni the Mañjuśrī school produced the Mahāyāna *prajñā* <sūtras>,[72] and in their exposition of 'emptiness' they emerged above the teaching of 'being' expounded by the Kāśpaya school who had produced the *Āgama* sūtras.[73] The Fugen school produced the *Lotus Sūtra*, the *Jinmitsu Sūtra* and so on,[74] teaching 'not emptiness but being itself', as if this were the message of the Buddha's sermons during the forty years after his enlightenment, but this again emerged over above the Mañjuśrī teaching of emptiness. Next came those who produced the *Kegon Sūtra*, saying that it was the teaching of the Buddha in the first two

67 'Non-Buddhist' is used here, following Katō, for the Japanese *gedō*, meaning 'external ways', that is, ways external to the Buddha-Way. Cf. also *Emerging from Meditation* Chapter 1 (especially note 9) and Chapter 22 (*passim*) where the term 'heterodoxy' is used.

68 Udraka: Udraka-Rāmaputra. 'Nor non-conception', is short for 'neither conception nor non-conception'.

69 On these concepts and those following below cf. the opening passage of *Emerging from Meditation*.

70 Mizuta's paraphrase and annotation brings in the expression *kajō* (cf. note 63 above), rightly linking up with the thought of *Emerging from Meditation* (Nakamura 1971, 161 and 164). Cf. also the same phrasing a few lines later.

71 'Self-abiding heaven': *jizaiten*. *Jizai* translates the Sanskrit Iśvara as a proper name for the presiding deity of the highest of the eighteen heavens of the world of form. However in this context the conceptual associations are of some significance and therefore a literal translation is given.

72 The ascription of the sūtras making a special virtue of 'the perfection of insight' (*prajñāpāramitā*) to the bodhisattva Mañjuśrī is of course non-historical.

73 These sūtras are the equivalent of the Pali *suttas*.

74 Fugen, Samantabhadra in Sanskrit, is a mythical bodhisattva who came to be associated with the *Lotus Sūtra* and the *Sandhinirmocana* (*Gejinmitsu*, abbreviated to *Jinmitsu*) *Sūtra*.

weeks after his enlightenment, like the sun's disc first illuminating the tops of the mountains. This too, while being ascribed to the time just after the Buddha's enlightenment, emerged on the basis of the teachings which had gone before. Next came those who produced the *Nirvāṇa Sūtra*, saying that it consisted of the sermons given in the one day and night of the Buddha's nirvāṇa, like the very ghee pressed out of the milk, while in fact it brought together the existing teachings and emerged above them. When Kongōsatta ascribed his teaching to the Tathāgata Dainichi,[75] putting the *Lotus Sūtra* at the eighth stage and the *Kegon Sūtra* at the ninth stage, and saying that Śākyamuni's teachings were only provisional teachings, this meant that it emerged above the very topmost by cutting loose from all the other teachings. Again, in the sūtras teaching sudden enlightenment we read things like, 'When all the passions disappear of themselves and not one discriminative thought arises, that is enlightenment'[76] and so on, while according to the Zen sect the sūtra scrolls representing forty years of the Buddha's teaching are just strips of toilet paper, and so on.[77] This amounts to emerging above the topmost by the destruction of all the other teachings.[78] When, being unaware of this, Bodhiruci[79] argued that one sermon uttered by Śākyamuni was heard in various ways, Tendai[80] argued that Śākyamuni changed his teaching

[75] Kongōsatta, Vajrasattva in Sanskrit (appearing as Kongōshu in Chapter 2 of *Emerging from Meditation*), is a mythical intermediary in the transmission of 'esoteric Buddhism'. Dainichi Nyorai, Mahāvairocana Tathāgata in Sanskrit, is the central deity (in effect, though a mythical Buddha) in Shingon Buddhism.

[76] The teaching of 'sudden enlightenment' arises on the basis of the idea that it is illogical to expect to achieve a qualitatively different state gradually. The point being made here is that this thought is bad news for those who have previously been expounding the need for steady progress along the religious path. The quotation is probably from the *Kegon Sūtra* (cf. Nakamura 1971, 165).

[77] This idea finds expression in *Rinzairoku* 10.

[78] Katō breaks off for a new paragraph here, which is not justified by the original edition of the text.

[79] Bodhiruci was an Indian monk active as a translator and teacher in northern China in the sixth century AD.

[80] Tendai (Chinese T'ien T'ai): honorific name for the founder of the T'ien T'ai school in China. Otherwise known as Chih-I (538-597) he was responsible for one of the most influential classifications of Buddhist scriptures, arranged to stress the preeminence of the *Lotus Sūtra*, against which Tominaga's historical criticism provides an irreversible antidote. On the details of Chih-I's

to suit the circumstances[81] five times during his lifetime, and Genju[82] said that the people understood what was passed down in various different ways according to their dispositions, these were all serious misunderstandings and distortions. Anybody wishing to know more about this should refer to the book entitled *Shutsujō <Emerging from Meditation>*.[83]

11 Similarly when Confucius regarded Yao and Shun[84] as his precursors and expounded the way of kings in admiration of kings Wen and Wu,[85] he was emerging above the current whole-hearted devotion to the way of the five nobles such as Huan of Ch'i and Wen of Chin.[86] When Mo Tzŭ[87] stressed the way of the Hsia <Dynasty> out of reverence for Yao and Shun he thereby emerged above Confucius' admiration of Wen and Wu. Next came Yang Chu[88] who expounded the imperial way in admiration of the Yellow Emperor,[89] and thus emerged above the way of kings taught by Confucius and Mo Tzŭ. When Hsü Hsing expounded Shên Nung[90] and when Chuang <Tzŭ>,

thought, magnificent in its way, see Petzold 1979 (posthumous), especially 1-37, and Hurvitz 1962.

81 Tominaga uses the term *hōben* (skilful means) here. See notes 110 and 115 below.

82 Genju (Chinese Hsien Shou) is another name for Hōzō (Chinese Fa Ts'ang) (643-712), identified in particular with the Kegon (Chinese Hua Yen) school.

83 The abbreviated form of the title (*Shutsujō* for *Shutsujōkōgo*) found in the text here is the basis for the convenient English title *Emerging from Meditation*.

84 Legendary rulers in ancient China (Hsia Dynasty). Yao is reckoned to have died in 2258 BC and Shun, his appointed successor, in 2208 BC. Shun is particularly revered as a model of filial piety.

85 'The way of kings' is a phrase implying virtuous government. King Wen is the posthumous title of the Duke of Chou (1231-1135 BC) whose son King Wu (1169-1116 BC) brought the Shang Dynasty to an end by conquest.

86 Two of 'the five nobles', rulers of the five major states in the Warring States period.

87 Mo Tzŭ (470-381 BC), otherwise known as Mo Ti, propounded a teaching of universal love as the basis for political organisation which, he believed, would lead to the elimination of strife and oppression.

88 Yang Chu was a thinker of the fourth century BC who is known, however, only through the works of others. Mencius contrasted his epousal of ethical egoism with the universal altruism of Mo Tzŭ.

89 Huang Ti, the celebrated legendary ruler supposedly of even greater antiquity (2698-2598 BC) than Yao and Shun. Tominaga's point is that successive thinkers sought models of ever greater antiquity to go one better than their forbears.

90 According to Mencius Hsü Hsing taught that ruler and subject should work side by side in the fields. Nung legendarily reigned before Huang Ti (previous note) and taught the arts of agriculture and herbal medicine.

Lieh <Tzŭ> and their set acclaimed the long distant times of Wu Huai and Ko T'ien[91] they were all trying to come out above each other. These latter were all heretics anyway,[92] but even within the way of Confucius it is said that scholars divided into eight, so that while they all appealed to Confucius they also sought to come out above each other. Kao Tzŭ taught that 'human nature is neither good nor bad', thus going beyond the teaching of Shih Tzŭ that 'human nature is both good and bad'.[93] Then again Mencius' teaching that human nature is good was an advance on Kao Tzŭ's teaching that 'human nature is neither good nor bad', and Hsün Tzŭ's teaching that human nature is bad came out beyond Mencius' teaching that it is good.[94] When Lo Cheng Tzŭ wrote the *Canon of Filial Piety* appealing to the oral teaching of Ts'eng Tzŭ and emphasising filial piety, he in turn was discarding all kinds of ways and bringing them down to filial piety.[95] The Sung Confucianists did not notice this and thought that all these teachings were consistent, while recently Jinsai said that only Mencius received the bloodstream from Confucius and all the other teachings were false, and then again, Sorai said that the way of Confucius came directly from the way of the ancient kings but that Tzŭ Ssu, Mencius and the rest had departed from it and

[91] Chuang Tzŭ and Lieh Tzŭ are post-Confucian Taoist thinkers whose writings are supposedly assembled in works bearing the same names, but compiled centuries later. Wu Huai and Ko T'ien are legendary rulers presumed to have predated Yao and Shun.

[92] This is typical of Tominaga's irony. Though not without acclaim in Japan, as Chinese wise men of old, they were Taoists and not Confucianists. Tominaga playfully nears the position of the official orthodoxy of his time by calling them 'heretics' (*itan*); then he turns on the Confucianists. The point is all but lost in Katō's translations.

[93] Kao Tzŭ is known via Mencius as a protagonist in the debate on good and evil in human nature. He argued, for example, that human nature would flow in any direction, just like water, to which Mencius replied that it would not flow uphill; see Mencius Book VI (Legge 1895, 394-9). There remains little evidence for the thought of Shih Tzŭ who was a second-generation disciple of Confucius (Forke 1964, 188).

[94] The thought of Hsün Tzŭ (third century BC) is preserved in the work bearing his name. The essential point of his pessimistic appraisal of things is that because human nature is bad, ethical regulation is all the more necessary.

[95] Ts'eng Tzŭ was an eminent disciple of Confucius who is particularly known for radical filial piety, expressed in actions such as divorcing his wife for serving up badly-stewed pears to her mother-in-law. *The Canon of Filial Piety* (*Hsiao-Ching*) has been ascribed to Ts'eng himself as well as to his pupil Lo Cheng Tzŭ.

were all thoroughly mistaken.[96] Anybody wishing to know more about this should refer to the book entitled *Setsuhei* *<Teachings Determine>*.[97]

Comment:

Although the Old Man argues like this, Confucius expounded the way of kings in admiration of kings Wen and Wu because he grieved that people only respected the utilitarianism of the five nobles and that everything was running awry. He was not purposely trying to come out above others. Similarly, when Śākyamuni, regarding the six buddhas as his precursors, exhorted people to depart *saṃsāra*, it was because he grieved that the heretical ways taught before him all failed to be the true way.[98] He was not purposely trying to come out above others. If they were purposely trying to come out above others, in the way the Old Man puts it, Śākyamuni and Confucius would not be worth taking seriously.[99]

12 As for Shintō, in semi-antiquity they all claimed that it went back as far as the age of the gods and gave it the name of the way of Japan, thus trying to come out above Confucianism and Buddhism. To offer analogies, at the time of the deva

[96] The differences among early Confucianists were not of great importance to the Chinese Neo-Confucianist Chu Hsi, who was more interested in developing his own system. However they resurfaced for the Japanese critics Itō Jinsai (1627-1705) and Ogyū Sorai (1666-1728) when they tried to go back behind the Sung Confucianists. Tzŭ Ssu: grandson of Confucius and presumed author of *The Doctrine of the Mean* (*Chung Yung*).

[97] Just as the preceding section on Buddhist tradition was a thumbnail sketch of the contents of *Emerging from Meditation* so we may presume that the lost work *Setsuhei* was a similar work on the Confucian tradition, of which this section is in turn a summary. It is not difficult to imagine how Tominaga must have set one line of interpretation against another. Section 15 below gives further indications.

[98] The phrase used here is *shinjitsu no michi*. Compare *makoto no michi* in Section 1 above.

[99] Tominaga is of course not arguing against 'the Old Man' on this point (as he would be arguing against himself). The implication seems to be rather that Confucius and Śākyamuni were sincere enough in their efforts and not mere manipulators. The mechanics of superseding (*kajō*) are unconsciously carried through, and thus the Old Man's, i.e. Tominaga's theory, is a meta-theory (worthy of the name *Religionswissenschaft*).

Kōon[100] in India, or at the time of P'an Ku[101] in China, there was no fully-fledged, defined way which could be called Buddhism or Confucianism. If Buddhism and Confucianism were made up by people on purpose in later times, Shintō too could not have existed in an ancient age of the gods. What was given out first was called 'twofold combination'.[102] This was made by combining elements of Confucianism and Buddhism and adding or subtracting as desired. Next to appear were the 'stories of origin and manifestation'.[103] These were the work of Buddhists of the time who, jealous of the rise of Shintō, taught Shintō on the surface while inwardly redirecting it towards Buddhism. After that came what was called 'single great source'.[104] This was a departure from the way of Confucianism and Buddhism and only taught pure Shintō. While these three kinds of Shintō are all from semi-antiquity, there has recently appeared something called 'kingly way Shintō'.[105] According to this there is no such thing as a separate way known as Shintō. It teaches that the kingly way *is* Shintō. Yet again, there has appeared a Shintō which teaches Shintō on the surface and

[100] *Kōonten* is the deva Ābhāsvara, one of the eighteen divinities of the world of form in ancient Indian pre-Buddhist cosmology, from whose mouth sound streams forth in the form of light (Nakamura 1981, 387).

[101] P'an Ku is the first personified being to appear in ancient Chinese cosmology. 'He is often depicted as wielding a huge adze, and engaged in constructing the world. With his death the details of creation began. His breath became the wind; his voice, the thunder; his left eye, the sun; his right eye, the moon; his blood flowed in rivers; his hair grew into trees and plants; his flesh became the soil; his sweat descended as rain; the parasites which infested his body were the origin of the human race' (Giles 1898, 613-14).

[102] *Ryōbu shūgō*: the best-known version of this is Ryōbu Shintō (Dual Shintō) 'a term derived from the equation made between the two maṇḍalas of Shingon Buddhism and the Inner and outer Shrines at Ise' (Tsunoda *et al.* 1958, 269).

[103] *Honjaku engi*: legends devised by Buddhists to show that Buddhas or bodhisattvas were the origin or essence (*honji*) while Shintō divinities were their manifestations or traces (*suijaku*). Thus this way of thinking, current from the tenth century onwards, is usually called *honji suijaku*.

[104] *Yuiitsu sōgen*: otherwise known as Yuiitsu Shintō, this school of thought is primarily associated with Yoshida Kanetomo (1435-1511) who tried to turn the tables on *honji suijaku* interpretations by treating the Shintō gods as prior and the Buddhist bodhisattvas as manifestations (cf. Tsunoda *et al.* 1958, 271-2).

[105] *Ōdō shintō*: this was the point of view espoused by Hayashi Razan (1538-1657) in his work *Honchō Jinja Kō* (Study of Our Shintō Shrines). Hayashi even claimed that the first civilised rulers of Japan were Chinese immigrants (Tsunoda *et al.* 1958, 358).

inwardly is identical with Confucianism.[106] None of these existed in the age of the gods, but as explained, each was expounded to come out above the others. When foolish people today fail to realise this and think that one or other of these teachings is the true way, they wrong themselves and argue disputatiously with each other. This seems to an old man to be vexing, pitiful and ridiculous.

13 So the three teachings all have their propensities. One should realise this clearly and not be led astray.

14 The propensity of Buddhism is magic, for which people nowadays use the world *izuna*.[107] Indian people like it, so if one is proclaiming a way and teaching people they will not believe and follow unless they are led with an admixture of magic. For this reason Śākyamuni was good at *izuna* and it was in order to learn it that he went to the mountains for six years and practised austerities. Many of the sūtras mention supernatural transformations, supernatural knowledge and supernatural powers, which are all a kind of magic; for example, when the Buddha lit up three thousand worlds in the light of the ray from his forehead, or stretched out his tongue so widely and so far that it reached the heavens of Brahman,[108] or again when Vimalakīrti produced eighty-four thousand lion thrones within his chamber, or when the goddess turned Śāriputra into a woman,[109] these things were all done by magic. Then came the teaching of the various mysteries of the round of birth and death and of action and retribution, the stories of former lives of the Buddha and his disciples, the marvels of the Buddha and various other wonderful teachings, all of which were clever devices[110] to make the people believe. This was the way of guiding people in India and it is not so necessary in Japan.

[106] This probably refers, for example, to the views of Yamazaki Ansai (1618-1682). Cf. Ienaga *et al*. 1966, 558, and Tsunoda *et al*. 1958, 363ff).

[107] Katō explains that the word *izuna* comes from Izuna Shrine on Mount Togakushi (Katō 1967, 32). His translation 'sorcery' has an unduly sinister nuance, but Tominaga probably picked on the word *izuna* to suggest a slightly queer image which his readers would not respect highly.

[108] These feats are part of the mythological scenario of various Mahāyāna sūtras such as the *Lotus Sūtra* (Chapter I).

[109] For these performances see *The Teaching of Vimalakīrti* in any version (e.g. Fischer and Yokota 1944, Lamotte 1962 or Thurman 1976), chs 6 and 7.

[110] The standard Buddhist term *hōben* is used here which normally means a skilfully adapted expression of teaching or, for short, 'skilful means' (cf. Pye 1978). However Tominaga uses it in a rather pejorative sense.

Comment:

The Old Man puts it this way but really there is a difference between supernatural knowledge and *izuna*. *Izuna* is derived from technique while supernatural knowledge comes from austerities.[111] However, what he says is true enough.[112]

15 The propensity of Confucianism is high-flown language, which we nowadays call eloquence. China is a country which likes this, so if one is proclaiming a way and guiding people they will not believe and follow unless it is cleverly used. This can be seen, for example, with the explanation of the word 'rites', which originally referred to the ceremonies of coming of age, marriage, mourning and veneration, but was extended to human relations[113] when it was said 'a man's son is his rite, a man's retainer is his rite'! then it was used for how to see, hear, speak and move; then it was even applied to the universe when rites were said to be the principle of heaven and earth. It was the same with the word 'music' which at first just meant the amusement of playing bells and drums but then was said to mean not just the playing of bells and drums but the harmony of heaven and earth. It was the same again with the word 'sage' which at first just referred to a wise man but then was extended to mean the highest kind of person, capable of supernatural transformations. Confucius emphasised benevolence. Ts'eng Tzŭ emphasised benevolence and righteousness, Tzŭ Ssu emphasised sincerity, Mencius expounded the four principles and the goodness of human nature. Hsün Tzŭ expounded the badness of human nature, the *Canon of Filial Piety* taught filial piety, the *Great Learning* taught where value should be placed, and the *Book of Changes* expounded the two principles of the universe;[114] all of these were simple

[111] 'Technique' or 'art' is *jutsu*, as in *genjutsu* 'the propensity of Buddhism', translated above as 'magic'. Supernatural knowledge (*jintsū*) stands representatively here for the supernatural transformations, knowledge and powers mentioned above.

[112] Tominaga has deliberately referred to supernatural powers in a Buddhist context as *izuna*. By using the device of a comment to say that there is some difference he merely emphasises the provocativeness of the comparison.

[113] *Hito no michi*: literally 'the way of man'.

[114] For the above mentioned persons see Section 11 above and the notes thereto. The term translated here as 'two principles of the universe' is *kenkon*, which refers to heaven and earth or to *yin* and *yang*.

matters set forth with mountainous rhetoric, clever devices[115] to make people think it interesting and make them follow. China's high-flown language, just like India's magic, is not so necessary in Japan.

Comment:

Although the Old Man argued that these things were all really very easy, he must have known that the way is not within easy reach. Also the Old Man surely knew that there are some mysteries which are not easily passed on. So one should not be led astray by the Old Man's words and lose sight of his main point.

16 As to the propensity of Shintō, it is mysteriousness, esotericism and secret transmission, the bad habit of simply concealing things. Concealing everything is the root of lying and stealing, so that while magic is interesting to see and high-flown language is pleasant to hear, and therefore more or less forgivable, just this habit of concealment is very much worse. Long ago, when people were honest, some secrecy may have been helpful in teaching and guiding them, but in these latter times of today[116] when the number of people lying and stealing has increased it is outrageous for people teaching Shintō to give perverse protection to such evils. Even in such wretched matters as farce acting and tea ceremony they all copy this secrecy, inventing certificates of initiation, even setting a price on it and generally making a business of it. It is quite deplorable. Moreover when asked why they make up all this, they say it is because it is too difficult to pass things on to those whose ability has not matured. Although this argument may sound plausible, we should realise that ways which are kept hidden, difficult to transmit, and passed on for a fixed price, are none of them the true way.

End of *Writings of an Old Man*

115 The term *hōben* (see Section 10, note 81 and note 110 above) is here transferred from the Buddhist to the Confucian context. Thus it appears to be one of the terms which enables Tominaga to perceive all phases of a tradition of religious teaching as relative.

116 Although Tominaga's phrase here is *sue no yo* the character for *sue* immediately suggests the Buddhist term *mappō*, the age of latter Dharma when mankind becomes increasingly decadent. Cf. p. 33 above.

Emerging from Meditation and then Speaking

Preface

When I was young and had time, I was able to read the writings of Confucianism, and later on when I had time I also read the writings of Buddhism.[1] Thus I can now say that the ways of Confucianism and Buddhism are both alike in that the point of them lies in establishing the good. Yet on the other hand when we try to trace the meaning of the Way in detail we find that we do not get the teaching at all.[2] We cannot do so because there are no writings which directly pertain to it. This state of affairs gave me the idea of 'Emerging from Meditation'.[3] I had this argument in my mind for ten years,

[1] On the justification for the renderings 'Confucianism' and 'Buddhism' cf., for example, the closing paragraph of Chapter 1 below, where the teachings identified with Confucius and the Buddha are clearly regarded as recognisable, extended sequences of tradition which are considered by the followers to be authoritative. Kyōdo renders the terms into modern Japanese as *jukyō* and *bukkyō*, respectively, without discernible hesitation. On the general question of the importation of modern, reifying concepts see also Pye 1983.

[2] The term *innen*, usually meaning karmic causality, is taken by all Japanese interpreters here as a verb meaning to trace in detail. Opinions diverge however as to whether the 'way' mentioned here is the common 'way' (i.e. the 'way of ways' referred to in *Writings of an Old Man*) or the Way in a more precisely Buddhist sense. Similarly, while the text simply refers to 'the teaching' or 'the expositions' (*setsu*), it is possible and even likely that it refers to the presumed teaching of the Buddha himself (*bussetsu*). *Setsu* frequently appears in the titles of sūtras purporting to be the Buddha's teaching. See further in the following sentence and the following note.

[3] 'Emerging from Meditation' (*shutsujō*) is Tominaga's own abbreviation of the title of his work. The term *shutsujō* is explained by him at the end of Chapter 18, the point being that expositions provided by various monks neither directly touch the Buddha's meaning, nor however do they impede it, and indeed there is much to be said for them. This relativism was inevitable as a consequence of the Buddha's 'emerging from meditation' and 'afterwards

and when I spoke to people about it they were all very vague. As the years accrued to my age, my hair began to whiten. Everybody took the Confucian and Buddhist way to be just as they appear, Confucian and Buddhist, and there seemed no point in discussing it.[4] Alas, my body is worthless and sick, and I cannot be of any help to anybody. As I am nearing my end, should this matter not be passed on? I am now already more than thirty years old, and I cannot refrain from reporting it. I hope that those who take it up will tell it to many, passing it on to Korea and China, from Korea and China to the peoples west of China, and on to the land of Śākyamuni's divine descent.[5] If it helps the people to be illumined by the Way, then my death will not be a mere putrefaction. It may be said on the other hand that this is a bad kind of wisdom, which is a difficult question.[6] As to this, I will await the combined efforts and supplementary work of later scholars.[7]

First Year of Enkyō (1744)[8] Autumn, Eighth Month,
Tominaga Nakamoto.

---

speaking' (*kōgo*), that is, on his reentering the world of articulated discourse. Thus arises the complete title of the work: *Shutsujōkōgo*. Cf. p. 64 above.

[4] This slightly bemusing sentence means that people all assumed a one-to-one relationship between the form of Buddhism or Confucianism known to them and the real meaning of these traditions, thus overlooking the conditioned character of their various phases and not understanding the problem which Tominaga perceived.

[5] By 'peoples west of China' Tominaga means the Central Asian lands through which Buddhism was transmitted from India to China, the oasis civilisation of the Taklamakan Desert based on towns such as Kucha, Khotan and Kashgar. The 'land of Śākyamuni's divine descent' is India, of importance in the Japanese perspective of Tominaga's time almost exclusively because the Buddha was born there. This geographical chain, stretching back through the countries of Buddhist transmission, is a frame of reference frequently met with in Japanese argument. The Tendai, Shingon, Pure Land, Zen and Nichirenite traditions all assume an Indian, a Chinese and a Japanese phase in the transmission of their teaching. By (commendably and realistically) including Korea and 'the peoples west of China' Tominaga gives a stronger sense of the historical particularity of this perspective than is sometimes found (even today when the Silk Road has been rediscovered but Korea has not, cf. Nosco 1984, 182).

[6] It is unclear whether this means that Tominaga would find such an accusation difficult to accept, or that he finds the matter difficult to judge.

[7] There is no reason to doubt the straightforward sincerity of these sentences. Tominaga realised that pious offence would be taken at the drift of his argument, but still hoped that it would lead to a better understanding of

EMERGING FROM MEDITATION: FIRST SCROLL
written in Japan by Tominaga Nakamoto

1. *The sequence in which the teaching <of Buddhism> arose.*

If we first consider the sequence in which the teaching <of Buddhism> arose we see that in effect it began among the heterodoxies.[9] People were advancing about ninety-six different theories, all emphasising heaven. They were each saying, 'If you follow this discipline you will be reborn in heaven.' The *Inga Sūtra* says:

> The prince thereupon went into the Himalayas and asked the hermits all around what result they were seeking: the hermits replied that they wished to be reborn in heaven.[10]

The most ancient of these heterodoxies was that of the Vaiśeṣika which existed eight hundred years before the Buddha.[11] The latest ones to appear were those of Ālāra and Udraka.[12] In the end there were twenty-eight heavens. In Udraka's teaching nor-non-conception was regarded as the ultimate, and one was born into it by transcending the realm of

---

Buddhism. 'Later scholars' have indeed done nothing but vindicate his basic position and hence sometimes feel the need to explain the strains and stresses of historical criticism to the faithful.

[8] As there are nearly three hundred era names for periods which are often of only three or four years' duration, the date is also given here in the western calendar, even though it detracts slightly from the flavour.

[9] Since the literal meaning of the term '*gedō*' is 'external ways', a Buddhist equivalent to the frequently used western phrase 'other religions', and as it has usually been used with a pejorative overtone from a Buddhist standpoint, the best translation is 'heterodoxies'. The irony is, as Tominaga sees it, that Buddhism arose just as the 'heterodoxies' did. The frequently used translation 'heresies' for *gedō* is inappropriate because it implies distortions of an already existing teaching, whereas some of the heterodoxies already existed before Buddhism. For further discussion of these heterodoxies see Chapter 22 below.

[10] The names of Buddhist writings are normally given in their Japanese pronunciation (see 'Conventions'). The index contains cross-references to the consolidated forms used. The location of quotations within the Buddhist texts may usually be found by consulting the modern editions.

[11] The Vaiśeṣika teaching was one of the 'six schools' in ancient Indian teaching, based on the *Vaiśeṣika Sūtra*.

[12] These two figures appear as contemporaries of the Buddha under whom he trained until dissatisfied. Cf. for convenience *Majjhima-Nikāya, Ariyapariyesana Sutta* and *Mahāsaccaka Sutta* in Horner (trans.) 1954.

non-existence. This arose by going beyond[13] Ālāra's regarding non-existence as the ultimate. Non-existence in turn arose by going beyond the realm of consciousness. The realm of consciousness in turn arose by going beyond the realm of space. The realm of space in turn arose by going beyond the world of form. The realm of space, the world of form, the world of desire, the six heavens, all came to be taught as a result of mutual superseding.[14] The realities are obscure and the rights and wrongs unknown; but it was because of this heterodox teaching, in which nor-non-conception was regarded as the ultimate, that it was hard for Śākyamuni to go further with another teaching of rebirth in a heaven. On this account he adduced the teaching of seven previous buddhas and taught detachment from the characteristics of birth and death,[15] adding to this the remarkable power of great supernatural transformations. Pointing out that this was very hard to achieve, he got the heretics to submit and converted the Indians. This was how Śākyamuni's teaching arose.

On Śākyamuni's death the monks met to assemble the teachings. First Kāśyapa assembled the three sets of teaching[16] but then the Mahāsāṁghikas assembled three sets of teaching. So the following was divided into two. Later on it split up into eighteen divisions. However, these are what are known as the Lesser Vehicle[17] teachings, which take the concepts of being as central, giving names and numbers to all things as if existent and quite lacking the subtle meaning of the 'articulated' teaching.[18] In this regard the disciple

13 Literally 'going above', but it implies an improvement or at least a supposed improvement on what went before. The same term is translated 'going further' in other contexts below when there is no direct object. On the significance of these expressions see also the following note.

14 Literally 'adding and going above' (*kajō*). This is a key term in Tominaga's view of religious development, introduced here right at the start of his presentation. Related terminology is used in *Writings of an Old Man* (Sections 9-11). The principle is that religious leaders regularly add something to that which they have received, thus contributing to religious change.

15 *Shōji*: saṃsāra.

16 Three sets of teaching: *sanzō*, i.e. the Tripiṭaka.

17 *Shōjō* hereafter also translated as Hīnayāna.

18 The term *hōdō*, 'articulated', originally stood for the Sanskrit term *vaipulya* which is usually explained as meaning broadly drawn out or extended. However it should not be forgotten that Tominaga was almost certainly not familiar with Sanskrit. In effect *hōdō* is a synonym for Mahāyāna in its early phase.

Mañjuśrī went further by producing the *prajñā* according to which things are all articulated while having the character of voidness. This is known as the Great Vehicle.[19] In the *Great Treatise* and the *Kongōsen Treatise* it says:

> The Tathāgata was on the outer side of Mount Tetsuchi with Mañjuśrī and the buddhas of the ten directions, and there the teachings of the Great Vehicle Dharma were assembled.

At that time there was still no explanation of the Hīnayāna and Mahāyāna arising over a period of years. Those who put out the Mahāyāna just said, 'From the night of attaining the way until the night of the Nirvāṇa he steadily taught *prajñā*.' This is confirmed in the *Great Treatise* which also speaks as follows of Śākyamuni's first attainment of the way:

> At that time the ruler of the world, Brahmarāja, named Śikhin, the gods of the world of form, Śakra the presiding deity, and the gods of the world of desire, all came to pay their respects to the Buddha and besought the world-honoured one to give the first turning of the wheel of Dharma. Thereupon, remembering also what he had originally vowed as a bodhisattva, and the principle of great compassion, because he received this request he proclaimed the Dharma. The depth of all dharmas is the *prajñāpāramitā* <the perfection of insight>, and for this reason the Buddha expounded the *Great Prajñāpāramitā Sūtra*.[20]

Those who spread the Hīnayāna say that from the *Tenbōrin Sūtra* <i.e. Sūtra of the turning of the wheel of Dharma> up to the *Great Nirvāṇa Sūtra*[21] the four *Āgamas* were compiled. In the *Great Treatise* it says:

> Mahākāśyapa spoke thus to Ānanda, 'From the *Tenbōrin Sūtra* up to the *Great Nirvāṇa Sūtra* the four *Āgamas* <*Agon*> were

[19] *Daijō*: hereafter also translated as Mahāyāna.

[20] *Prajñāpāramitā*: in general the translation 'perfection of insight' is preferred (to perfection of wisdom), but the Sanskrit term is kept here and in many contexts below because it reflects the transliteration in Tominaga's text (Japanese *hannyaharamitta*).

[21] Although the text does not say 'sūtra' this is probably implied to complement the Sūtra of the Turning of the Wheel of Dharma (cf. Kyōdo, ad loc). At the same time the whole teaching span of the Buddha's life is implied which ended with his Great Nirvāṇa or Great Decease, to which Mizuta takes this to be a direct reference.

compiled, the *Zōichi-agon, Chū-agon, Chō-agon* and *Sōō-agon*. These are known as the Sūtra Dharma Store'.

These all refer to the beginning and the end but contain no statement about the numbers of years and which came before and which after. Thus too when the preface of the *Ninnō-Prajñā Sūtra* says, 'First the world-honoured one expounded the four *prajñās* and then at New Year in the thirtieth year he proclaimed the *Ninnō-Sūtra*' it is still putting it only very vaguely and not saying that it was precisely thirty years after the *Āgamas*. The *Hokkaishō Treatise* in explaining this says, 'For twelve years he expounded the *Āgamas*, for thirty years he expounded the *Great Prajñā Sūtra*, and for eight years he expounded the *Lotus Sūtra*.' This is merely stated in a changed way to make out that the *Lotus Sūtra* was expounded after more than forty years. The reality is otherwise. The *Lotus* school itself gave rise to this, saying,

> For more than forty years after my enlightenment, using countless skilful means, I guided living beings along. Of all the sūtras which I have expounded the Lotus is the greatest. However this is for the benefit of bodhisattvas, not for the sake of the Lesser Vehicle. Seeing the true character of all dharmas is called the practice of the bodhisattva.

The *Murgōyi Sūtra*[22] also says: 'For more than forty years I have not yet revealed reality, but have been expounding the Dharma variously by my power of skilful means.' From this we can see that claiming the teaching was given after more than forty years was to make the teachings of others up till then seem foolish, and claiming to teach the true character of things was to refute the previous teachings of existence and voidness. These supporters of the *Lotus* were a distinct group within the Great Vehicle who rejected both of the two existing vehicles alike.[23] However later scholars have all been unaware of this.

[22] The *Muryōgi Sūtra* is usually associated with the *Lotus Sūtra* as a kind of introduction. However no Sanskrit original is known.

[23] The two existing vehicles are the vehicle of the hearers (*śrāvakayāna*) whose enlightenment depends on the teaching of a Buddha, and the vehicle of the *pratyekabuddhas* (*pratyekabuddhayāna*), who attain enlightenment in solitude and do not transmit to others. Although there is certainly a polemical aspect in the *Lotus Sūtra*, as Tominaga points out, there is also a complex exegetical problem about the relationship between the three vehicles, i.e. the

Those who make the *Lotus Sūtra* the main point, and regard it as the greatest of all the truly real teachings of the world-honoured one, are making a vain error. The argument about the number of years, and about which came first and which after, really began in the *Lotus Sūtra* itself. The argument about the provisional and the real also really began in the *Lotus Sūtra*. With this expansive power of skilful means, where is the end of misleading people past and present? Where is there anyone who will object to it? It is impossible except for a Tathāgata emerging from his meditation![24] The *Gejinmitsu Sūtra* says: 'First there was the Lesser Vehicle, in between there was the teaching of voidness and lastly came the teaching of non-voidness.' This takes the side of the *Lotus* party. Furthermore it is to be considered that the division into three sets of teaching first arose with Kāśyapa. However the text of the *Lotus Sūtra* refers to 'scholars of the three sets of teaching' from which we know that the *Lotus Sūtra* appeared afterwards. It is also to be considered whether the *Lotus Sūtra* was compiled by disciples of the Bodhisattva Fugen. As to this see Fugen's commendation of it in the *Great Treatise*.[25]

This is where the Kegon school statement arises. That is, by claiming that the perfect and complete sūtra was expounded up until the twenty-seventh day[26] they played down the previously existing Hīnayāna, and then, by saying it was like the sun first illuminating only the tops of the mountains, they played down the previously existing Mahāyāna; in so doing they created a special king of all the sūtras. Thus they were truly trailblazers in superseding others. Later generations who

---

two mentioned above and the *bodhisattvayāna*, and the relationship between all of these and the 'sole vehicle' (*ekayāna*).

[24] In the modern Japanese translation Kyōdo glosses 'Tathāgata emerging from his meditation' with 'that is, I, Nakamoto' while Ishida simply translates 'the author', relegating the original idea to brackets. Of course Tominaga implies that he himself can expose these misleading perspectives; but his own way of putting it here, without the gloss, is quite ironic and intended to be thought-provoking.

[25] Kyōdo adduces *Great Treatise* (T25, 127a): 'Henkitsu (= Fugen) Bosatsu himself says, "If anyone should recite the Lotus Sūtra I will appear riding a white elephant and give him guidance".'

[26] I.e. the twenty-seventh day of Buddha's presentation of Dharma. Since it was so mysterious he then dropped down to elementary teachings and gradually worked back up again towards the highest Mahāyāna teachings, according to the Kegon theory.

believed in this device, declaring the <Kegon> sūtra to be the highest pinnacle, – the sudden of the sudden <enlightenment>,[27] are also mistaken.

<The *Kegon Sūtra* says that> Śāriputra and Maudgalyāyana both entered the Buddha-dharma at different times and places, yet at their meeting Śāriputra already had an entourage of five hundred *śrāvakas* <hearers>. At that time the Gion grove and the Fukōhottō were not yet built, yet the text mentions them in detail. These are all expedients for those attached to the passions.[28] Consider also that the *Kegon Sūtra* contains the teaching of the real character of all dharmas[29] and of the *prajñāpāramitā*.[30] This indicated that this sūtra appeared after the other two.[31]

Then comes the teaching of those who associated the *Daijū* and *Nirvāṇa Sūtras*, and by setting up these two combined the two vehicles of Mahāyāna and Hīnayāna, though they put the emphasis on the *Nirvāṇa Sūtra*. Saying that the *Daijū Sūtra* was expounded from the sixteenth year <of the Buddha's teaching>, and indirectly claiming that this was before the *Prajñā*, they made it out to have emerged between the two vehicles. Thus too they explain the Vinaya, saying that although the five divisions are different none is inconsistent with the Dharma-worlds of the Buddhas or with the great nirvāṇa.[32] This is an attempt to smooth out differences between the five divisions of *vinaya*. However the five divisions

[27] Sudden enlightenment came to be regarded as superior, indeed the only true enlightenment, because a gradual attainment of enlightenment is based on discriminated phases of development which are ultimately subverted by the Mahāyāna logic of identity. The 'sudden of the sudden' means the ultimate gist. Cf. note 179.

[28] Tominaga's point is that such inconsistencies in the story-telling, though making for attractive reading, betray the later composition of the *Kegon Sūtra*.

[29] 'The real character of all dharmas' (*shohōjissō*) refers not to a theory of phenomenal existence but to the ultimately identical nature of the elements of existence in terms of suchness.

[30] I.e. the teaching of the 'perfection of insight', the leading feature of the sūtras bearing the name.

[31] I.e. the *Kegon Sūtra* appeared after the *Lotus Sūtra* and the *Prajñāpāramitā Sūtra*, a historically correct judgment.

[32] That is, variations in the vinaya regulations fade into insignificance in the light of the ultimate goals of Buddhism.

of *vinaya* all emerged from the eighty sections of recitation.[33] Five later teachers divided it into five versions some time after the Buddha's nirvāṇa, and this shows that this sūtra appeared later. The *Nirvāṇa Sūtra* was created by the same hands, for which reason it displays many similarities of language. This claims to relate the Buddha's decease, and thus to show that this sūtra emerged in the last years of his life. It is compared to ghee, which illustrates that the meaning of this sūtra is the most pure. Furthermore they adduced the problem as to whether the precepts in the Vinaya were light or hard to argue that it was difficult to separate the two vehicles of Hīnayāna and Mahāyāna. When people later referred to this as the realised teaching they did not know that it was this combining school.[34] Consider the *Fa Hsien Record* which says,

> In some lands they study the Hīnayāna, in some lands they study the Mahāyāna, and in some countries they combine the Hīnayāna and the Mahāyāna.

The word 'combine' here refers to the Combination School. Consider also the Aitan Chapter <of the *Nirvāṇa Sūtra*> which compares a secret set of sūtras to a new form of the Sanskrit letter 'I'. From this we can tell that the *Nirvāṇa Sūtra* too emerged later.[35]

Then comes the statement of the Sudden School. Its preferred sūtras number about twenty, among which the *Laṅkāvatāra Sūtra* is outstanding. They said that previous sūtras were all tiresome, their contents being circumlocutions as numerous as a cow's hairs. For this reason they came out with terse expressions, such as:

> All passions originally depart of themselves. There should be no talk of cutting them off and not cutting them off. All beings are

[33] Tradition has it that after the Buddha's decease the rules of discipline were recited in the course of one summer in eighty sessions. Later divisions into five or four parts are therefore secondary.

[34] The question of the relative ease or difficulty of precepts is formulated in various places, e.g. *Makashikan* (T 46, 39a) (cf Kyōdo n. 92). In retrospect those who failed clearly to separate Hīnayāna and Mahāyāna were referred to as Kunjukyō.

[35] A late variation of the Sanskrit letter I is used as an esoteric analogy for three aspects of nirvāṇa, namely dharma-body, insight and release, thus indicating the late compilation of the sūtra. Cf. Kyōdo, p. 183, n. 95.

themselves the universe, and in short unborn. If we detach ourselves from nomenclature then all dharmas are but one true mind. When not one conception arises, this is Buddhahood. There is no coming from one land and going to another land. The first land is all eight lands.

These are direct words, not complicated talk. With these they tore through the Indra's net of those before them. The ultimate outburst was that of Bodhidharma whose coming to the east impressed the *Laṅkāvatāra Sūtra* on the minds of the people. However this was a sign, for he relied on meaning, not on text. From beginning to end he did not expound a single letter. He was the true originator of the Zen line. It ended up with weird transformations such as being awakened to the buddha-nature by a dried bottom-wiper. They came round to rejecting the sūtras like scraping off boils and warts. These all belong to what is known as the Sudden School.[36]

Then comes the teaching of the secret maṇḍala of Kongōshu <i.e. Vajrasattva>. In the *Rokudo Sūtra* it says:

After my decease, Ānanda is to preserve the Sūtra Piṭaka which I have expounded, Upāli is to preserve the Vinaya Piṭaka which I have expounded. Kātyāyanī is to preserve the Abhidharma Piṭaka which I have expounded, and the bodhisattva Mañjuśrī is to preserve the Mahāyāna Prajñāpāramitā which I have expounded. This bodhisattva Vajrasattva is to preserve the deep and subtle mantras which I have expounded.

In this teaching it says,

The world-honoured one achieved all wisdom and distributed it broadly for the countless multitude. He proclaimed all wisdom in accordance with various tendencies, various desires and various expedient paths. Now <he taught> the path of the *śrāvaka* vehicle, now the path of the *pratyeka-buddha* vehicle, now the path of the great vehicle, now the path of the five wisdoms, now the vow of rebirth in heaven, or among men, dragons, *yakṣas*, or *gandharvas*, and so on up to teaching the dharma of rebirth as *mahoragas*. Each of these <beings> has its own kind of speech and they abide at different levels of dignity, but the wisdom path of all wisdom has a single flavour.[37]

[36] On the principle underlying the 'Sudden School' see note 27 above.

[37] In principle the understanding of the relation between different forms of Buddhist teaching which is illustrated by this quotation is common throughout

It also says:

> The Sūtras are like the milk, the Vinaya is like the whey, the Abhidharma is like the fresh curds, the Prajñā is like the mature curds, and the mantra gate is like the ghee.

Observe that this teaching subsumes the various schools under 'all wisdom' and identifies this with what is known as the maṇḍala. In the long run this puts the emphasis back on what is known as Vairocana's Gate of the Letter A. This king of the sūtras <the *Dainichi Sūtra*> appeared last. Master Fukū <i.e. Amoghavajra> said, 'The sūtra was stored between the others in an iron tower for several hundred years, and Nāgārjuna was the first to find it'. However there is not a word about this in what Nāgārjuna taught. The story came about simply because the term 'mystery' appears in Nāgārjuna's works and later generations revered him greatly.

Thus the appearance of divisions among the various teachings came about because they all first arose by superseding others.[38] If it had not been for this relationship of superseding, how would the path of Dharma have been extended? This is natural for a path of Dharma, whether old or new. However, the scholars of later generations vainly say that all the teachings came directly from the golden mouth <of the Buddha> and were intimately transmitted by those who heard him frequently. They do not realise that, on the contary, there are many gaps and connections.[39] Is this not foolish?

---

the Mahāyāna. However it is sandwiched between two others which interpret it as a hierarchy of teachings within Buddhism, with the mantra school (sometimes referred to as esoteric Buddhism) at the top.

[38] Literally 'mutual superseding'; however one only supersedes what has gone before. Tominaga is speaking of a continuous process of development, although these English words are not directly justifiable in a cautious translation.

[39] Tominaga means that the Buddhist scriptures are a network of inconsistent but nevertheless interrelated writings.

2. *Differences in what the sūtras say.*

The *Great Treatise* says:

> One hundred years after the Buddha's decease, King Aśoka convened a five-yearly council and because the positions of the leading teachers of Dharma differed the various divisions of teaching acquired their names. [It also says:] When five hundred years had passed from the beginning of the Buddhadharma, the various schools of thought numbered five hundred.

In the Preface to the *Vibhāṣā Treatise* it says:

> Early in the four hundredth year after the decease of the Tathāgata (the old treatise makes it the six hundredth year) the King of Gandhāra was assiduously studying the sūtras. Each day he called a monk into his room to expound the Dharma, but there were discrepancies in what the monks said. The king had grave doubts and enquired of Pārśva. Pārśva replied, 'After the Tathāgata left this world, many months and years passed and his disciples split up, making contradictions about what they had heard and seen.' So the king asked, 'Which is the best among all these divisions?' He answered, 'Nothing surpasses the Sarvāstivāda.' The king said, 'The Tripiṭaka of this school must be compiled at once. Virtuous men must be assembled to discuss it in detail.' Upon this, Vasumitra and five hundred others commented on the Tripiṭaka in some three hundred thousand verses, now known as the *Great Vibhāṣā*.

The *Great Treatise* also says:

> Question. In the sūtras five places of rebirth are preached, so why do you speak of six? Answer. The sūtras have been transmitted for a long time after the Buddha's departure, and after five hundred years there are many differences and the various schools do not agree. Some tell of five places of rebirth and some tell of six. Those who expound five read through the text of the sūtras to make it five, and those who expound six read through the Buddha's sūtras to make it six. Among the Mahāyāna writings the *Lotus Sūtra* says that there are six kinds of living beings. Considering all those opinions, there must be six places of rebirth.

The *Fa Hsien Record* says:

> Fa Hsien was seeking the original Vinaya. However in all the countries of northern India he found that it was passed on orally from teacher to teacher and was not something to be written in books. So he travelled far until he came to Middle India, and here he was able to obtain the Vinaya of one school, namely the Vinaya of the Mahāsāmghikas. He was also able to get an abbreviated Vinaya of one school amounting to seven thousand verses. This was the Vinaya of the Sarvāstivādins. Again everybody received it orally from teacher to teacher and it was not written down in letters. [It also says:] At that time Fa Hsien wanted to copy down this sūtra, but the person said there was no written sūtra and it was only recited.

Now from these six statements we can conclude as follows. We can tell that for long after the Buddha's decease there was no fixed exposition among his followers and there were no writings upon which one could depend. Everybody renewed the teaching according to their opinions and passed it on orally. Thus it is that the differences in the teachings of the canonical sūtras cannot be overcome, and this again is why they cannot be trusted. When the Zen school say 'No setting up the written word', perhaps that is what they mean! Again, when we review the *Vibhāṣā Treatise* we find that it sets out various lines of interpretation, saying 'this is because of so-and-so, that is because of so-and-so', so that in short there is no fixed teaching. Again, from the fact that the *Great Treatise* refers to Kāśyapa's compilation of the Tripiṭaka as being based on a recitation, we can tell that it is based on oral recitation only.

The *Diamond Sūtra* says: 'All Buddha-dharmas arise from this sūtra.' The *Muryōgi Sūtra* says 'I am expounding this sūtra, which is most profound, so that beings may swiftly achieve supreme enlightenment.' The *Sūtra of Golden Light* says: 'The Buddhas of the ten directions are constantly thinking of this sūtra.'

The *Great Prajñāpāramitā Sūtra* says:

> All good dharmas and all assisting dharmas, the three vehicle Dharma and the Buddha-dharma, all these dharmas are taken up in the *Prajñāpāramitā* <*Sūtra*>. [It also says:] Those who

> wish to learn the *śrāvaka* vehicle should learn *prajñā*, those who wish to learn the *pratyekabuddha* vehicle should learn *prajñā*, and those who wish to learn the *bodhisattva* vehicle should learn *prajñā*.

The *Kegon Sūtra* says:

> Of all the people in the whole world there are few who seek to achieve the *śrāvaka* way, those who aspire to the *pratyekabuddha* way are particularly few and those who turn to the Great Vehicle are hard to meet with. Turning to the Great Vehicle is relatively easy but believing this <Kegon> Dharma is extremely difficult.

The *Lotus Sūtra* says: 'Of all the sūtras which I have expounded the Lotus is the greatest.' The *Dharma Drum Sūtra* says:

> The teachings of all the voidness sūtras leave something lacking. There is only this sūtra which has the highest teaching.

Where is the end of all the statements of this kind? They are all teachings in which each school emphasises itself.

Again, when the *Shōman Sūtra* says: 'The Great Vehicle gives birth to the other two vehicles, just as Lake Anoku gives birth to the eight rivers', and the *Monjumon Sūtra* says: 'The eighteen schools and the two main divisions all arose from the Great Vehicle', this makes the Mahāyāna include the Hīnayāna. Again, when the *Lotus Sūtra* says: 'For more than forty years I have not revealed the truth', this implies that the Mahāyāna regard the Hīnayāna as a provisional teaching. Again, when the *Kegon Sutra* says: 'On the twenty-seventh day after attaining the way, the Buddha proclaimed the rounded and complete sūtra', this means that the Hīnayāna was expounded after the Mahāyāna. The reality of all these is that they are teachings by which the Mahāyāna provokes the Hīnayāna. The scholars of later times did not realise this, so although they said various things they were mistaken. As I have said before – both the Mahāyāna and the Hīnayāna schools compiled their own sūtras and all tried to prove them to be the work of Śākyamuni, which was just a clever expedient.

There was once a doctor named Kan <i.e. Huan>, during the Ch'in dynasty <of China>, who died. His eldest son acquired his arts and a reputation equal to that of Kan. The second and third sons could not bear this, and therefore they thought up various novelties and imputed them to their father, seeking thereby to outdo their elder brother. It was not that they did not hold the elder brother in affection but it seemed as if they had to have something different from the elder brother to claim it to be similar to the arts of their father. There was no way for people in general to resolve which was which until one day the father of a neighbour to the east, who had acquired a book from Kan's bedside, brought it out as proof. After that the elder son's art extended for the first time all over the world.[40] This matter is found in Mō Gan Ni's *Kankeifu*. It is similar to the above state of affairs.

3. *Thus I have heard.*

In the expression 'Thus I have heard', who is the 'I'? It is none other than the expositor of a later time. What is the 'heard'? It is that the later expositor has heard something passed on. What is the 'thus'? It is the later expositor's having heard it passed on 'thus'. A sūtra says, for example: 'Ānanda went up to this seat and claimed "I have heard" ...The audience cried out with emotion' (*Shotai Sūtra*). This is wrong in that Ānanda was the bosom companion of the Buddha and so it is not appropriate for him to use the words 'I have heard on such and such an occasion'. Or again, in interpretation, it is said:

> Ānanda was born on the night in which the Buddha attained the Way and he served the Buddha for more than twenty years, but he cannot be said to have heard him during the time before he served him.[41]

This is also wrong. Why would he <later> have to repeat

[40] The point here, slightly obscured by Kyōdo's conflated rendering in modern Japanese, is that a school can establish itself by bringing out a relevant document which supposedly proves authenticity, and that this is far more effective than simply presenting one oral tradition among others.

[41] The point of the interpretation, rejected by Tominaga, was that since Ānanda was only just born at the time of the Buddha's enlightenment he did not hear the earlier years of the Buddha's preaching activity, recorded to have extended over some forty years in all. He only attended to the Buddha's needs for the latter twenty years or so.

saying 'I have heard' after he had already heard <the teaching> before? This is an inconsistent argument.[42] The *Hōon Sūtra* says: 'Ānanda four times entreated: "May the Buddha please expound again the sūtras which I have not yet heard." ' It also says: 'A secret teaching was expounded from the Buddha's mouth.' It also says: 'The sūtras which Ānanda had not heard, he either heard by following the other monks or had expounded to him by the devas.' Moreover the *Shotai Sūtra* says: 'The Buddha stretched forth his golden arm from within the golden coffin, and repeated his preaching <for Ānanda>.' The *Kongōge Sūtra* says:

> Ānanda attained the royal *samādhi* of the Dharma-nature-enlightenment of self-abiding, and therefore he was able to recall all the sūtras which the Tathāgata had expounded before, exactly as if he had heard them intimately.

And the *Nirvāṇa Sūtra* says: 'After my nirvāṇa, let the bodhisattva Gukō spread widely all the teaching which Ānanda has not yet heard.' Ah, how inconsistent this is with salvation! Expounding it at length and expounding it in brief does no more than to preserve this error. It is laughable. Many of the sūtras were compiled by people five hundred years after the Buddha, so they contain many words from these five hundred years. This is what it means when the *Great Treatise* also says: 'After five hundred years they split up in various ways into five hundred divisions.'

To think that there should be some particular words at the head of the sūtras was a common theory of the time. It originally appeared in the *Great Treatise*, and the *Nirvāṇa Sūtra* took it up in particular. We can see that the *Nirvāṇa Sūtra* in fact came after the *Great Treatise* because the *Great Treatise* adds not a word to the *Nirvāṇa Sūtra*. Scholars of later times did not know this. They all seem to have idly thought that thousands of sūtras were all collected up by Ānanda. What foolishness! The *Great Treatise* says:

[42] Tominaga's point seems to be that nevertheless it is a fiction to make Ānanda say 'Thus I have heard' when he had just spent at least twenty years in the Buddha's presence. His underlying assumption is that the Buddha's teaching may have been given on various occasions, but that it did not vary so notably that hearing the last twenty years would not suffice.

> Question. If the Buddha related this Prajñāpāramitā <Sūtra> to Ānanda, why is it not found in the Tripiṭaka compiled by Ānanda and Mahākāśyapa after the <Buddha's> nirvāṇa? Answer. The Mahāyāna is extremely profound, hard to believe and hard to practise. When the Buddha was in the world there were monks who heard the Mahāyāna but did not believe it or understand it. They therefore left their seats, and that is why it was not recited after the Buddha's nirvāṇa.

It also says:

> Just as Mahākāśyapa collected up the Tripiṭaka with all the other monks on Mount Vulture Peak, so did Mañjuśrī and Maitreya and all the other bodhisattvas, together with Ānanda, collect up this Mahāyāna <Tripiṭaka> after the Buddha's decease.

Again:

> Ānanda knew how to weigh up the minds and hearts of men, and therefore he did not expound the Mahāyāna among the *śrāvakas*. If he had done so he would have confused them to no advantage.

Thus we should note that these doubts already existed at the time. Even the wise men of the time themselves could not appreciate the Mahāyāna Dharma though it was intimately heard from the Buddha. Doubt should be cast if it is said that it was handed down by later people. If it is as they say, Ānanda must have been a soft-head, knowing how to attain the way himself, but not expounding it among the *śrāvakas*, that is, secretly keeping silent but outwardly flattering and praising them. What kind of a disciple to the Buddha is that? These are all inconsistent arguments. They are clearly decorative words of explanation. The reality of it is that the sūtras collected by Ānanda were just a few chapters of the *Āgamas*. On this argument see below. As to the rest, not only do they not stem from Ānanda, but they represent the claims of later parties. For this reason it is also said in this connection:

> At a later time Mañjuśrī called together all the bodhisattvas and great *arhats* and compiled the Mahāyāna Tripiṭaka, each one of them saying that he heard a certain sūtra from the Buddha.

> Subhūti said, 'I heard the *Diamond Sūtra* from the Buddha.' Therefore we know it was not Ānanda's responsibility.

This is somewhere near the truth. However the sūtra teachings are all things claimed by later parties. Why does it say that they are from bodhisattvas and great *arhats*? This is also a mistake.

Furthermore, the *Shotai Sūtra* says:

> The first sūtras given out by Ānanda were the Womb Collection, second came the Intermediate Collection, third the Mahāyāna Expanded Collection, fourth the Discipline Collection, fifth the Ten Bodhisattva Realms Collection, sixth the Miscellaneous Collection, seventh the Diamond Collection, and eighth the Buddha Collection; and this makes up the complete sūtras.

Thus according to this the Mahāyāna and the Hīnayāna both appeared at the same time. It is also the most exaggerated case of 'Thus I have heard'!

4. *Mount Sumeru, the heavens and the cosmos.*

The teachings about Mount Sumeru were all handed down by brahmans. Though Śākyamuni used them to expound his Way, they are to be regarded as cosmic theory. Later scholars however have made much of this teaching while criticising others, and lost sight of the Buddha's intention. This is because the Buddha's intention is not to be found in such matters. He was urgently seeking people's salvation and had no time for such petty matters. What he did is what is known as skilful means. The Confucianists are also unaware of this and say, 'Śākyamuni taught about Mount Sumeru, but the teaching is inapposite.' Ah! Why should we expect Śākyamuni to be like the Confucianists? When Confucius wrote the *Spring and Autumn* was he not unaware that there were eclipses from time to time? How can this be explained? The progression of the sun and moon is dealt with by the stargazers, but there is no harm in not knowing about it. Those who discuss the rights and wrongs of such things are all small-minded people. Recently there have been people who have indulged in taking this up again when putting together theories about the universe. It is extremely squalid, indeed ridiculous. Those discrepancies between what the sūtras and treatises say are just there for the sake of giving names to the various divisions and providing sayings for each school.

Take, for example, what is asserted about the depth of the earth. The *Zōichi-agon* makes it 68,000 *yojanas*, the *Kusha Treatise* makes it 800,000 *yojanas*, the *Kise Sūtra* makes it 600,000 yojanas, the *Bosatsuzō* makes it 6,800,000 *yojanas*, the *Dairōtan Sūtra* makes it 8,000,000,000 *yojanas*, and the *Sūtra of Golden Light* makes it 168,000 *yojanas*. Why is there no settled teaching? It is the same when they refer to the diameter of Mount Sumeru. The *Chō-agon*, the *Kise Sūtra*, and the *Great Treatise* make it 4200 yojanas, while the *Taihō Treatise* and *Kusha Treatise* make it 40,000 yojanas. Again, why is there no settled teaching? It is the same again when they refer to length of life in the four continents. The *Chō-agon*, the *Dairōtan Sūtra* and *Kusha Treatise* are all different on this point. They also disagree on the four precious stones of Mount Sumeru. It is the same with the residential hall of the Asuras, which the *Kise Sūtra* puts at the east of Mount Sumeru and the *Jūji Treatise* puts at the north. It is the same again when they expound the hells. The *Vibhāṣā Treatise* discusses it but is not consistent. One place says, 'The eight hot hells and the eight cold hells each have their locations.' On this the *Great Treatise* says, 'The eight cold hells belong together with the eight hot hells.' The sūtras and treatises do not agree on their whereabouts and names. In short, these are all different statements by different schools and it is not essential to harmonise them.

It is the same when they teach about the formation of the world. The *Vibhāṣā Treatise* says that there was first a circle of water, while the *Shuryōgon Sūtra* says there was first a circle of gold. Again, the usual order of the five rings is air, wind, water, gold, earth, but the *Zōichi-agon* makes it earth, water, fire, wind, gold. As for the devas of golden sound, the *Chō-agon* puts it that when their life is ended they are reborn in this world, and the *Zōichi-agon* has them discussing their hopes of coming to see the lie of the land in Jambudvīpa. Other sūtras say that when they die they are reborn in the Great Heaven of Brahman and then gradually descend until they are reborn as humans. Or again, take the teaching about the three disasters.

The *Chō-agon* and the *Kise Sūtra* say that they are weapons, famines and epidemics, the *Kusha Treatise* and the *Vibhāṣā Treatise* say they are weapons, epidemics and famines, and the *Yuga Treatise* and the *Taihō Treatise* say they are famines, epidemics and weapons. So the order is different each time. In short this is just different nomenclature in each school, and it is beyond dispute that they are hard to reconcile.

It is the same when they teach about the heavens. The Sarvāstivādins say there are sixteen, the Sautrāntikas say there are seventeen, the Sthaviravādins say there are eighteen, the *Vibhāṣā Treatise* says there are thirty-two kinds altogether including the heaven of the sun, moon and stars. The *Nirvāṇa Sūtra* has four kinds and the *Great Treatise* has three kinds. It is the same when they teach about the palaces of the four heavenly kings. The *Dairōtan Sūtra*, the *Kusha Treatise* and the *Great Treatise* are all different. It is the same again with the three Brahmans. In the *Kise Sūtra*, the *Taihō Treatise* and the *Vibhāṣā Treatise*, these are doubled up with a dwelling assigned to each, while in the *Kusha Treatise* and the *Vibhāṣā Treatise* of the Sarvāstivādins they are all put together in one place. Again, the *Ninnō Sūtra* has eighteen Brahmans, while the *Yōraku Sūtra* has Brahmans in each of the *dhyāna* heavens, and so this is different from other sūtras which have one Brahman king. In the same way the *Great Treatise* regards Māra as the ruler of the world of desire, Brahmarāja <King Brahma> as the ruler of the three worlds, but also Maheśvara as the ruler of the three worlds. Similarly, when it discusses the ruler of the great thousand-fold world, it is said to be Brahmarāja of the first *dhyāna*, but then the *Kegon Sūtra* said it was Maheśvara. Similarly, when teaching of Maheśvara, they place him in the sixth heaven or else place him in the ultimate heaven of form. It is the same when they make of Brahman, Nārāyaṇa and Maheśvara one body with three parts. It is the same again when the *Shuryōgon Sūtra* and the eighty-chapter *Kegon Sūtra* put the Sudarśana heaven first and the Sudṛśa heaven last, while the *Kusha Treatise*, the *Junshōri Treatise* and the sixty-chapter *Kegon Sūtra* have it the other way round.

Similarly, in discussion of the nature of existence in the formless world, the *Vibhāṣā Treatise*, the *Kusha Treatise*, the *Yuga Treatise*, the *Sautrāntikas* and the *Jōjitsu Treatise* define it as non-being and the *Kise Sutra*, *Zōichi-agon*, the *Kegon Sūtra*, the *Ninnō Sūtra*, the Keji School and the Mahāsāṁghikas define it as being. Similarly, with the discussion of humans and non-humans, the *Sūtra of Golden Light* classifies them in eight groups. Similarly in discussing the Asuras, the *Butchi Treatise* says they are devas and the *Taihō Treatise* says they are demons, the *Shōbōnen Sūtra* says that some are demons and some are animals, and the *Kada Sūtra* says they are to be taken as the aggregate of the three types. It is the same when the *Vibhāṣā Treatise* says, 'Some other schools set up the Asuras in six types, but this is mistaken because the sūtras expound them as five'; while the *Great Treatise* says:

> Question. In the sūtras it says there are five places of rebirth, so why do you speak of six? Answer. Long after the Buddha's decease some differences came about between the sūtras. Only the *Lotus Sūtra* teaches that there are six places of rebirth. Thus that is the position.

In short these are all things enjoined by different schools, and were not originally proclaimed by a single voice.

There was a teacher in the Ming period named Shi Ban[43] who gave three reasons in explanation of this, first that what the Buddha taught was varied to suit the occasion, secondly that there were differences between the groups which compiled the teachings, and thirdly that there were differences between the times of the translation. Ah! What extreme delusion! If it is because the Buddha had suited his teaching to the occasion he would have been giving delusory words, in which case how could he have presented people with the Vinaya? If there were differences between the groups which compiled the teachings, how can these be regarded as what the Buddha taught or how can the teachings of the sūtras be believed? How does this confusion arise? Or again, if we regard it as a matter of differences between the times of the translations, this makes the translators difficult to trust. There is no disputing that referring to nirvāṇa <*nehan*> as *metsudo* <extinction> or as *enjaku* <perfect rest> shows differences in the understanding of the translators. If the nomenclature and numeration are to

[43] Shi Ban was a thirteenth-century T'ien T'ai monk. Ming is a mistake for Sung. Cf. Kyōdo, p. 221, n. 95.

be explained as different because they appeared in sequence, this is very vague. How can this be considered a sufficient explanation? In short, he only says this because he fails to understand it. The reality is otherwise.[44]

The *Shakafu* also says:

> The sūtras are sometimes different within and without China only because the translators think differently and those who published the sūtras had their way of receiving them. Even recent Chinese works such as the *Historical Records* and the *Han Writings* are contradictory, so it is not surprising in works from beyond the Great Wall thousands of miles away, and a thousand years old. Those well informed about ancient matters should select what is good and follow it.

Ah, what delusion again? This selecting what is good and following it amounts to elevating onself and issuing sūtras. Then again, how could such <selections> be regarded as sūtras? These arguments are just prevarications. They are just things said out of embarrassment over the inconsistencies. This has in fact been one Great Wall of doubt in ancient and recent times alike. It has been cleared up for the first time with the publication of this 'Emerging from Meditation Sūtra'.[45]

There are five theories about the cosmos. The first one, that of the Sumeru world, was propounded by the brahmans and is the basis for the others. When they speak of the small thousand-fold world, the medium thousand-fold world and the three thousand-fold great thousand-fold world, or again of ten worlds apart from the three thousand-fold world, these are all later supersedings. The *Bonmō Sūtra's* teaching of the lotus world is another superseding layer. This went on, until we get

[44] The second and third of these two explanations are in fact quite close to Tominaga's own view of the matter and one might incline to suspect a little 'superseding' on his part. However there is a significant difference in that Tominaga finds these efforts at explanation inadequate because they fail to address the motivation of those responsible for differences in the teaching. Hence the vigour with which he questions the trustworthiness of the tradition. The older explanations were essentially harmonising and eirenic in intention whereas Tominaga wishes to lay bare historical motivation.

[45] *Shutsujōkyōten*. With this ironic comment Tominaga emphasises the loss of external religious authority resulting from a fully historical view of the development of scriptures.

to the world sea in Kegon teaching. Teachings about the cosmos are in actuality quite vague and do no more than tell us of the inner working of the mind.[46] There is no way of knowing whether they are right or wrong. Hence I say that the cosmos arises on the pattern of people's minds.

5. *Tripiṭaka, Abhidharma, Sūtras, Verses.*

Tripiṭaka is a Hīnayāna designation which originated with Kāśyapa. The *Great Treatise* says: 'When the Buddha was in the world the term Tripiṭaka did not exist. Mahākāśyapa and others compiled the Tripiṭaka'. It also says, 'The Tripiṭaka is the Dharma of the *śrāvakas* and the Mahāyāna <Sūtras> are the Dharma of the Great Vehicle.' The *Lotus Sūtra* is referring to this when it speaks of 'scholars absorbed in the Hīnayāna Tripiṭaka'; in Nāgārjuna's time the term Tripiṭaka referred to the Small Vehicle; and this is what was meant when 'Piṭaka' was listed as one of the 'four teachings' in the Tendai account.[47] However, when the teacher Chō Kan said, 'The Great Vehicle also has its Tripiṭaka', this is an independent meaning given at a later time, and it is a case of 'language being conditioned'.[48] Again, when the *Fuchō Sūtra* and the *Nyūdaijō Treatise* refer to the Three Vehicles as the Tripiṭaka, this is another, quite different meaning. We may reflect that in the introductory chapter of the *Zōichi-agon* it says, 'The sūtras are the first Piṭaka, the Vinaya is the second Piṭaka and the Abhidharma is the third Piṭaka.'

[46] 'Inner working of the mind': *shinri*. The *ri* used here is the well-known term used to refer to the inner principle or 'logic', as people sometimes say, of anything, *Shin* (mind) is another key term in Buddhist thought, but also in wider reaches of Chinese philosophy. 'Shinri' eventually came to be used as the modern Japanese term for 'psychology', and indeed what we have here is a projectionist theory of myth in embryo form. The implication that truth-claims are thereby relativised is also clearly present in this terse conclusion.

[47] The 'four teachings' in the T'ien T'ai system are: the sudden teaching, the gradual teaching, the secret teaching, and the undetermined teaching. Cf. Petzold 1979 (posthumous), pp. 10-11.

[48] This may seem a rather speculative translation, but it is (using modern vocabulary) what Tominaga actually meant here. His cryptic phrase *gen ni butsu aru nari* is developed at some length in Chapter 11 where it is clear that he considered language to be conditioned by a variety of factors external to itself. A modern Japanese translation such as Kyōdo's unashamedly interprets this without further ado, but Tominaga did not in fact explain himself further at this point.

The *Shutsuyō Sūtra* says,

> The Buddha announced to the five monks in the Deer Park the basic cause of suffering, which <teaching> had not been seen or heard before. This Dharma is expounded at length in the Sūtra-Piṭaka. When the Buddha was at Rājagṛha, Sudinna of Kalandaka left his home to learn the Way, and because he was the first to transgress the ordinances the Buddha thereupon expounded the Vinaya-Piṭaka. When the Buddha was in Vaiśālī he saw the past and future karma of Vajjiputtaka and announced it to the monks, explaining that those who are free from the five fears and from anger and malice would not fall into an evil rebirth and also would not be reborn in a purgatory. This kind of thing is expounded at length in the Abhidharma.

The *Great Treatise* says:

> Ānanda explained that when the Buddha was at Benares he taught the Dharma in four truths to the five monks. This is called the Sūtra-Piṭaka. Upāli explained that when the Buddha was at Vaiśālī Sudinna first gave way to sensual desire, for which reason the Buddha first defined the major sins and so delivered the Vinaya-Piṭaka in eighty divisions. Ānanda explained that when the Buddha was at Śrāvastī, he announced to the monks that if the five fears, the five sins and the five hatreds were not cut off and extinguished then the living body and mind would suffer anguish and in the next world they would fall into an evil rebirth. Teachings of this kind are called the Abhidharma.

From these writings we can see what the meaning of Tripiṭaka is. Tripiṭaka was after all originally the name of a book and then everybody favoured similar writings with the same name. First were those recited by Kāśyapa and his companions which consisted only of sections numbered one to three called for separately and divided provisionally. This was not like the later practice of distinguishing between the four *Āgamas*, the five sections of the Vinaya and various Abhidharmas, and calling them by this name <Tripiṭaka>. The classifications into four *Āgamas*, five sections of Vinaya and various Abhidharmas are all expansions by the monks of later times. Hence the *Vibhāṣā Treatise* says,

> In the sūtras are mainly expounded teachings about the mind, in the Vinaya are expounded teachings about ordinances, and in

the Abhidharma are expounded teachings about wisdom, and although these sometimes overlap with each other we follow the majority in using these names.

From this we can see that 'Tripiṭaka' was originally the name of one book which was then divided because each recited the place assigned to him. In reality the meanings are mutually related. Later people who have worried because only the Abhidharma is without a sūtra were unaware of this. Thus the *Vibhāṣā Treatise* says,

> Question. Who composed this treatise? Answer. The Buddha, the World-honoured. Question. If so, why is it recorded that Kātyāyanī composed it? Answer. Because the sage received it, preserved it, expounded it and spread it widely abroad. That is why the name of this treatise assigns it to him. However, it is the teaching of the Buddha.

This gets it just right! Originally it was merely designated as a teaching for the Vajjians, but afterwards Kātyāyanī and others expounded it for the benefit of a wider circle. So if doubt is cast on it as being of later origin, then all the sūtras and vinayas must be of later origin too.

The *Great Treatise* says,

> There are three kinds of Dharma Gate. The first is the *Konroku* Gate, the second is the Abhidharma Gate, and the third is the Voidness Gate. The *Konroku* has 3,200,000 words. In the Abhidharma, compiled by Kātyāyanī while the Buddha was in the world, the Buddha himself explains the meaning of the various dharmas and the names of the dharmas.

It also says,

> The Buddha directly expounded the world's greatest Dharma, but he did not explain the meaning of the characteristics <of existence>.[49] The detailed analysis of the meaning of the characteristics is named the Abhidharma Gate.

We can now conclude from this writing that Abhidharma is indeed the name given to the interpretation of the meaning of

[49] That is, the meaning of the characteristics of existence which lies in their interrelations: the classic subject of Abhidharma.

the characteristics. Translating it as *Taihō* refers to analysing them with respect to Dharma, and translating it as *Ehō* refers to analysing the meaning of the characteristics with respect to wisdom. The *Yuga Treatise* also says, 'Because it questions, determines and identifies the nature and characteristics of all dharmas, it is called the Abhidharma.' This gets it just right! Hence although it was the teaching of the Buddha, this analysis of the meaning of the characteristics was originally called Abhidharma, so that <the teaching of the Buddha> was not restricted to the sūtras. Hence the *Shuryōgon Sūtra* says, 'This Abhidharma is the single gate to nirvāṇa for the Bhagavants of the ten directions.'[50] That the *Upadeśas* are contained within the twelve divisions of the teaching has the same implication. The *Great Treatise* says,

> The *Rongi Sūtra*, taught by the Buddha, the sūtras explained by Kātyāyanī, and those taught as a substitute Dharma by the common people of the second millennium, are called the Upadeśas.

We can see the same meaning again here. When later translators of the *Rongi Sūtra* thought that only the sūtras were to be assigned to the Buddha, this is rather like the Confucianist's view of their spiritual transmission, but it does not get to the truth.

The word 'sūtra' is taken to mean 'thread'. A thread is something which leads along very well. What is behind this? Probably because the main body of a sūtra consists of verses, the term verse (*gāthā*) is used to count the sūtra. Thus the *Nirvāṇa Sūtra* says, 'Apart from the sūtras and ordinances (vinaya) the rest of the four line verses are called *gāthās* (verses).'

The sūtras are seen as threads, in the sense that they lead along with the order of the verses depending on them. When the *Butchi Treatise* speaks of 'collecting up' and the *Zōjū Treatise* speaks of 'binding together' they are making the same point. The sūtras are being regarded here as threads. Thus when 'sūtra' is translated as *kaikyō* this is by analogy with the books of Confucianism, but there is a great difference in the

[50] I.e. if the Abhidharma is the gate to nirvāṇa it must be identified with the Buddha's teaching.

meaning. 'Sūtra' has a general meaning and a particular meaning. As one of the twelve divisions of teaching 'sūtras' are distinguished from *gāthās* (verses) and other parts. This is the particular meaning. When the whole collection of Buddhist writings is referred to as 'sūtras', this is the general meaning. Why is this?

Verses are only there for the convenience of chanting, while the content pertains to sūtras. So why does the main part of the sūtras consist of verses? This is because Chinese doctrine necessarily relies on the accompaniment of music. The Book of Odes, the Book of Documents, the Book of Changes, the Kuan Tzŭ and the Lao Tzŭ all make their statements rely on rhyming words. The old sayings and prayers[51] in this country also all make use of recitation. The three countries are all alike in this. Why is it? It is because there was originally no other way but to pass things down from mouth to mouth by chanting. Moreover it gave happiness to the gods of heaven and earth.[52] The *Ninnō Sūtra* says,

> Fumyōō, in accordance with the Dharma of the seven Buddhas, invited one hundred Dharma masters, set up one hundred high seats for them and in the course of two days lectured on *prajñā* in eight hundred thousand million verses.

This indicates it. It tells us that the main body of the sūtras in fact consists of verses, but that this should be understood as a convenience in recitation.

Master Jō Sui said in explanation of this,

> There are about eight reasons why the sūtras have many verses: first, they contain many meanings in few letters, second, the reverent usually rely on stanzas, third, for explaining things repeatedly to dull-witted people, fourth, for the benefit of those who come after, fifth, to follow people's inclinations, sixth, because they are easy to remember, seventh, to clarify what was expounded before, and eighth, to cover what was not taught in prose.

[51] Prayers: *norito*.

[52] This was believed to be so, but it is not really a part of Tominaga's serious argument. With this passing comment he captures something of the spirit of Shintō, but the sting is in the 'moreover'. He viewed recitation as having a transmissional function, whatever the country and whatever the religion.

Of these the fifth and sixth are right and the rest are all rhetoric.

We may reflect on what the *Fuhōzō Sutra* says:

> Memyō <ie Aśvaghoṣa> was going about teaching in Pāṭaliputra. He made exquisitely entertaining music and called it Rāṣṭrapāla. The sound being clear and elegant, he proclaimed the meaning of suffering, voidness and non-self. At that time five hundred princes of the city were enlightened at once, left their homes and practised the way.

The *Zōichi-agon* and the *Gengu Sūtra* say,

> At the time of the Buddha Mahākāśyapa, the monk Mahācunda's youthful voice was well-liked, so he skilfully made up songs which people enjoyed hearing.

The *Binimo Sūtra* says,

> It is not permitted to chant the sūtras by singing songs in a loud voice. This involves five errors, just as when those following other ways teach using songs.

From this we can tell that at that time sūtra exposition usually relied on singing. It was not only for convenience in recitation.[53]

6. *The Nine Divisions, the Twelve Divisions and the Extended Vehicle.*

'The Nine Divisions' and 'The Twelve Divisions' are both terms indicating the whole Tripiṭaka.[54] In later times they have sometimes been used to distinguish the Mahāyāna and the Hīnayāna, but that is mistaken. How do we know this? The *Nirvāṇa Sūtra* says (in the Shōgyō Chapter), 'The Twelve

[53] The point about the use of singing is a little different from the explanation of recitation and the use of verses. It was a further device employed because it gave pleasure and led people to follow Buddhism.

[54] Nine divisions, twelve divisions: these divisions refer to ancient classifications. *Lotus Sūtra*, Chapter 2, for example refers to sermons, verses, former things, birth stories, marvels, origins, parables, mingled prose and verse, and expositions (T IX 7c), but the point is that the lists vary. On the interpretation of these various *genres* as skilful devices, admitting their diversity, cf. Pye 1978, pp. 29-30.

Divisions were imparted by the Buddha', which is as much as to say that the Buddha imparted the whole Tripiṭaka. More specifically the passage below says, 'He imparted the Extended Sūtras.'[55] Similarly, the Shisō Chapter contrasts the Nine Divisions with the Extended <Sūtras>. Again, the *Lotus Sūtra* says (in the Hōben Chapter), 'I expounded the Nine Divisions of Dharma in accordance with living beings, with the intention of bringing them into the Great Vehicle.' It should be noticed that this refers to the whole Tripiṭaka without yet distinguishing the terms for the Great and Small <Vehicles>. Therefore the *Great Treatise* still teaches that both the Great and Small Vehicles have the Nine Divisions, which is enough to show how the matter lies. When the *Nirvāṇa Sūtra* also says, 'The Small Vehicle does not have a section of Extended <Sūtras>' the statement that the Small Vehicle is alone in lacking Extended Sūtras is made to pour scorn on the Small Vehicle. Although it is called the Small Vehicle it does <in fact> have Extended <Sūtras> in accordance with the capacity <of the hearers>, as later people recognised when they said that the Small Vehicle also has Twelve Divisions. This <*Nirvāṇa Sūtra*> is merely saying that the Extended Sūtras were the sole property of the Great Vehicle. The *Nirvāṇa Sūtra* also says, 'The sūtras in Eleven Divisions belong to both vehicles while the Extended Division belongs to the bodhisattvas'. The *Matoroga Treatise* also says, 'Only the Extended Division is the Bodhisattva Collection, the Eleven Divisions are the Śrāvaka Collection', which comes to the same thing.

The terms *Hōdō* and *Hōkō* <Extended Sūtras> are not different in meaning. *Hōdō* is simply used to distinguish the Great Vehicle <Sūtras> within the Twelve Divisions. They are not separately existing sūtras. The *Nirvāṇa Sūtra* says (in the Shōgyō Chapter),

> From the Buddha there issued the Twelve Divisons, from the Twelve Divisions there issued the sūtras, and from the sūtras there issued the Extended Sūtras. It also says (in the Shisō Chapter), 'The incomplete script is called the Nine Divisons

[55] Extended Sūtras: cf. note 18 above.

> Sūtra, while the complete script is called the Extended Great Vehicle Sūtra.'[56]

In the *Great Treatise* it says, 'Why were the *Lotus Sūtra* and other Extended Sūtras entrusted to the bodhisattva Kiō?' The *Fugen Sūtra* says, 'This Extended Sūtra is the eye of the buddhas.' There are also places which refer to the Extended Great Vehicle Sūtras. Again, the *Nirvāṇa Sūtra* has the phrase 'Great Extended Great Nirvāṇa <Sūtra>'. These are all terms which praise the Great <Vehicle>. There is no question of a separate sūtra. It is the same when the *Kegon Sūtra*, the *Engaku Sūtra*, the *Shōman Sūtra*, and the *Shishiku Sūtra* are called Extended, and again when the *Great Treatise* refers to 'those following the Extended Way'. These are also all terms which praise the Great <Vehicle>. There is no difference in the meaning. Later scholars perhaps did not know this when they suggested a reason and a time for the promulgation of the Extended Sūtras, but it is a mistake. Of the two vehicles the Śrāvaka Dharma is the Small Vehicle and the Bodhisattva Dharma is the Great Vehicle. The theory that beyond the Great Vehicle or Bodhisattva Vehicle there is another Buddha Vehicle or Sole Vehicle, is also an idea put up by a particular school. The *Daijōdōshō Sūtra* says,

> The Dharma of the *śrāvakas*, the Dharma of the *pratyekabuddhas*, the Dharma of the Bodhisattvas and the Dharma of the Buddhas, all flow into the great sea of Vairocana's store of knowledge.

The 'great sea of the store of knowledge' is a name for the tenth stage, the Buddha stage. Thus here there is a special Buddha Vehicle. The *Laṅkāvatāra Sūtra* says, 'There is no setting up of vehicles. What I teach is a Sole Vehicle. I distinguish and expound the vehicles for the guidance of living beings.' The commentary on the *Ryōyakushō Treatise* says,

[56] 'Incomplete script': literally 'half-lettered', an epithet for the Hīnayāna as opposed to the 'full-lettered' Mahāyāna. Referring to the latter the text actually carries the Sanskrit term *vyākaraṇa* meaning here not 'prediction' as often in Buddhist writings, but 'knowledge of words'. Cf. Kyōdo, p. 244, n.18.

> The Tathāgata has three ways of establishing the true Dharma, first the Small Vehicle, second the Great Vehicle, third the Sole Vehicle. The third is the supreme, and is therefore called the superior establishment.

Thus here there is a special Sole Vehicle. Above the Sole Vehicle there comes the Non-Vehicle. The *Laṅkāvatāra Sūtra* says,

> Even if I teach all the *deva* and *Brahman* vehicles, the *śrāvaka* and *pratyekabuddha* vehicles and all the buddha-tathāgata vehicles, if there is no turning of the mind all the vehicles fail to reach the ultimate. If this mind is extinguished there is no vehicle and no rider.

Thus here there is a special Non-Vehicle. These are all teachings superseding each other layer by layer. Again, we can reflect on the T'ang translation of the commentary on the *Ryōyakushō Treatise* which says, 'The Bodhisattva Vehicle is the Buddha Vehicle, and above it there is no other.' This again is the individual saying of one school. It is not the same as those mentioned above. We may also reflect on the *Lotus Sūtra* which says (in the Hōben Chapter), 'There is only One Vehicle of Dharma, no second and no third.' and 'By the way of the One Vehicle only I teach many other bodhisattvas', and 'I expound this Great Vehicle Sūtra for the sake of sons of the Buddha; whether *śrāvakas* or bodhisattvas, there is no doubt they will attain buddhahood.' Here the distinction between the Bodhisattva Vehicle, the Buddha Vehicle and the Sole Vehicle is done away with. Consider also the *Nirvāṇa Sūtra* which says, 'All living beings equally have the buddha-nature. They are all equally in the One Vehicle.' This is the One Vehicle teaching of the Combination School.

7. *Two analogies in the Nirvāṇa Sūtra and the Kegon Sūtra.*

The *Nirvāṇa Sūtra* says, in the Shōgyō Chapter,

> It is like a cow, for example, giving out milk, the milk giving whey, the whey giving curds, the <fresh> curds giving mature curds, and the mature curds giving ghee, the ghee being the

supreme. Buddhism[57] is similar to this. From the Buddha there come the scriptures in Twelve Divisions, from the scriptures in Twelve Divisions come the Sūtras, from the Sūtras come the Extended Sūtras, from the Extended Sūtras comes the *Prajñāpāramitā* <*Sūtra*>, and from the *Prajñāpāramitā* <*Sūtra*> comes the *Great Nirvāṇa* <*Sūtra*> which is like the ghee.

This is a story to illustrate the Buddha-nature. This analogy was originally from the Buddha's affirmation of King Mukuza's <i.e. Vimalakīrti> praising the *Nirvāṇa* <Sūtra> teaching as the supreme, saying that the *Nirvāṇa Sūtra* is like the best of the five flavours in the parable. 'Twelve Divisions' refers to the Tripiṭaka, 'Sūtras' does not yet distinguish between divisions and between the Great and Small Vehicles, 'Extended Sūtras' refers to the scriptures of the Great Vehicle, distinguishing within the Sūtras, and the *Prajñāpāramitā Sūtra* is the pith[58] of the Extended Sūtras. Furthermore, redoubling wisdom, the *Great Nirvāṇa Sūtra* is the 'great perfect peace'[59] and the pith of *prajñā*. Each one distinguishes the pith of the one preceding. This is the basic meaning. However later scholars have all misinterpreted it saying, 'The Twelve Divisions are the *Kegon* <*Sūtra*>, the Sūtras are the *Āgamas*, the Extended Sūtras are the *Vimalakīrti Sūtra* and the *Shiyaku Sūtra*.' This makes it fit in with Tendai Daishi's 'Five Teachings'.[60] The Twelve Divisions and sūtras are as explained above, so why should they be limited to the *Kegon* and the *Āgamas*? The milk is

[57] Kyōdo's modern Japanese reads 'the Buddha's teaching' while Tominaga's text simply has the character for Buddha. Some addition is necessary to complete the sense but actually what it means is the whole of Buddhist teaching as a received system, i.e. Buddhism. The usage is close to Tominaga's own as found in the opening lines of the preface to *Emerging from Meditation* (cf. also note 1 above, thereon). The present quotation from the *Great Treatise* is a good example of the tendency to objectify the tradition while reflecting on it, an essential prerequisite (here current in Asian thought) for Tominaga's ideas.

[58] On the background and meaning of the 'pith' metaphor cf. Pye 1978, pp. 133ff.

[59] I.e. nirvāṇa.

[60] The influential Tendai (Chinese T'ien T'ai) classification of the Buddhist scriptures divided them into the following five sections: *Kegon Sūtra*, the *Āgamas*, *Vaipulya Sūtras* (various Mahāyāna sūtras), *Great Prajñā Sūtra*, *Lotus* and *Nirvāṇa Sūtras*. Cf. Hurvitz 1962 and Petzold 1979. Tominaga's point is that there was development and creativity in the elaboration of such schemes.

coarser than the whey, but the *Kegon* is superior to the Deer Park teaching. This does not fit at all. The original purport of the sūtra was to distinguish the strength or lightness of the five flavours as a parable to indicate the highest teaching. However they fit it together with the 'five teachings' and end up saying things like 'This is meant for lower natures', and 'This refers to the order of appearance', thus losing sight of the meaning.

The *Kegon Sūtra* says, in the Shōki Chapter,

> It is like the rising sun which first illumines the peaks of the great mountains, then the great mountains, then the diamond mountain[61] and then the plains. The light of the sun does not conceive of it so. It is just that the difference between high and low exists on the earth, and this gives the sun's illumination its before and after. It is similar with the Tathāgata. The sun-disc of his wisdom is always sending forth light. First it illumines the mountain tops of the bodhisattvas, next it illumines the *pratyekabuddhas*, next the beings with good disposition, and finally all beings in general. The Tathāgata does not fundamentally conceive of it like this. It is just that the good dispositions of the living beings vary and this gives rise to these various distinctions.

This analogy originally meant that there was from the first no distinction between shallow and deep in the Tathāgata's teaching, but that while the first, supreme teaching was actually received by the assembly of bodhisattvas or above, those below, namely the *pratyekabuddhas* and *śrāvakas*, received it in a varied form and matured at their own level. However if the highest is to be sought there is no getting away from the first teaching, and if the most exquisite is sought there is no getting away from the Kegon. This was the original purport of the sūtra. However later scholars have again misinterpreted this saying,

> The *Kegon* <*Sūtra*> was the first illumination, the *Āgamas* were the second illumination, the Extended Sūtras were the third illumination, and the *Lotus* and *Nirvāṇa Sūtras* were the fourth and fifth illuminations.

This was also to make it fit with Tendai Daishi's 'five

[61] This refers to Mount Tetsuchi, see also Chapter 1.

teachings'. There is no argument about regarding the *Kegon Sūtra* as the first illumination, but it is quite inadequate to regard the *Āgamas*, which are the most elementary Dharma, as the second illumination, and then again to regard the *Lotus* and the *Nirvāṇa Sūtras*, which are the most exquisite, as the fourth and fifth illuminations. This shows that the analogy is also not adequate. In addition, the sūtra only gives a sequence of four illuminations, but they make it fit in with the 'five teachings', thus again losing sight of the meaning.

The long and short of these two analogies is that the *Nirvāṇa Sūtra* puts its trust in the last <teaching> and supports the purest ghee, while the *Kegon Sūtra* puts its trust in the first <teaching> and praises the sun's first illumination of the mountain tops. They set up analogies which show a contradictory order, each making out its teaching to be the most exquisite, but being poles apart – as far apart as Ko and Etsu <i.e. north and south>.[62] Tendai Daishi must have known this when he combined these two analogies and used them to demonstrate his 'five teachings'. He saw that these analogies had it in them to make it easier for people to understand, and so he took them up as a convenience and gave them that meaning. It did not amount to a proof of his teaching. He certainly did not mean the same as scholars who have taken this up in the sense that the 'five periods' were entirely based on these two analogies. Tendai's original intention is as stated above. Thus later generations who criticise Tendai Daishi are not right.[63] It is the same thing with those 'four proclamations' in the *Chō-agon*, or the four kinds of *sūtra* in the *Gattōzanmai*, or the four *bodhi* <enlightenments> in the *Nirvāṇa Sūtra*. The setting up of 'four teachings' on this basis is also just a provisional way of putting it. Later people such as Shō An and so on all stretch the argument and, while explaining the meaning, fall into inconsistency. The *Myōgenshinki* says, 'It does not amount to proof, but it does give the feel', and that is right.

[62] Ko and Etsu: two Chinese states.

[63] This does not mean that Tominaga supports the whole Tendai system. He means that Tendai Daishi (Chih I) knew that it was a contrivance at the time, but that later it turned into a dogma which is at odds with the realities of historical development. It should not be overlooked that Tominaga has great respect for some of the towering figures of the Buddhist tradition.

8. *Supernatural abilities*.

The common people of India are very fond of magic, and similarly the people of China are fond of literature. All those who establish a teaching and expound a Way find they must put it forward in terms of such things, for if they do not, the people will not trust them. This is clear from the following. The *Vibhāṣā Treatise* says, 'He is not like the *pratyekabuddhas* who can only make living beings rejoice by using supernatural abilities, but cannot preach Dharma.' The *Great Treatise* says,

> The bodhisattvas attain supernatural abilities for the sake of living beings and manifest fantastic marvels to get the living beings to purify their minds.

It also says,

> If birds had no wings they could not fly up high, and if bodhisattvas had no supernatural abilities they could not teach living beings in accordance with their inclinations.

As the other teachings of the time all made use of magic in their promotion, even though Śākyamuni surpassed them in his teaching, he could not avoid using magic provisionally when making it known.

The *Great Treatise* says,

> There was once an evil heretic whose heart ached with envy and who slanderously said, 'The Buddha's wisdom does not surpass that of others. He merely misleads the world with magic.' In order to put a stop to this conceited arrogance the Buddha displayed countless feats of supernatural ability and also countless powers of wisdom.

It also says,

> All things are patent of transformation, but while the changes performed by the pundits of other ways cannot last for more than seven days, the transformations enjoyed by the buddhas and their disciples have no time limit.

Thus we read in the *Hōshaku Sūtra*, 'The *Tathāgata* displays supernatural transformations in order to tame living beings of their conceit.' The other ways call it magic and the Buddha called it supernatural ability, but the reality is identical. The disciples transmitting their respective ways all relied on it and used it to promote their teachings. Nine-tenths of the teachings given in the sūtras are nothing but this.

If we consider this with regard to the Twelve Divisions of teaching we find the *adbhutadharma* or 'unprecedenteds', which are true magic, and the (*itivṛttaka*) or 'original matters', the (*jātaka*) or 'birth stories', the (*vyākaraṇa*) or 'predictions of destiny', and the (*nidāna*) or 'cause and occasion', which are all things to do with magic. The *vaipulya* or 'extended <sūtras>' are magical sermons. So half of <the Twelve Divisions> amounts to magic. Then again the *Mahāsāṁghikas* have compiled a book of spells as well as the Tripiṭaka. When the *Jiji Treatise* says, 'Among the four *dhāraṇīs* there is a spell which can work sorcery because it has supernatural power', this too is magic. Moreover there are many illustrative stories based on magic in the sūtras, either because in India many such things have been seen and heard, or else because they like it. It is similar when the disciples claimed sayings of Śākyamuni and set them up to supersede each other and take each other over. This too is magic. The teachings of thirty-two heavens and of birth and decease in six different states are also magic. Saying that seven buddhas previously surpassed the other ways is also magic. Bonten's <i.e. Brahman's> coming to call for the Buddha to teach is also magic. These things are all magic.[64] The learning of Indian people really consists in using magic to propound a way. If they do not use magic in their exposition the people will not believe it or follow it.

This is why I already said, 'If all the monks in the world know that the Buddha made provisional use of magic, and if all the Confucianists in the world similarly know that Confucian teaching is built on literary form, why do they have such a petty understanding of the way?[65] As Shiki once put it to me, 'The Indians like words such as "innumerable" and "unlimited"

[64] Tominaga includes various forms of teaching here which might not normally be thought to come under the English word 'magic'. His point is that all of these things, such as claiming alternative sayings of the Buddha, require the credulity of others to be effective.

[65] Kyōdo arbitrarily introduces the technical phrase *makoto no michi* ('Way of truth') here, which is otherwise found in the *Writings of an Old Man*. This may be misleading.

and that is indeed their nature.' That the Chinese like words which are difficult to explain, while eastern people like words which are straightforward and honest, is also indeed their nature. Analogies like that of Mount Sumeru in the poppy seed and Indra's net are also things which find favour in the mind of that people. There are many analogies of this kind, and they are rooted in magic. Although the Chinese go in for 'mountains lying in the plains' and 'elephants having three ears', this is rooted in literary form. Eastern people[66] do not like such story-telling and limit themselves to plain speaking. (Shiki's surname was Miyoshi and his given name was Muneaki. He was an Ōsaka man and a respected friend, but now he has died.)

Teachings like karmic retribution and heaven and purgatory, originally started in non-Buddhist schools, are also things liked by the Indian character. Śākyamuni used them to lead people with, thereby winning over people of the lower kind. He then set up the teaching of attaining Buddhahood by detachment from particulars, and leaving the lower level he won over people of the higher kind. This was possible because those teachings were not originally bad, and moreover the Indian people liked them. Nevertheless the reality is that it was a skilful means. It is similar to the people of In revering demons and the king of In referring to gods and heavenly beings in his proclamations. The Confucianists scold others for duping people, but it must be said that they do not realise they belong to the same ilk. At the same time the Buddhists complain that the Confucianists lack such teachings, which just shows that they themselves do not know it is a skilful means.

Since ancient times, therefore, those expounding a way or setting up a teaching have always had to depend on common custom and use it to guide people. Not even wise men can avoid this. Whether magic for the Indians, literary form for the Chinese, or plain speaking for eastern people, all are common customs. To quarrel over such customs always arouses manly vigour. What is wrong with manly vigour? It is all right if it serves the good.[67] Some people ask how to acquire supernatural abilities. The answer is that it originally begins in the perception

[66] Eastern people means people who live east of China. In effect Tominaga's Japanese readers will have thought of themselves.

[67] I.e. such debate is also part of the religious life, but the question is whether it serves to establish truth and promote the true Way.

of ideas. This is fully explained in the *Great Treatise*.

The *Great Treatise* says,

> Question. How do supernatural abilities come about? Because a bodhisattva is detached from the five passions, acquires all *dhyānas* and has compassion, he takes supernatural abilities for the benefit of living beings, and manifests fantastic marvels to get the living beings to purify their minds. Why is this? If they performed no marvels they could not bring the multitude to salvation. With this idea the *bodhisattva-mahāsattvas*[68] link the mind with the space inside the body, try to extinguish the sense of weight and hold voidness and lightness in view. There will arise a great desire for the mind to advance, wisdom will reflect on whether the power of the mind can raise the body, or not yet, and it will be realised in oneself that the power of the mind is greatly able to raise the body. To illustrate, it is like a cripple learning to walk. If one constantly breaks down the sense of weight and trains in voidness and lightness, one will then be able to fly. The second step is to be able to transform things, turning earth into water, water into earth, wind into fire and fire into wind. All the elements of the cosmos can command such transformations, making gold into rubbish and rubbish into gold. They can change anything like this. When changing earth to have the characteristics of water, they train steadily in the idea of water and concentrate on not letting thoughts of earth return again, and then the characteristics of earth become those of water in accordance with their thoughts. In this manner they are able to transform all things. Question. If so, what difference is there between this and entering all dharmas?[69] Answer. Entering all dharmas is the first step towards supernatural abilities. If one has first already entered all dharmas, this entails the deliverances and victories and makes the mind supple, and after this it is easy to enter supernatural abilities. Then, next, in the case of entering all dharmas, one sees oneself that earth is transformed into water, but other people do not see it, whereas in the case of supernatural abilities

[68] 'The bodhisattvas, the great beings': this is a common epithet in Mahāyāna Buddhism.

[69] I.e. attaining enlightenment. In Mahāyāna terms attaining enlightenment involves recognising the equivalence of all elements of existence. Hence if such transformations are possible this must presuppose penetrating the true character of all these elements or factors (dharmas). To the enlightened person this simply means not being caught in the differences of things (which is however a spiritual as well as an intellectual attainment). To the unenlightened person this may be communicated as a transformation of elements into other elements.

> one sees that in reality it is water, and others see that in reality it is water.

Nevertheless this is difficult for eastern people. Why so? Because customs are different. Ō Jū's *Ronkō* says this quite clearly. He argued that when Zen monks in later times interpreted supernatural abilities as fetching water and so on, this theory was inevitable.[70]

In the Gendoku Chapter of the *Ronkō* it says,

> In sunny lands the people are restless. Restless people have poison on their tongues. For this reason the people of So and Etsu are restless and aggressive, and when they speak with people they spit at them and their veins stand out, causing injury. In the lands of the extremely hot southern region, if the people there pray towards a tree it withers and if they spit at a bird it falls. Mediums, who can use prayers to alleviate people's illness and smooth over their misfortunes, when born south of the Yangtze have temperaments of fire.

Again, we may consider Chō's *Hintairoku*, which says,

> Tō Ba was guarding Yō Shū. He dreamed he went into the mountains where a tiger came and attacked him, but a Taoist who was there scolded the tiger, which ran off. The next morning a Taoist enquired of him, 'Did you not go out last night and get frightened?' Tō Ba exclaimed, 'You rascal! I would still like to put a cane to your back. Do you pretend I do not know you gave me a magic dream?' Whereupon the Taoist went off in surprise.

If we think about it, this too is magic. When they make people experience dreams in most cases they are this type of magic: Ka Sen Nen bewitching King Ki Ra, the Ming Emperor dreaming he saw a golden man, Gen Sō of the T'ang dreaming of graceful golden letters in the sky, Shuku Sō dreaming of a monk chanting to Hōshō Nyorai, Dai Sō dreaming that he was at play in a mountain temple. Ki Sō of the Sung dreaming of a supernatural sky, and Shin Sō dreaming that a supernatural monk was riding through the sky on a horse. These are all in the long run nothing but magic.

[70] I.e. it was inevitable because their customs and exceptations were completely different from those of Indians.

9. *Stages.*

Originally no use was made of the terms *shōmon* <*śrāvaka*> and *engaku* <*pratyekabuddha*> in the Small Vehicle. They were terms of contempt used by the Great Vehicle school to add importance to bodhisattvas. Hearers <*śrāvakas*> are those who follow the Buddha, hear his voice and understand, but are not yet fully enlightened. This can be seen from the following. The *Kegon Sūtra* says,

> Aspiring to the topmost ten goodnesses they discipline themselves for their own benefit. Having an inferior wisdom they are afraid of the three worlds and they lack great compassion. They follow others, hear their voices and attain understanding and hence they are called Hearers.

The *Jūji Treatise* says, 'They became proficient by hearing others and that is why they are called Hearers.' It also says, 'We living beings only have names for things, and therefore it is thanks to the voice that we understand. That is why we are called Hearers.' Or again it says, 'By the voice of the Buddha-way we make all the people hear, and therefore we are called Hearers.' These are all mistaken. We should recognise that these were various kinds of interpretation in India.

The word *engaku* <*pratyekabuddha*> means to be enlightened as a result of karmic attainment. It is similar to the Confucian idea of attaining virtue oneself. It means not following or hearing the Buddha, and is no less than independent enlightenment which is achieved alone by the individual. The *Great Treatise* says, 'There are two kinds of *pratyekabuddha*,[71] the first is said to have solitary enlightenment and the second to have enlightenment as to cause.' The *Shuryōgon Sūtra* says the same. The *Kusha Treatise* also says that there are two kinds of solitary enlightenment. The first is called a caused enlightenment obtained through perseverance in group practice with mutual guidance. The second is known as the rhinoceros horn solitary enlightenment which is obtained through solitary study. These are all solitary enlightenment and similar in that they do not extend to the

[71] A different term is used here for *pratyekabuddha*, but this does not affect the argument.

conversion of others. This is what is meant when the *Kegon Sūtra* says,

> He does not follow the teaching of others because he attains enlightenment by himself, and because he is not yet furnished with the skilful means of great compassion.

The *Nirvāṇa Sūtra* says,

> The *pratyekabuddhas* only manifest supernatural abilities when converting living beings, and on the last day they are silent, with nothing to proclaim.

The *Yuga Treatise* says, 'They only display their own characteristics, and because they utter no words of teaching for them they display the various realms of supernatural ability.' The *Great Treatise* says, 'The *pratyekabuddha* people can also expound one or two verses.' They are all giving it their own meaning here, and are mistaken when they extend it to include not teaching others. It is also a mistake when the *Great Treatise* understands solitary enlightenment as meeting in the Buddha-world. In the Tendai Chapter of the first part of the *Prajñā Sūtra* there is the saying, 'Solitary enlightenment envisaged and solitary enlightenment achieved.' Again Ji On quoted the *Ninnō Sūtra* as saying there was a band of *pratyekabuddhas* and said, 'When Śākyamuni left the world five hundred *pratyekabuddhas* came out of the mountains.' Everyone should see the original text. It is also a mistake to explain the word 'cause' as in 'caused enlightenment' by reference to the law of cause and effect. This does not lead to that word.

Bodhisattvas are those who have already reached the level of enlightenment and are able to give enlightenment to others. The *Great Treatise* says, '*Bodhi* refers to the Buddha-way and *sattva* refers to bringing on living beings.' This is what is meant when the *Vibhāṣā Treatise* says, 'Being enlightened oneself and enlightening others is called bodhisattvahood.' The bodhisattva is the highest and the ultimate. The Buddha is also a bodhisattva-buddha and apart from the bodhisattvas there is no Buddha. It is for this reason that in the *Muryōgi Sūtra* the bodhisattva extols his own virtue by saying, 'At the Tathāgata stage he is firm and immovable.' That is its underlying meaning. However, in the *Zenkai Sūtra* we find reference to Myōjibosatsu <Bodhisattva-In-Name>, Higibosatsu <Bodhisattva-No-Meaning> and Bosatsu Cāṇḍāla <Bodhisattva-Low-Class>.[72] In the *Mukushō Sūtra* we find Ushitsubosatsu (Bodhisattva-With-Sickness).[73] The *Great Treatise* has Shoshinhaiebosatsu (Bodhisattva-Defeating-The-First-Mind). The *Yuga Treatise* has Bosatsu-Tōshugetai (Bodhisattva-Falling-Back-With-Laziness), and also both dull-witted and sharp-witted bodhisattvas. These are all terms given by different groups. The reality is that they are expositions building up in layers on the term bodhisattva.[74] While 'Buddha' has the meaning of enlightenment, *śrāvakas* and *pratyekabuddhas* have already experienced it in themselves, and bodhisattvas have already experienced it in themselves but can go on to extend it to others. Thus 'Buddha' is a comprehensive name. However, the *Lotus Sūtra* says, 'There is no doubt that *śrāvakas* and bodhisattvas will all become Buddhas.' It also says, 'All the practices which you perform belong to the bodhisattva way. If you steadily pursue them you will become Buddhas.' The *Kegon Sūtra* says,

> If people's dispositions are bright and sharp, if they have the mind of great compassion, if they bring abundant benefit to all living beings, I will expound for them the bodhisattva way. If they have the unsurpassed mind and are resolved to delight in great things, I will show them the Buddha-body and expound the inexhaustible Buddha-dharma.

According to this there is a further distinct Buddha<-stage>

[72] *Sendara* stands for Sanskrit *cāṇḍāla*, a despised class below the four main castes. Tominaga's adducement of *higibosatsu* is said to be based on a mis-reading of the text (Kyōdo, p. 282, n. 42 and Mizuta, p. 44, note ad loc.). However the point is that bodhisattvas are not always regarded as equal to a Tathāgata.

[73] This is a reference to Mañjuśrī's characterising Vimalakīrti as a sick bodhisattva on account of his feigned illness. This condition of Vimalakīrti is not really a stage in the bodhisattva's own development. It is simply a mode of being which he adopts as long as there are creatures living in conditioned existence. This distinction does not matter for Tominaga's argument because he is concerned in a general way with the variety of aspects under which a bodhisattva may be conceived.

[74] At this point Kyōdo, reprehensibly, introduces Tominaga's semi-technical term *kajō* into the modern Japanese translation (p. 102), although it is not in the original text.

beyond the bodhisattva level. It is similar again when the Hossō school expounds a sequence in the practice of bodhisattvas, again giving the terms of one group, making a special virtue of them, and putting pressure on the Small Vehicle. The Great Vehicle originally had no Books of Discipline <Vinaya>, and that it now does is the same story all over again.

Master Gen Ju got the point when he explained it thus,

> It is in order to draw them along by skilful means like a shadowy resemblance, because if the teaching is completely different they would have difficulty in trusting and believing it.

In the *Ryōyakushō Treatise* the ten <stages of> faith are spoken of as those of the ordinary bodhisattvas and the ten <stages of> release are spoken of as those of the saintly bodhisattvas. Why should there be a distinction between ordinary and saintly bodhisattvas? It is only to make a name for a group. The four fruits of the *śrāvakas* are the basis of it. Dividing them up into ten stages, as in the *Butsuji Sūtra* and the *Daijōdōshō Sūtra*, is a superseding doctrine. *Pratyeka-buddhas* and bodhisattvas originally had no stages. How do we know this? The *Muryōgi Sūtra* says, 'There are three Dharmas, four fruits and two ways.' The three Dharmas are the illustrious Dharma, the superior Dharma and the World's First Dharma, the four fruits are the four fruits of the *śrāvakas*, and the two ways are the *pratyekabuddha* and bodhisattva ways. The *pratyekabuddha* and bodhisattva ways are named side by side, which is how we can tell. Dividing them up into ten stages, or expounding a sequence of disciplines, are all teachings of different groups superseding each other. They are not the original truth.[75] The superseding teachings of different groups went so far as to divide up the Buddha into ten realms (as in the *Butsujūji Sūtra* and *Daijōdōshō Sūtra*), three enlightenments (as in the *Treatise on the Awakening of Faith*), and even a Buddha of the original mind (as in the *Dainichi Sūtra*). If the Buddha had already

[75] 'Not the original truth': Kyōdo puts 'teaching' rather than 'truth', and indeed this is consistent with Tominaga's general standpoint. However the text does say 'truth', another indication that he felt there was a truth within Buddhism as well as its mere formulations.

attained the utmost, why do they have to go on to make distinctions between realms and grades, and former and latter? These are just cases of different groups superseding each other and stretching out the teaching. As to the 'four fruits' the <idea of the> *srotāpanna*, or stream-winner, kept the original meaning. The *sakṛdāgāmin*, or once-returner, is similar to the Confucian idea of progressing by the day and by the month, and the *anāgāmin* or never-returner is similar to the Confucian idea of not lapsing from benevolence for three months; but to interpret these in terms of rebirth is a mistake. The (*arhat*), who is not subject to rebirth and is thus equivalent to a buddha, is similar to the Confucian idea of the sage.

The *Shibunritsu* and *Gobunritsu* both say, 'After the Buddha had brought across the five <ascetics> there were six *arhats* in the world.' This is what is meant when the *Zōjū Treatise* says, 'The *arhats* and the Tathāgata attained instantaneously.' That later people reduced them to *śrāvakas* was a case of teaching by different groups superseding each other. In the *Kegon Sūtra* there are ten Brahma-practices but not the ten <stages of> faith. In the *Ninnō Sūtra* there are no realms of enlightenment. In the new *Sūtra of Golden Light*, the *Shōtennō Prajñā Sūtra* and the *Great Prajñā Sūtra*, only ten Buddha-realms are expounded and there is no setting out of realms of enlightenment in terms of thirty states of mind. The *Laṅkāvatāra Sūtra* adds a 'wisdom of self-enlightenment' as well as having 'exquisite enlightenment'. The *Nirvāṇa Sūtra* provides for 'five practices'. However in the Myōji Chapter the ten abodes come after the ten <stages of> faith, while in the Shakugi Chapter the order is the usual one. What in the *Ninnō Sūtra* is called 'giving the mind' is referred to in the *Yōraku Sūtra* as 'abandoning the mind' and in the *Kegon Sūtra* as 'not retreating' but it does not teach 'seeing and discipline'. The *Mirokumon Treatise* says,

> The Hearers first cut off the delusions of seeing and afterwards cut off the delusions of discipline, but bodhisattvas at their first stage instantaneously cut off all the passions in the Way of seeing and in the Way of discipline.

In the *Ninnō Sūtra* there are three wisdoms and ten saintlinesses while in the Sarvāstivādin teaching there are three wisdoms and four saintlinesses. In the *Ninnō Sūtra* there are fifty-one levels. In the *Yōraku Sūtra* there are fifty-two levels, in the *Kegon Sūtra* there are forty-one levels, in the *Great Prajñā Sūtra* there are forty-two levels, and in the *Shuryōgon Sūtra* there are fifty-seven levels although it also speaks of sixty saintly levels. The *Jiji Treatise* makes the first stage the Way of seeing, and the *Ninnō Sūtra* puts the first fruit in the fourth stage, but later generations explained this by setting up a common and a separate set <of stages>. Again in the Kyōe Chapter of the *Ninnō Sūtra* <the delusions of> seeing are cut off at the third stage and thoughts are exhausted at the sixth stage, while in the Juji Chapter seeing is cut off at the fourth stage and thoughts are exhausted at the seventh stage. Later generations saved the situation by coming up with the 'common teaching' and the 'separate teaching'. Both the *Yuga Treatise* and the *Ryōyakushō Treatise* teach twelve abodes for the *śrāvaka*, but these are now found in the Sarvāstivādin scriptures. In the *Nirvāṇa Sūtra* the *arhats* abide at the tenth stage, but the *Hongō* links the seventh stage with the bodhisattvas. The *Ninnō Sūtra* puts *arhats* at the seventh stage and bodhisattvas at the eighth stage. The *Ryōyakushō Treatise* assigns the eighth stage and onwards to the Sole Vehicle. The *Great Treatise*, the *Laṅkāvatāra Sūtra* and the *Consciousness only Treatise* differ about the placing of compassion and wisdom from the first bodhisattva stage onwards. However the *Treatise on the Awakening of Faith* makes it 'equality in discipline and in cutting off, training in both moment by moment'. Master Gen Ju explained it by distinguishing the beginning and the end. Although there were originally seven wisdoms and saintlinesses taught, the *Jōjitsu Treatise* makes them twenty-seven. Although there were originally eighty-eight passions taught, the *Jōjitsu Treatise* makes them ninety-eight. Although fifteen minds of the Way of seeing were taught, the *Jōjitsu Treatise* makes them sixteen. The *Great Treatise* gives two varieties of the ten stages, one has the 'common' series, *kenne* and so on, and the other has the 'separate' series, *kangi* and so on. The ten bodhisattva stages in the *Laṅkāvatāra Sūtra* are the same as 'the separate', except that the eighth stage and upwards are regarded as 'superior' and the seventh stage and below are regarded as 'common'.

The present writer considers that even this 'Great Vehicle' and 'Combined Teaching' are both just the names given out for different groups, each insisting on its own teaching, superseding each other and thrusting each other aside. Of course there were discrepancies from the beginning. Later scholars who twist and distort things in many directions to fit them together are all mistaken. It is the same again when the various schools are numbered from the superior to the next best. Originally there were no graduations. If the sixth grade is the right one, why would anyone stop with the third, fourth and fifth? Sayings such as that of the *Kusha Treatise* that the *arhat* is at the perseverance stage,[76] are just so many conjectural view-points. Again, when expounding 'irreversibility' <of a bodhisattva's progress>, the *Kusha Treatise* puts it at the time of attaining endurance, the *Jōjitsu Treatise* puts it from the first two roots of goodness onwards, and the *Jūji Treatise* puts it from the realm of vision and above. The *Bussho Treatise* regards the *śrāvakas* as <at the stage of> suffering and enduring, the *pratyekabuddhas* as supreme in the world, and the bodhisattvas as a tenfold transformation of merit. All of these are the designations of different groups. Similarly, when expounding the passing over of the four fruits, some speak of instantaneous detachment and passing over of the two intermediate fruits, while others negate this, others negate the wisdoms and the saintlinesses altogether, others regard the transformation of merit as indispensable, or see the streamwinners and *arhats* as indispensable, or only the once-returner and the never-returner fruits as essential? but these are all the designations of different groups. Why should it be necessary to make all these fit together? Why should a harmonious interpretation be essential? Then again there is the theory of conversion <to the Mahāyāna>[77] which is nothing but a take-over theory. Why so? The Sarvāstivādin <or Existence> School asserts itself as the Sarvāstivādin School, and the Emptiness School asserts itself as the

[76] It is not clear whether a direct quotation is intended here. The statement has not been identified.

[77] The theory of drawing together the *śrāvakas, pratyekabuddhas* and bodhisattvas into one Buddha-vehicle, described graphically by Mizuta as 'drawing the water into one's own paddy-field' (Mizuta, pp. 47-8, note ad loc.).

Emptiness School, each one putting forward proofs for its way. Why do they put forward the idea of conversion? This is for the Great Vehicle to make itself important. Consider also what the *Kegon Sūtra* says about Buddha-stages: 'When he first raised the mind <of enlightenment> he immediately attained true enlightenment.' However, when it then goes on to expound the various 'abidings', these are nothing but polemical teachings.

10. *Seven buddhas and three aeons.*

We cannot now know the names of the seven <previous> buddhas mentioned by Śākyamuni. The *Āgamas* and the *Vibhāṣā Treatise* are mistaken when they include Śākyamuni to make up the seven. How do we know this? We know it from many sources such as the following. The *Ninnō Sūtra* when referring to Fumyō-ō says, 'He performed this in accordance with the Dharma taught by the previous seven buddhas.' The *Daijū Sūtra* also has a saying about 'coming after the seven buddhas'. The *Kegon Sūtra* refers to 'the seventh hermit'. The *Daihōdōdarani Sūtra* says, 'In order to explain this to Mañjuśrī the world-honoured One said, "This is the *dhāraṇī* <i.e. spell> which was made by the seven buddhas of the past".' Then again, those who sought to match the seven buddhas in their discipline <of reviewing> characteristics[78] set up the teaching of the three aeons[79] and thus came out one level ahead.[80] Then after the three aeons came an additional one hundred kalpas as in the *Āgamas* and the *Vibhāṣā Treatise*. As to the three aeons, these are distinguished by writings such as the *Ubasokukai Sūtra* and the *Great Treatise*. The *Treatise on the Awakening of Faith*, the *Yuga Treatise* and so on simply assert the three aeons without teaching about the discipline <of reviewing> characteristics. These are all designations made by different groups and it presents difficulty if they must be harmonised.

[78] Mizuta says (p. 48, note ad loc.) that this discipline implies 'cutting off' the characteristics (the distinguishing features of phenomenal existence); so it does, eventually, but first the characteristics have to be reviewed or rehearsed and it is this which gives rise to the expansion of their range.

[79] 'Aeon' stands for *asaṃkhyeya kalpa*. As various abbreviations appear for this term in the text the English usage is standardised to aeon and kalpa.

[80] Here too the term *kajō* is unwarrantably introduced into the modern version by Kyōdo.

Consider also the *Great Prajñā Sūtra* which says, 'Nentō Buddha said of me that I would become a buddha after one aeon.' The *Diamond Sūtra* says, 'I received the prediction <of future buddhahood> at the feet of Nentō Buddha.' Here we can manifestly see that Nentō Buddha is being regarded as the very first and greatest buddha. The *Diamond Sūtra* also says, 'I was able to meet all the buddhas before the time of Nentō Buddha.'[81] This therefore is a superseding teaching. Of that there is no doubt. The *Lotus Sūtra* also says, 'In the meantime I have taught of Nentō Buddha', and so on, 'but they are all differentiated as a skilful means', which is enough to give rise to the same idea.[82] Or consider the *Laṅkāvatāra Sūtra* which says, 'At those times I was the Buddha Kuruson, Kunagon and Munikashō.' This makes these identical with Śākyamuni. This is also a saying from one school. Or consider the *Zuiō Sūtra* which says, 'Jōkō Buddha received his prediction from Śākyamuni for ninety-one kalpas hence.' This is a confusion with the Bibashi <Buddha> spoken of in the *Inga Sūtra* and the *Hongō Sūtra*, though they make it one aeon. These teachings are all quite unsettled. Such statements as that there was a further <Buddha> Keinashiki beyond Nentō <Buddha> or that a separately existing Śākyamuni would say, 'A buddha vowed that I would in future become a buddha with a name like the presently existing buddha', are superseding teachings of different groups. Similarly, when the *Kegon Sūtra* teaches of ten buddhas, the *Butsumyō Sūtra* teaches of twenty-five buddhas, the *Ketsujōbini Sūtra* teaches of thirty-five buddhas, and the *Yakuō Sūtra* teaches of fifty-three buddhas, these are also designations made by different groups. Saying that these were really there before Śākyamuni is just to make use of it as magic.[83] The reality is that he experienced pain and well-being for ten years and then beneath the tree obtained true enlightenment. The talk of three aeons is just magic. The talk of countless kalpas is magic within magic.

[81] Kyōdo says (p. 106): 'Before the time of Nentō Buddha all the other Buddhas existed.'

[82] Kyōdo gives the full quotation from the *Lotus Sūtra* inserting the phrase 'and how they entered into nirvāṇa', and once again he completes the sense by adding the semi-technical term *kajō* which is not found in Tominaga's text at this point.

[83] 'Magic' is used here, as earlier in Chapter 8, with the implication of techniques which prey on people's credulity.

The *Hōun Sūtra* says, 'For the sake of shallow-minded beings I teach that I trained for three aeons, but in reality I have trained for countless aeons.' In the *Kegon Sūtra* it says, 'Inconceivable ķalpas have passed since I saw Śākyamuni attain the Buddha-way.' The *Lotus Sūtra* says,

> All the whole world, gods, men and *asuras* all consider that the present Śākyamuni Buddha left the palace of the Śākyas, sat in meditation not far from the city of Gayā, and attained supreme enlightenment. However, good young men, there have in reality passed innumerable, infinite, hundreds of thousands of ten thousands of billions of *nayutas* of kalpas, since I became a buddha.

These all make the <Buddha's> length of life incalculably long in order to go beyond the three aeons. This is truly magic within magic. The limits having been reached, it became unavoidable to teach the attainment of buddhahood in one thought, to beat the others. This is the teaching of the Sudden School. Hence the *Treatise on the Awakening of Faith* fits it together by saying,

> Training for countless aeons is taught for the sake of lazy beings, and attainment of Buddhahood in one thought is taught for the sake of the cowardly, but the reality is that all the bodhisattvas pass through three aeons.

Again it is like when the *Lotus Sūtra* tells of the eight-year-old dragon girl becoming a buddha in the southern quarter. This saying means that if there is the slightest occasion for it the fruit can be achieved without it necessarily depending on age or sex. Thus the previously existing Indra's net of doctrine was destroyed. Some commentators might explain this case by saying that she was a goddess, but this is to miss the point. It is similar with the teachings about missing out kalpas. The *Kusha Treatise* and the *Vibhāṣā Treatise* say, 'To praise Teisha <Buddha> is to pass over nine kalpas', the *Great Treatise* says, 'To praise Bussha <Buddha> is to pass over nine' but the *Inga Sūtra* makes it Bibashi <Buddha>. Others say 'Teisha and Bussha are one Buddha', while the verses of the *Kegon Sūtra* regard them as distinct buddhas. However the *Nirvāṇā Sūtra* makes it twelve kalpas. On Kō's commentary says, 'In the three aeons, passing over three kalpas', so adding them up as twelve is wrong. The *Shinjikan Sūtra* says, 'In the first aeon, passing over twelve kalpas, in the second aeon, passing over eight kalpas, in the third aeon, passing over eleven kalpas.' Again, the *Shibunritsu* makes the nine kalpas eight, and the *Sūtra of Golden Light* makes them eleven. These are again the designations of separate groups. Why do they all necessarily have to be harmonised?

I, Nakamoto, have already said that all the names of the buddhas and bodhisattvas which appear in the sūtras by no means have to be pushed through one chiselled hole.[84] If one thinks about it, many of them are the names of people from ancient times, such as, in China, Mu Kai, Katsu Ten and Son Ro, or again, for there is no settled teaching, such as Ka Haku, Hyō I, Shin To or Utsu Rui (as in the *Yakakusōsho*). In the end they all come from somewhere. For example, the name Shiki refers first to the one Śākyamuni met on completing the first aeon, secondly to the second of the seven buddhas, and thirdly to Brahmarāja Shiki. Or take Kanzeonjizai for example, which refers first to Kanjizai Bodhisattva, secondly to Kanjizai Buddha, and thirdly to Kanzeonjizai Brahmarāja. Again, Makeishura, for example, refers to the lord of the three worlds and secondly to the god Yakusha. Again, Zengen refers first to the great general of the western quarter, and secondly to the fourth *dhyāna* of the world of form. These are all nomenclature of the time, and therefore the exponents of the teaching used them provisionally one by one.

11. *Language has three conditions.*[85]

The *Prajñā Sūtra* does not have the word 'Buddha-nature' and the *Āgamas* do not have the word *dhāraṇī*. When the *Sūtra of Golden Light* refers to three bodies <of the Buddha> the *Butsuji Sūtra* and the *Hongō Sūtra* refer to two bodies, the *Laṅkāvatāra Sūtra* and the *Ryōyakushō Treatise* refer to four bodies, the *Kegon Sūtra* refers to two kinds of ten bodies, the *Great Treatise* refers to four demons, the *Mei Sūtra* refers to five demons, the *Great Treatise* refers to three heavens, the

[84] I.e. no one unified conclusion about them is required. It is acceptable to recognise the diversity of historically conditioned terminology.

[85] The simple term used here has to be translated 'conditions' because of its meaning in the subsequent text. Cf. Mizuta, p. 51, note ad loc.

Nirvāṇa Sūtra refers to four heavens, the *Vimalakīrti Sūtra* refers to the inconceivables, the *Diamond Sūtra* refers to non-abidings, the *Kegon Sūtra* refers to the Dharma-world, the *Nirvāṇa Sūtra* refers to the Buddha-nature, the *Prajñā Sūtra* refers to all-knowledges, the *Sūtra of Golden Light* refers to the Dharma-nature, and the *Lotus Sūtra* refers to all dharmas having the characteristic of reality, all these are words of a school. When each one emphasises its points, this is what is meant by words being conditioned by the person.[86] Then there are many differences in the scriptures over the transmission of Sanskrit words, which the present writer sees as the Ch'u and Hsia <different dynasties> of Sanskrit. Kumārajīva's Gōga <i.e. Ganges> is Hsüan Tsang's Gōga <with different characters> and Kumārajīva's Shumi <Sumeru> is Hsüan Tsang's Someiro <also Sumeru>. Where is the end to differences of this kind? They are sometimes referred to as out-of-date dialects. How language changes to suit society, and sounds change with the ups and downs of time! Such so-called dialect is not a true dialect, but rather it is what is meant by words being conditioned by period.[87] The *Vimalakīrti Sūtra* says, 'Knowing all dharmas in one thought is the seat of enlightenment.' The *Zenyō* says, 'When one's essential nature is determined and of itself detached, this is the seat of enlightenment.'[88] This is a teaching which magically transforms and expands.[89] The seat of enlightenment itself is the seat of enlightenment! It has no <longer any> original connection with thought or disposition. This is like the Shintoists[90] regarding *Takama-ga-hara* as the mind and body. Again it is like the four foods referred to in the *Zōichi-agon* and the *Kise Sūtra*, where fasting means only to eat the food of which people usually partake and then rinse the mouth. This argument is extended to costume, incense and flowers, and so on. Mental food consists of what is considered, what is perceived, what is thought and so on. The food of consciousness has the meaning of what one is conscious of. Thus

86 Or 'conditioned by the individual'.

87 'Period' may be considered to be a little too modern in tone, but 'generation' would scarcely do justice to Tominaga's point.

88 According to Mizuta this statement is not to be found in the text cited.

89 That is, it transforms and expands the original meaning in a manner dependent on the credulous readiness of readers to follow.

90 'Shintoists': *shintōsharyū*.

consciousness is regarded as a food. Yet none of these <expressions> is the true meaning of food. They are an expansion of food. They are like eating as in, popularly speaking, 'eating rods' or 'eating fists'. Again it is similar when the *Great Treatise* treats sūtra scrolls as relics of the Dharma-body. Relics are themselves relics. They originally had no connection with sūtra scrolls. This again is an expansion[91] of 'relics'. It is the same when they speak of putting Mount Sumeru inside a mustard seed, or displaying the bejewelled <Buddha->land on the edge of a hair. This is an expansion of the meaning. All <teachings> of this kind are expanded teachings.[92] All statements which do not run loose from the reality of the teaching are what are known as 'close' <meanings>.[93] The close <meanings> are the real ones. There are many cases of expanding the teaching among the expositors of ancient and recent times alike. If scholars know this why do they bother with trifles? The meaning of Tathāgata is 'coming thus'. This originally referred to the essential mind,[94] without distinction of good or evil. As to type we can regard this as 'general'.[95] Hence the *Laṅkāvatāra Sūtra* says, 'The Tathāgata-womb is the seat of good and evil.' The *Prajñā Sūtra* says, 'All beings are the Tathāgata-womb.' Or again it can be regarded as a term for virtue achieved, in the sense of stopping all delusions and coming (*gata*) in a state of thusness (*tathā*). As to type this can be regarded as 'fundamental'.[96] Examples are when the *Shōman Sūtra* says, 'The Tathāgata is the Dharma-body, and the womb undetached from the

[91] 'Expansion': *chō*, the first of Tominaga's five types of language.

[92] By relating it to 'expanded teachings' it is made clear that the starting point of this typology of language is the same as that for the alteration or development of religious tradition.

[93] 'Close <meanings>': *hen*. Close meanings and expanded meanings belong together as a pair of opposites, though one might regard the prior existence of close meanings as a condition for the development of expanded meanings and hence expect them to have been listed the other way round.

[94] 'Essential mind': *shintai*, that which fundamentally constitutes the mind. A further occurrence is identifiable at note 103.

[95] 'General': *han*. This is the third type in order of appearance in the text, but it refers to a general or original meaning prior to the division between 'close' and 'expanded'.

[96] 'Fundamental': *ki*. This fourth type refers to language which goes beyond 'general' in the sense of bringing out the meaning in a forthright and effective but not antithetical way.

passions is the Tathāgata-womb' and the *Nyoraizō Sūtra* says, 'All living beings have the Tathāgata-womb within the angry and foolish passions.' Again, in cases like translating *prāvaraṇa* as *jishi* ('self-indulgence' or 'confession'), the word *jishi* originally had a bad meaning, but was turned into a good meaning.[97] As to type we can regard this as 'opposite'.[98] All these five types together are what is called 'words being conditioned by type'.

All words are conditioned by type, by period and by the person, and this may be known as 'language has three conditions'. To explain all language in terms of these three conditions is my standpoint in scholarship. At any rate, looking at it in this light, I have not yet found any Way of Dharma in the whole world, or any language, which cannot be approached and interpreted in this way. This is why I say that three conditions and five types are the basis of the creation of language. Another example of words being conditioned by period is the difference between the old and new terms Locana and Vairocana <Buddha>. That this was originally a word of praise for Śākyamuni, and then became a name, is like when the Confucianists spoke of Gyō and then turned it into Hō Kun. Such later scholars as take the new and the old as a basis for distinguishing the three bodies are mistaken.[99] There are also two different ways of writing *naraku* <i.e. infernal regions> in Chinese characters, and the *Vibhāṣā Treatise* and the *Junshōri Treatise* have no agreed text in this respect. Later scholars have sometimes given different interpretations based on these characters, but that is mistaken. It is the same with the words *shintan* and *shina* <each being written in two different ways>.[100] Master Rin says, 'The eastern quarter belongs to

[97] Though basically meaning 'self-indulgence' the term *jishi* refers to the ceremony of *prāvaraṇa*, including confession, or self-reflection, at the end of the rainy season.

[98] 'Opposite': *han*. According to Mizuta (p. 52, note ad loc.) this fifth type of language involves meanings antithetical to the 'close' meanings. However this may be a misunderstanding, for the text makes it clear that the complementary type to 'close' is 'expanded' (cf. also note 93 above). It seems more likely that Tominaga meant both 'fundamental' and 'opposite' meanings to be regarded as extrapolations from 'general' meanings, but in contrary directions.

[99] I.e. it is a mistake to take terms which have arisen for the different 'bodies' of the Buddha at different times and use them to create a new systematic doctrine as if they were all equally authoritative or original.

[100] Both are words for China.

shin <using a character found in *one* of the ways of writing *shintan*>, thus again giving rise to an interpretation based on the characters. It is ridiculous. Then again the words *lakṣa* and *koṭi*, which refer to large numbers, have both been translated as *oku* <one hundred million> on the basis of a provisional harmonisation.[101] Some people have been perplexed by the difference and explained it thus: 'In the western country there are three kinds of *oku*.' But as *oku* is a Chinese term, why should there be three or four kinds of *oku* in India? This is also mistaken. Indeed, like the aeons and the expanded numbers, these are all just words preferred by different groups improving on each other and doing people down. Why should these necessarily be harmonised? Again, when Hsüan Tsang discussed five kinds of words which cannot be translated, and said that the word Bhagavān has six meanings, those who are ill-informed say that Sanskrit words have many meanings and that other <languages> cannot be equal to it. Yet this is a great error, for Chinese also has many meanings. This can be seen by looking at a dictionary. The explanations always give so-and-so, then so-and-so. These are all various meanings which cannot be brought down to one only. Nor do we need to stop at Chinese, for our own language also has many meanings. For example. when people say *tawake* <fool> to mean *hōtōsha* <profligate> there is no question of this one meaning exhausting the word *hōtō*. We can tell this from the analogies <considered above>.

12. *Eight consciousnesses*.

The original teaching told of six roots and six consciousnesses. The *Shōman Sūtra* still taught six consciousnesses, and in the *Ryōyakushō Treatise* it says, 'In the Śrāvaka Vehicle they do not teach calling this mind the *araya* <i.e. *ālaya*> consciousness or calling it the *adana* consciousness;[102] the reason is that they depend on what can be obtained from this profound and delicate realm.' Here we see it again. Speaking of there being seven consciousnesses or eight consciousnesses is

[101] *Lakṣa* should be 100,000 and *koṭi* should be 100,000,000.

[102] *Araya, adana*: alternative transcriptions for *ālaya*, 'storehouse', as in *ālayavijñāna*, 'storehouse-consciousness', a teaching associated with the (Mahāyāna) 'consciousness-only' school.

the teaching of different groups superseding each other. The *Yuga Treatise* and the *Taihō Treatise* thus make seven consciousnesses the ruling idea, saying, 'People say that the eye and so on make up six realms of consciousness to which is added the realm of meaning', and 'the eighth consciousness draws upon the realm of meaning'. The *Jinmitsu Sūtra* and the *Consciousness Only Treatise* make eight consciousnesses the rule, and say, 'If we depart from the consciousness of meaning, there is no other consciousness left. However, there is still the *ālaya*-consciousness.' This is also the saying of a different group. There is no need to harmonise it. Again, similarly, the *Laṅkāvatāra Sūtra* puts up eight or nine consciousnesses and teaches them to fit in with cause and effect, and in the *Ryōkakushō Treatise* we find one more level set out by emphasising the *amala* <consciousness>. These are also the preferred points of different groups. Why should we necessarily find it strange? Master Jō would not admit it and said, 'The ninth is another name for the eighth.' This has to be called inflexibility. Again, in the *Shakumakaen Treatise* there are ten consciousnesses, while in the *Dainichi Sūtra* there are countless consciousnesses of the mind. This is a teaching to supersede consciousness of the mind. One may reflect that *ālaya* means storehouse. *Adana* and *manas* mean attachment. They have traditionally been translated as mind and will. The *Kusha Treatise* says,

> Assembling and producing <is the work of what> is called the mind, reflecting and weighing <is the work of what> is called the will, and understanding and distinguishing <is the work of what> is called the consciousness.

The *Shōdaijō Treatise* says,

> The *ālaya*-consciousness is the essential mind.[103] As the seeds <of ideas> are produced within it, it is transformed into will and consciousness. For what reason is this also called mind? It is because it is the place where the impregnating seeds of various dharmas are planted and assembled.

One should take note of all these things.

[103] Essential mind: *shintai*. Cf. note 94.

However, 'mind' and 'will' are Chinese words, while *araya* <i.e. *ālaya*> and *adana* are Sanskrit words. Originally they had different tendencies. They could not easily be harmonised. <The Sanskrit words> did not necessarily fit directly with Chinese words. It was enough if it fitted the intention of the speaker. Why should *ālaya* be 'storehouse' and *adana* be 'attachment'? 'Attachment' and 'storehouse' are both to do with the mind. Originally it was not appropriate to distinguish between mind and will with respect to these two. If they have to be distinguished, then *ālaya* and *adana* have the meaning of will, and *ālaya*-consciousness and *adana*-consciousness have the meaning of mind. Why is this? Attachment to something and storing something are the activities of the mind, or dynamically, the will. When we name them consciousness, it refers to the essential mind, or mind understood statically. If this is not so then why do the sūtras and treatises distinguish between *ālaya* and *ālaya*-consciousness. This is clear from the *Gejinmitsu Sūtra* which says,

> Otherwise a bodhisattva, neither within nor without, does not see abiding in the storehouse, does not see the impregnation <of seeds>, does not see the *ālaya*-consciousness, does not see the *adana*, and does not see the consciousness.

The *Ryōyakushō Treatise* makes this just 'not seeing the fundamental consciousness and not seeing the *adana*-consciousness'. The translators have simply not met the meaning here. It is most unfortunate.

It is apparently acceptable to regard the *adana* as the eighth consciousness. We see this when the *Yuga Treatise* and *Zōjū Treatise* say,

> The mind is the place of the constituents[104] and the dharma-worlds,[105] and where the dispositions are framed. The *ālaya*-consciousness containing all the seeds is named the *ijuku*-consciousness[106] as well as the *adana*-consciousness.

[104] The five constituents of phenomenal existence.

[105] The eighteen worlds made up of the six senses, their fields of perception, and the resultant six consciousnesses. Kyōdo says that it refers to ten worlds (p. 111).

[106] A synonym for *ālayavijñāna*: 'storehouse-consciousness'.

Again the *Laṅkāvatāra Sūtra*, when explaining the *ālaya*, makes it the Tathāgata-womb which is linked together with the seven consciousnesses of ignorance. This draws it out and expands it,[107] giving it the same meaning as Tathāgata. So when things are pushed to the limit by setting up a further *anmara* <-consciousness>, this is a superseding teaching. We should also consider that the *ālaya*-consciousness was originally the teaching of non-Buddhists.[108] For this one should see the thirty wrong views listed in the *Dainichi Sūtra*. It is just that Buddhists made a special point of teaching it. Consider also that the Sarvāstivādins simply call the *ālaya*-consciousness mind-and-will[109] without further argument. In the *Ryōyakushō Treatise* it says,

> As it says in the *Zōichi-agon*, in order to extinguish the *ālaya* in which the world delights, the *ālaya* of love, the *ālaya* of desire, the *ālaya* of attachment, the Tathāgata expounds true Dharma.

Mu Shō, in his *Shō Treatise*, speaks of the *ijukuālaya* in the same sense.

In short, putting 'mind' and 'will' for the seventh and eighth consciousnesses is a mistake of the translators of antiquity.

13. *Four truths, twelve causal relations, six perfections.*

When the *Zōshin Treatise* says 'suffering, cause, way, extinction', the *Great Prajñā Sūtra* says 'cause, suffering, way, extinction', and the *Kegon Sūtra* says, 'suffering, cause, extinction, way', these are the phrases of different groups.[110] Calling these 'truths' is like calling *shintai* <observing the truths> the way. This refers to the way of dealing with them. Compare the statement in the *Great Prajñā Sūtra*, 'when there is suffering, truth is absent'. 'Suffering' lies in the passions of the mind. When ordinary people take pleasure in their attachments it is not true pleasure. 'Cause' is the mind's ignorance. When foolishness and obscurity combine in the

[107] These are two of the terms, *ki* and *chō*, used in Tominaga's typology of language (see Chapter 11) but here they are used as verbs.

[108] *Gedōshosetsu*: cf. Chapter 22, Heterodoxies.

[109] *Shin-i*, a single concept linking both ideas.

[110] These are variations on the order of the 'four noble truths' of Buddhism which are most commonly given as in the third example.

mind the passions arise: 'Extinction' is the extinguishing of that ignorance, or, that is, nirvāṇa. The 'way' is the warding off of passions, or, that is, enlightenment. Thus the *Yuigyō Sūtra* says,

> The Buddha teaches the truth of suffering as real suffering. One cannot make people happy with it. The constituents are real cause, apart from which there is no other cause. If suffering is extinguished, this means that its cause was extinguished. If the cause is extinguished then the result is extinguished. The way of the extinction of suffering really is the true way, and apart from it there is no other way.

This is the basic meaning of the four truths. Statements such as 'ordinary people have suffering but not the truth', or 'the two vehicles have truth but it is not yet fully realised', or 'bodhisattvas do not have <suffering> but only the truth', or 'the noble truth does not lie in suffering, nor in cause, nor in extinction, nor in the way' (as in the *Shiyaku Sūtra*), or 'there are four kinds of four truths' (as in the *Nirvāṇa Sūtra* and the *Shōman Sūtra*), all these are the terminologies of different groups. They each determine their own meaning, but they are not the original truth. The *Vibhāṣā Treatise* says, 'When the mind itself is foolish and dark, its lack of clear wisdom is called ignorance.' This is the true meaning. The *Jōjitsu Treatise* says, 'The discriminations of the heretical mind, lacking the true clarity of wisdom, are called ignorance.' This statement itself appends a heretical word, <i.e. it adds 'true' to the phrase 'clarity of wisdom'> and is therefore not the true meaning. Mental activity[111] is carried out in dependence[112] <on ignorance>. Being so dependent it leaves its impregnations in the mind,[113] and this brings about consciousness. Name-and-

[111] Mental activity: *gyō*, standing for Sanskrit *saṁskāra*, and often translated more or less meaninglessly as 'aggregates'. The term refers to the whole range of mental movement, including 'everything that may come into the mind, permanent qualities like memory, ideas, good and bad impulses or dispositions, as well as unconscious habits' (Thomas 1951, p. 61).

[112] With the introduction of this term Tominaga enters on a brief explanation of 'causal arising' (pratītya-samutpāda). The list does not match up neatly with other accounts because 'craving' and 'grasping' (*tṛṣṇā* and *upādāna*) are represented here by three terms: loving, taking and having.

[113] Mind: *shinshiki*, which represents Sanskrit *citta-vijñāna*. As this is immediately followed by *shiki* (consciousness) the translation 'mind' is required here.

form[114] consists of adding forms and naming, and is similar to what is called the will. The six fields of sense correspond to the six sense-organs,[115] and they are similar to what is called feeling. Contact and sensation mean <respectively> touching things and being aware of them. Craving and grasping mean craving things, taking them and possessing them. Birth, old age and death refer to one's being born, growing old and dying. Being born in ignorance we grow old and die, and this is what is called 'birth is intoxication and death is a dream'. Every single act is a cause, until all are completed with old age and death. This is the original teaching that every cause in the present life has an effect. The teachings that cause and effect arise in the three worlds, or in the two worlds, are teachings of mystification. (See *Kusha Treatise*, *Great Treatise*, and so on.) Again, teachings which bring it down to one instant (*Daijū Sūtra*), or which view it in reverse order (*Āgamas*), or which make sensation the starting point of vision, are all designations of different groups.

There are also some who say that the twelve causal relations go round and round continuously like a wheel, always beginning all over again, but the difficulty with this is that ignorance is without a cause and old age and death are without a result. For this reason the *Vibhāṣā Treatise* says, 'Ignorance having a cause refers to a previous ignorance, and old age and death having a result to a later old age and death.' Further teachers say, 'Ignorance having a cause refers to previous old age and death, and old age and death having a result refers to later ignorance.' The *Nirvāṇa Sūtra* and the *Shugokokukai Sūtra* say, 'False views may be seen as the cause, and ignorance as the relation.' However none of these realise the original intention, and they just speak like this because they are groping about in the black lacquer tub. After all, when the Buddha made up twelve causal relations he was saying that the origin of all karma lay in ignorance. If only ignorance could be avoided there would be no mental acitivity, no consciousness, and so on up to no old age and death. This is referred to as

114 Name-and-form: *myōshiki*, which represents Sanskrit *nāmarūpa*, sometimes translated mind-and-body. Assigning name and form is an activity which is affected by human intention and will.

115 These are six because they include the physical five senses plus the willing mind (*i*).

achieving nirvāṇa. It is like the four truths, where, if there is cause there is suffering, and if suffering is extinguished that is the way. The four truths summarise it and the twelve causal relations spell it out in detail, but the reality is the same. When the various schools assign them to the *śrāvakas* and *pratyekabuddhas* respectively this is but a pattern of words. Therefore the *Great Prajñā Sūtra* says,

> Know that the noble truths are of two kinds; the *śrāvakas* and *pratyekabuddhas* are at the medium <level>. [It also says,] Of the four kinds of beings who view the twelve causal relations, those with supreme knowledge are the Buddhas.

This shows that they are not limited to the *śrāvakas* and *pratyekabuddhas*.

Only the six perfections have to do with the conversion of others and are thus the works of the bodhisattvas. However it is a mistake to think that they are limited to this, as we can see from the following. The *Great Prajñā Sūtra* says, '*Arhats* and *pratyekabuddhas* depend on the six *pāramitās* <perfections> to attain the other shore', and the *Laṅkāvatāra Sūtra* says, 'The two vehicles of men and gods are both called *pāramitā* <perfection>.' If we reflect on it we can see that the six perfections are all things practised by students of olden times, and that donation, morality, perseverance, courage, *dhyāna*, and insight are all given a place to fit in with the teaching of the sūtras. Reviewing the *Vibhāṣā Treatise*, we find only four *pāramitās*, and it says, 'Six *pāramitās* are taught by foreign masters.' This suggests that the four perfections were the original teaching and that adding two more was a superseding teaching. The *Great Prajñā Sūtra* says, 'It is because of the *prajñā-pāramitā* <perfection of insight> that the other five perfections get their name.' The *Great Treatise* also says, 'The five *pāramitās* are embraced within the *prajñā*.' From this we can tell that there was a view-point which counted five *pāramitās* at the time, and that the addition of *prajñā* was the work of the voidness school. We should also realise that *dhyāna* was added by the *zenjō* school. The present Zen people belong to this tradition in the long run, and it is a mistake to say that they go back to Kāśpaya. Kāśpaya belonged to the Courage <*vīrya*> school of the Dhuta religion, and does not fit

<their interpretation>. Zen people have felt uncomfortable with the fact that *zen* is the same as the *dhyāna* of the six perfections, and hence said,

> Ancient men of virtue called the Buddha-mind sect the Zen sect, but this *zen* is not the *dhyāna* of the six perfections. It arises from the words making up 'simple transmission and direct pointing'. <*Seihokushu*>.

They teach 'no setting up of letters and words', and yet they name it after the way the words are written! How astonishing!

The four Perfections mentioned above are similar to each other and are the original ones. *Dhyāna* and *prajñā* alone are to do with the workings of the mind and are different from the others. Therefore it is evident that these were added by others later.

End of first scroll of *Emerging from Meditation*.

EMERGING FROM MEDITATION: SECOND SCROLL

14. *Precepts*.

The *Great Treatise* says,

> The ten goodnesses are *śīla* <morality> and even if the Buddha had not appeared in the world there would always have been morality; so we call them the old precepts.

After all, that good should be done and that evil should not be done, that good actions bring justice and evil actions bring injustice, is the natural law of heaven and earth. This did not originally wait for the teachings of Confucianism and Buddhism. The essence of the precepts arose in resistance to evil. If there were no evil there would be no precepts. That is why the *Great Treatise* says,

> If the Buddha had appeared in a good world <period> we would not have had these precepts. Even though appearing in a bad world <period> as Śākyamuni did there were no precepts for twelve years.

Accordingly the *Sōgiritsu* says, 'After five years the precepts were widely established.' The *Shibunritsu* says the same as the *Great Treatise* and again these are the statements of different groups. The precepts were originally precepts about things, that is, about actions and speech. However, the Great Vehicle school related them to the mind, in order to ward off three kinds of karmic effect together. This is another example of a superseding teaching. Don Mu Toku's *Jōjitsu Treatise* describes the essence of the precepts as 'non-production <of karma>'. The *Zōshin Treatise* and the *Vibhāṣā Treatise* describe it as 'mind'. The Great Vehicle school describe it as the body and mind of <Buddha->nature. These again are the statements of different groups. The *Great Treatise* says,

> The bodhisattvas appear in the five states of rebirth by the power of skilful means, take upon themselves the five passions and guide along living beings.

It also says,

> There are two kinds of bodhisattvas, those who leave household life, and those who remain in household life.

Those bodhisattvas make the expansive teaching their way and salvation their work. Their minds are vast and their acts are full of virtue, so how should they be restricted only to the precepts? For bodhisattvas therefore, what counts as precepts or disciplinary procedure is not what originally held true. In the *Yuga* and the *Jiji Treatise* there are four major rules and forty-five minor rules. In the *Hōdō Sūtra* there are four major rules and twenty-eight minor rules. In the *Bonmō Sūtra* there are ten major rules and forty-eight minor rules. The severity of the precepts more or less reaches its limit with the *Bonmō Sūtra*. These all depend on the Small Vehicle but come out beyond it.

That Buddhism has the precepts is like Confucianism having etiquette. Etiquette is determined by the Way in accordance with the time. Actions, speech and intentions are all part of etiquette. If this is discarded there is no Confucianism, and if the precepts are discarded there is no Buddhism. Therefore the *Yuigyō Sūtra* says, 'As to after I am gone, respect and revere the *pratimokṣa*. It is your great teacher. Just as if I were residing in the world do not diverge from it.' That the Buddhist Dharma was respected is due solely to the Vinaya <School>. However it was neglected from the *Prajñā* School down to the Sudden School, all of which thus departed from what was held true. Therefore only the Nirvāṇa and Combined Schools revered the precepts and thus truly kept Śākyamuni's intention.

When Master E On was approaching his end, Ki Toku told him to take some rice wine with soya to overcome his illness, but the master replied, 'The *Vinaya* has no statement to justify it.' He told him to drink some rice gruel, but the master replied, 'The day has passed noon <and hence the permitted hour is past>.' Then he told him to drink some honey mixed with water, so the master asked him to open the *Vinaya* to see if it was permitted, but before he had got halfway through the master died. Because he did not change the rules in a matter of life and death, it must be said that he kept the *Vinaya* well. Yet how petty it is to say that rice gruel cannot be drunk because the day has passed noon. The *Gobunritsu* says,

> Although I instruct you thus, if in another quarter it is considered impure, it will not be a mistake not to do it; and although something is not my instruction, if in another quarter it is considered pure it should be done.[116]

This is the true position. Well-versed men have determined the *Vinaya* in accordance with time and place, so why should one be restricted to early form alone?[117] Did not Master On know this? It is because of this that when determining funeral rites for teachers who have received the precepts he made them the same as for parents, with three years of mourning dress for all, and in the case of teachers of the newly ordained mourning dress was to be worn for a while after the funeral. This is not laid down either in the *Nirvāṇa Sūtra* or in the *Vinaya* and hence he determined this rite for the first time. It is really quite absurd that he had already not been able to avoid setting

116 This quotation also occurs in *Writings of an Old Man*.

117 Previously Tominaga was arguing that some schools had neglected the *Vinaya*. Here he is arguing for its adaptability in changing circumstances. In both cases the underlying assumption is that various documentable modes of dealing with the *Vinaya* stem not from the Buddha but from the monks and schools of the time.

up regulations which were outside the *Vinaya*, and yet he could not himself discard a regulation within the *Vinaya*. So what is this having no special ethos of purity?

Furthermore, if we reflect on the five precepts we see that stealing, adultery and lying have always belonged to evil, but that taking life and drinking intoxicants have been undetermined. Taking life has been seen as not sinful, while drinking intoxicants has been considered evil if it leads to a disturbance. The five precepts were originally precepts against evil, yet it is not possible to say that there should be absolutely no taking of life or drinking of intoxicants. This was the meaning of Ku Doku Gai's answer to Emperor Bun of Sung about the taking of life. When the *Laṅkāvatāra Sūtra* also says, 'There are various kinds of debauching intoxicants', it shows that intoxicants are wrong in so far as they are debauching. Consider also that the *Zōichi-agon* refers to eight kinds of precepts <for householders>, while the *Great Treatise* divides them into nine. The various schools have variations of sequence, and these too are statements made by different groups.

15. *Marriage.*

Of the four castes in India, the *kṣatriya* are the kings who rule the people and perform government and the brahmans are the legal class who provide teaching and guide the people; the *vaiśya* are the merchants and the *śūdra* are the peasantry, and these receive government and teaching from the two upper kinds. The *kṣatriya* are like what the Confucianists call the son of heaven, kings and princes, high stewards, and gentlemen. The brahmins are like what the Confucianists call instructors and village Confucian masters. Those who govern are the kings and princes and those who teach are the instructors. It is like here <i.e. Japan> where the Buddha-Dharma and the Kingly Dharma are ranged together and the Tendai is in the position of administering the Buddha-Dharma. In the Brahman Dharma they study in the home from the age of seven onwards, from fifteen onwards they receive the Brahman Dharma and travel elsewhere in pursuit of learning; on reaching forty, for fear of losing the succession at home, they return and marry a wife until they are fifty, when they withdraw to a mountain to practise the way (*Rinki*). The Brahmans, through succeeding generations, make studying the way their task whether in the household or away from the household, and in many cases they seek the arts of the Way for themselves and become conceited people. (Master Jō). Buddhism also provides a teaching and guides the people, and is thus a kind of Brahmanism, but one in which they leave home and do not marry. This is just the custom of the Indian Confucianists <i.e. Brahmans>, except that only those who are teaching the people do not marry. There is no question of urging the whole population not to marry and not to have issue. We can see this when the *Vinaya* says, 'Leaving the household life is not allowed without parents' consent.' This is all there is to Śākyamuni's first having had a wife. After all Śākyamuni was originally a *kṣatriya*, a royal personage. However, many sons of the Buddha[118] have disliked the fact that Śākyamuni had a wife and son. They said that Kui was Yasha <Yaśodharā> or that Zenshō <Rāhula> was the son of <Śākyamuni's> younger brother. However the names of three wives are already clear as they come in the three sūtras, *Gomu Sūtra, Butsuhongyō Sūtra*, and *Jūniyu Sūtra*. That the monk Zenshō (Rāhula) was the child of the Buddha when he was a bodhisattva comes in the *Nirvāṇa Sūtra*. This is all we need to see.

Furthermore the *Daizengon Sūtra* says,

> Why does the bodhisattva have a wife? Because the bodhisattva is without passion he displays a wife and son to prevent people from suspecting that he is not a man but only a eunuch. For this reason he took the Śākya woman Kui as a wife who bore Rāhula. The latter, through a heavenly transformation, was born in appearance without depending on the union of father and mother, and thus grew up. This too is achieved by the original vow of the bodhisattva.

Ah! This is a mystification of the teaching. If it said, 'I married a wife in accordance with the law of the world before I knew the way', that would be all right. However it says, 'to prevent people from suspecting that he is a eunuch'. Why this extreme of pettiness? It also says, 'without depending on the union', but unless it was the work of a demon it is quite weird, indeed laughable. The *Nirvāṇa Sūtra* also says,

[118] 'Sons of the Buddha' is a set phrase meaning Buddhists.

> Kāśpaya asked: 'If the Buddha has already crossed the sea of passions, why did he take Yaśodhāra and give birth to Rāhula?' The Buddha answered Kāśyapa, 'Countless kalpas ago I discarded the five passions; however in order to follow the law of the world I deliberately display these characteristics.'

There is something repugnant about this having the Buddha attain the way many kalpas ago and then taking a wife again. Therefore they again mystify the teaching to make it hang together, but the reality is that it is a provisional teaching. Again, consider the saying, 'If you had a son, I would let you depart the household life.' Reviewing this text, it seems as if he had no children before departing the household life. That a child was born six years later is recorded in the *Zuiō Sūtra* and the *Fuyō Sūtra*. But then again, saying that the son was born on the day on which he attained the way is strange if it means he was in the womb for such a long time. If one assumes that the Buddha's wife and son were there during his five years of pleasurable existence and interprets in this way there is no difficulty.[119]

Consider also that the sons of the Buddha strongly dislike the female body. This originally arose out of debate with popular customs. In India the popular attitude is to respect women highly. In Shi Ba Sen's *Historical Records* it says, 'Westwards from En as far as An Soku, women are held in respect, and whatever the women say the men hold to be right.' The southern barbarians are even more this way inclined. The red-haired people in all their countries marry into the wife's family and make women their rulers.[120] If we think about it, India was like this too. There are many places in the sūtra teachings where the mother's name is taken and used as an appellation, for example Furanakashō, Makkarikushari, and very many others. Thus Master Jō also said, 'In India many children are named after their mother.' Then again the *Shōbōnen Sūtra* explains four kinds of blessings, 'The first is one's mother, the second is one's father, the third is the

119 Mizuta and Kyōdo disagree on the interpretation of this passage. Mizuta thinks it refers to a time before the Buddha left the household life whereas Kyōdo thinks it refers to a pleasurable state which he experienced for five years under the tree of enlightenment.

120 This is Tominaga's only reference to civilisations outside those influenced by Buddhism in the whole of his extant work.

Tathāgata, and the fourth is a teacher of the Dharma.' This lists the mother first. The *Kanmuryōju Sūtra* also says,

> Since the beginning of the kalpa there have been various evil kings, and those who killed their own fathers to achieve this status number eighteen thousand, but nobody has yet heard of a mother being wrongly killed.

Here we see that it fits the national custom to respect one's mother but to vanquish one's father. Thus I conclude that the custom of India is to pay high respect to women.

The Buddha, therefore, came out in rejection of this, saying in extreme cases that bodhisattvas were not born of women and calling those who did not know the Buddha-nature women. These statements were all made on purpose to make the men feel proud. The reality is that things have both their ins and their outs, that human-kind has both men and women, and that this is the logic of heaven, earth and nature. If humankind is between heaven and earth how can women alone be detested?[121] Again, when the Buddha forbade licentiousness it was perverse sex and desires with respect to the *arhats* which he forbade.[122] This was meant from the standpoint of those who remain in the household life. The reason why those who enter the monastery have no wife is that there are many who fail in the holy life[123] because of these things. Thus there is also a Confucian saying which runs, 'Do not regard women's form with the eye' (Hsün Tzŭ). This is all that is meant. Therefore, if there is no *arhat's* desire in the mind, what need is there to detest the existence of women?[124] Therefore the Buddha also said, 'A madman commits no crime', (*Gobunritsu*) and 'You already have no mind, so how shall we speak of transgression?' (*Jōshogōshō Sūtra*). That is all that is meant. However he also said,

[121] These two sentences provide one of the few examples in *Emerging from Meditation* of a personal standpoint with respect to a matter of substance, as opposed to method.

[122] The meaning of this sentence is not beyond dispute, but (although Kyōdo says there is no such word!) '*arhat*-desire' probably has to be understood here as desire directed towards an *arhat*.

[123] 'The holy life': *bongyō*, which represents Sanskrit *brahmacarya*.

[124] In this case '*arhat*-desire' means desire on the part of an *arhat* and as this would be contradictory it can only appear in a negative formulation, as here.

> If all you monks take wives and arrange marriages like worldly people and trample down the Vinaya among the multitude, that will be a sign of the extinction of the Dharma. (*Maya Sūtra*)

and

> If there is a *śramaṇa* whose mind is concentrated and who does not turn back to the <female> voice and form, then he is my disciple and follows my teaching. (*Zōichi-agon*)

This therefore was Śākyamuni's intention. He only wanted monks not to marry, and said that monks who had no wives would be able to preserve his intention. However later generations often found monks taking wives, so this meant nothing less than the extinction of the Dharma. Again, the *Shuryōgon Sūtra* and the *Kanzeondarani Sūtra*, referred to before, both have spells with which to release one from sins of passion or from the five sharp vegetables.[125] Those monks of later generations with wives must have made good use of these spells!

16. *Eating meat.*

In forbidding killing and abstaining from meat Buddhism is just the same as Confucianism. Gentlemen do not themselves kill anything which has blood or breath. When King U thinned down his food and drink and regarded fine rice-wines as bad this was just the same kind of thing. Thus in the *Jūjuritsu* three kinds of meat are declared pure, and in the *Nirvāṇa Sūtra* there are nine. They both allow these to be eaten. The *Laṅkāvatāra Sūtra* also says, 'At times I have taught the prohibition of five kinds of meat and at times I made it ten kinds.' It should be observed that while both taking and rejecting meat are provided for, only pure meat is allowed. This was how it was originally. However in later times the prohibitions became more severe. The *Laṅkāvatāra Sūtra* says, 'In the *Bakuzō*, the *Daiun*, and the *Ōkutsurimara* (all names of sūtras), as well as in this *Ryōga*, I have decreed

[125] The five sharp vegetables (*goshin*) include leeks, onions, garlic, shallots, and ginger. In Chapter 16 below the belief is documented that they lead to sensual desire when eaten cooked and to anger when eaten raw.

abstinence from meat.' From this we can tell that previous sūtras permitted it. The *Nirvāṇa Sūtra* also says, 'Beginning from today meat is not permitted to the *śrāvaka* disciples.' From this we can tell that the Sarvāstivādins permitted eating meat. Of the seventeen <causal> relations listed in the *Laṅkāvatāra Sūtra* many are to do with a dislike of smell or impurity. Only in the first one does it say,

> All living beings have always circulated from the beginning in causal relations and hence have formed the six relationships <of affinity>,[126] and bearing these relationships in mind it is not appropriate to eat meat.

The *Laṅkāvatāra Sūtra* also says, 'If a sheep is eaten by a man, when the sheep dies it will become a man and when the man dies he will become a sheep.' Master Myō Kyō took the meaning of this as follows:

> Men eat animals and animals eat men. First they bear it reciprocally and then they make up for it reciprocally. This is what makes karma. We may say this is the nature of things, but why should heaven remain unfair?

He also says,

> When we now see a cow or a sheep we just fear that it is where the spirit of our former father or mother has gone to. Thus to forbid killing and to command that no harm be done to the tiniest thing is to show warmth of feeling towards our relatives.

Oh, what an extremely confused teaching! If people eating animals leads to unfairness in heaven,[127] are not cereals and vegetables also living things? If he understood this and yet discriminated, was the Buddha himself not unfair? If our father and mother may have become a cow or a sheep, then why should they only not become cereal or vegetable? The non-Buddhist Ba Ta in his estimation says,

[126] The six relationships referred to here are father, mother, elder brother, younger brother, wife and child.

[127] I.e., presumably, until fortunes are reversed through rebirth.

> The plants of the ten directions all have feelings and are no different from people; plants become people, and when people die they return to the plants of the ten directions.

And how are we to know that this is not so? The *Shuryōgon Sūtra* also says, 'Pure monks and bodhisattvas, when walking on pathways, do not tread on living plants and certainly do not pull them out with their hands.' The *Shōgon Treatise* also describes how a monk was being choked with grass but could not tear it off for fear of committing a transgression. Oh, are cereals and vegetables not grass? Now we can neither tread on it nor remove it and yet we are permitted to eat it. How is this possible without some special manipulation? Now we are allowed to eat cereals and vegetables and only meat is forbidden. Why are the Buddha and the bodhisattvas so unfair? We can tell therefore that the intention of the Buddha's prohibition of meat-eating is not to be found in this. Again the *Hōō Sūtra* says, 'The seven kinds of followers are not to eat meat or strongly smelling plants, except that if they are ill they may eat them.' To say that it is all right to eat them in the case of illness surely indicates that it is permitted in that the meat is not really regarded as one's father or mother. This is an inconsistent teaching, and therefore we can tell that the intention of the Buddha's teaching is not to be found here. The *Laṅkāvatāra Sūtra* says,

> Because it would prevent the birth of a compassionate mind among the adepts, it is not appropriate to eat meat; because it would prevent the accomplishment of all the spells, it is not appropriate to eat meat; because it makes the breath smell badly, it is not appropriate to eat meat.

Thus there are these reasons too. However the original intention of the Buddha's prohibition of meat was to avoid killing life. The prohibition of taking life was to avoid damaging benevolence and compassion.[128] The *Laṅkāvatāra Sūtra* did not know that it stemmed from there and vainly explained the seventeen <causal> relations, producing irrelevancies from the start. The *Shuryōgon Sūtra* says,

128 Kyōdo unaccountably omits this sentence in his modern Japanese version.

> The five kinds of strong-smelling vegetable in general should be disallowed. These five kinds of sharp vegetable give rise to sensual desire if eaten cooked, and if eaten raw they increase anger.

This was the original meaning of the Buddha's dislike of the five sharp vegetables.[129]

17. *Sarvāstivāda*.

The *Great Treatise* says,

> One hundred years after the Buddha's decease, King Aśoka convened a five-yearly council and, because the positions of the leading teachers of Dharma differed, the various divisions of teaching acquired their names.

This is known as the schism of Mahādeva. Before this time the Buddha-dharma was of one consistent flavour and there were as yet no discrepancies. As a matter of fact the first discrepancies appeared one hundred and sixteen years after the Buddha's decease. Between two hundred and four hundred years after that the various divisions brought about twenty-one schools, and in five hundred years they had become five hundred schools. These were all Hīnayāna Tripiṭaka scholars who made 'existence' their chief point. At that time there was still no such thing as Mahāyāna. The first mention of Mahāyāna was actually five hundred years after the Buddha's decease. The *Great Treatise* says,

> After The Buddha-dharma had endured for five hundred years the various divisions amounted to five hundred schools. From then on, because they strove to determine the dharmas they themselves became caught up with the dharmas, and, not realising that the Buddha expounded Dharma for the sake of release, they became firmly attached to words. Therefore, when they heard that *prajñā-dharmas* all conclude in emptiness, it was like a sword cleaving the heart.

See also all the other places where Mahāyāna sūtras refer to a period of five hundred years.

[129] Cf. also Chapter 15 above, and note 125.

The *Vinaya* however split into five schools, as can be seen from the list in the *Daijū Sūtra*. It says the *Donmutoku (Hōmitsu)*, the *Sabbata* (*Issaiu*), the *Mishasoku (Fujakuumukan)*, and the *Basafura (Tokushi)* are the Mahāsāṁghikas (Daishū). The sūtra says, 'Far and wide we see the five divisions of the sūtras which are called the Mahāsāṁghikas.' This is what is known as the Combination School. It is the broad linking of the five schools which makes the combination. Those who created the *Daijū Sūtra* called themselves this. However, later generations were unaware of it, and mistakenly took the Tokushi <Basafura> *Vinaya* book to be the Mahāsāṁghika *Vinaya*. The Mahāsāṁghika Combined School used the *Vinaya* of the five schools as their text. So how can there be a separate *Vinaya* book? When Fa Hsien said that the original Mahāsāṁghika *Vinaya* was the Basafura *Vinaya* and called them <the Basafura> the Mahāsāṁghikas, it was a mistake. This mistake first appeared in the *Yuigyōzanmai Sutra* which lists the *Donmukutsutaka*, the *Sabbata*, the *Kashōyui*, the *Mishasoku* and the *Makasogi* <Mahāsāṁghika>. Here the Mahāsāṁghika is included but the Basafura is omitted. It is easy to see how later diddlers once wrongly identified the Mahāsāṁghika and then spun this web together. It should therefore be clear that to say that the five schools already existed at the time of the Buddha is quite wrong. It is the same with the *Monjumon Sūtra*, and also the *Bushū, Shūrin* and *Jūhachibu Treatises*, all of which list schools, whether eighteen, twenty or twenty-one. They all give different terminology, different sequences, and different numbers of years. Each one gives different names to the schools, to suit the argument of its own tradition but without recognising its own beginnings. Later generations were unaware of this and made various distortions of the facts to try to fit them together. Again, making out that to speak of twenty-one schools is a mistake in translation is just obstinacy. The divisions of the Tripiṭaka tradition[130] into eighteen schools, as in the *Gobunritsu*, is just what is passed down in one school, and there is no need to be surprised at the variations. Similarly it is quite possibly not the case that the *Gobunritsu* <i.e. Five

130 Tradition: *ryūden*. Two sentences previously the term translated 'tradition' is *den*. Cf. also note 131.

Vinayas> goes back to the five disciples of Ubakikuta, as some argue. Note that *Basafura* is *Tokushi*. The *Great Treatise* says,

> When the Buddha was in the world Śāriputra explained the word of the Buddha and hence created the Abhidharma. Afterwards the follower of the way Tokushi chanted it, and it became known as the Śāriputra Abhidharma.

Shindai also says,

> Rāhula was a disciple of Śāriputra, and Kajushi was a disciple of Rāhula. Kajushi spread the Śāriputra Abhidharma, and that school consists of Kajushi's disciples.

We can infer from this that Tokushi was in the Śāriputra tradition,[131] Sabbata was of the Kataenishi, and Donmutoku was the disciple of Mokuren. This is what Shindai really indicates. That Mishasoku would have been one of Shanoku's tradition, if he had not been caught up on existence and non-existence, and that Kashōyui was a Sāṁkhya are all things which make sense, but are as yet insufficiently appreciated.

18. *Emptiness and existence.*

The teachings of emptiness and existence are very old. However they did not yet exist at the time of Śākyamuni. How so? The matter has little real sense. The ones who say that they did exist are making special pleas. The twenty Hīnayāna schools all made 'existence' the main point of their teaching, and it was the Mahāyāna followers of Mañjuśrī who produced the *Prajñā Sūtra* and made 'emptiness' the main point of their teaching. Followers of the *Jinmitsu Sūtra*, the *Dharma Drum Sūtra* and the *Lotus Sūtra* all made non-emptiness and absolute reality the main point of their teaching. The followers of Makakasennen <i.e. Mahākātyāyana>, who produced the *Konroku Treatise*, made 'both-emptiness-and-existence' the main point of their teaching. The followers of Shanoku <i.e. Cuṇḍaka>, who produced the *Riumu Sūtra*, made 'neither-

[131] Tradition: here *ryū* (= *nagare*).

emptiness-nor-existence' the main point of their teaching. The two latter schools were not transmitted to China. The teachings of emptiness and existence were worked out at this point. There is really not much sense in all this. All the schools just point out each other's short-comings in order to dominate. The *Great Treatise* says,

> If the slanderous Shanoku would submit with his mind he should teach the *Nadakasennen Sūtra* and attain 'the way'. [It also says,] When the Buddha was in the world Makakasennen interpreted the Buddha's words and compiled the *Konroku Treatise*. In China this is called the *Kyōzō*, and it is handed down in southern India to this day.

If we consider this, it means he was leading off with a sect. This matter of not being transmitted to China should also be treated with caution, for it says in the *Great Treatise*, 'Hōkōdōnin also made emptiness the main point of his teaching'. Hence we see that all the schools were based on the teachings of emptiness and existence.

However these things have little real sense. Why do we say that these things have little real sense? Well, it is like the teaching on human nature among the Confucianists. Seishi <i.e. Shih Tzŭ> said, 'In human nature there is good and there is evil.' Kokushi <i.e. Kao Tzŭ> said, 'Human nature is without good and without lack of good.' Mōshi <i.e. Mencius> said, 'Human nature is good.' Junshi <i.e. Hsün Tzŭ> said, 'Human nature is evil.' Yōshi <i.e. Yang Tzŭ> said, 'In human nature good and evil are mixed.' Kanshi <i.e. Han Tzŭ> said, 'Human nature has three aspects.' Soshi <i.e. Su Tzŭ> said, 'In human nature there is not yet <any distinction between> good and evil.' With this the teachings on human nature and its good or evil were worked out. Yet the reality is that these are so many empty words. Why? If it is natural for the body to perform the good, then what need is there to choose between good and evil in human nature? And if it is natural for the mind not to do evil, what need is there to judge the emptiness or existence of the nature of things <*li*>? All the vain, mutual disputation about these teachings is quite useless. Hence I say that in reality there is little real sense in them. The real teaching of Confucius was, '<Good and evil are> close in human nature, but far apart in training.' The question of good and evil in human nature did not yet exist at that time. Not to do evil but to work at the good, purifying one's intention, is the teaching of all the Buddhas, and this was the real teaching of Śākyamuni. The question of the emptiness or existence of *li* did not yet exist at that time. If we sincerely compare these things they are illustration enough.

We should note also that saying that the *Prajñā Sūtra* teaches emptiness and the *Lotus Sūtra* non-emptiness makes them out to be originally different. However when Nāgārjuna wrote the *Great Treatise* to explain the *Prajñā Sūtra* he said, 'The true *prajñāpāramitā* is called the mother of the buddhas of the three worlds and is able to display the true dharma of all dharmas.' Moreover he described the *Kegon Sūtra* as uncommunicated *prajñā*, but this was to effect a combination of different teachings. The reality is otherwise. On the contrary, he wrote the *Middle Treatise* to clarify the eight negations which are what truly made dharma-nature the main point of teaching and represent the climax of superseding in the Dharma-way. Dharma-nature teaching was started by Shōben and taken up by Chikō, but they made the *prajñā* term 'emptiness' the main point of the teaching. In the *Sanzōden* it says,

> In the night-time Mujaku <i.e. Asaṅga> ascended to the Tushita Heaven where Jishi <i.e. Maitreya> was, and received the *Yugashiji Treatise*, the *Shōgondaijō Treatise*, and the *Chūhenfunbetsu Treatise*, and in the daytime he descended from heaven and preached them for the people.

This is just an elevated way of putting the matter. The reality is that these treatises were all compiled by Asaṅga himself, and that unless he had ascribed them to Maitreya the people would not have believed them.[132] (In Ryoshi's Hakushi Chapter <of his *Shunjū*> it says, 'Kōkyū and Bokuteki read aloud and pursued learning in the daytime and at night had private meetings with the King of Bun <i.e. Wen> and Prince Tan of

[132] Kyōdo glosses: 'he thought the people would not believe him'. He may have 'thought' so; however Tominaga's point is that it was objectively so. In other words, while religious leaders knowingly advance their doctrines in certain ways, the psychology of reception by the people is in fact such as to require this.

Shū <i.e. Chou>.' This is the same kind of thing).[133]

The meaning of all this is that he <Asaṅga> received the *Lotus Sūtra*, the *Laṅkāvatāra Sūtra* and the *Jinmitsu Sūtra*, and pronounced the principle of non-emptiness and consciousness-only. This was called the Hossō <i.e. Dharma-characteristics> School. Thereupon each one set up his line and they disputed with each other. Master Rei said,

> These references to the characteristic of existence and the characteristic of non-existence eliminate hindrances, but it is not a question of things severally not existing as if in a great emptiness.

Master Gaku said,

> On no-characteristics or non-characteristics the Small Vehicle says that there is no life in the great emptiness, while the Great Vehicle says that it is like the image in a brightly polished mirror.

Or again some say 'the three thousand worlds are empty, provisional and middle', while others say 'the three thousand worlds are only provisional, so why call them empty and middle?' Thus the arguments are not consistent. This is all no more than the dance of the six dragons.

I have already settled this as follows. If a school declares for emptiness they all emphasise emptiness, and if a school declares for non-emptiness they discard it and deny emptiness. The reality is that they just set up some particular term and then aggravate each other. The argument over the affirmation or denial of form is just the same. Why? Because if form is discarded there is no emptiness, and if emptiness is discarded there is no form. Mountains, rivers and towers are originally things in emptiness and if it were not for these things there would be no emptiness. We can call this emptiness, or we can call it non-emptiness, but both emptiness and non-emptiness are the designations of men, and the great way is comprehensive. As the *Great Treatise* says,

133 I.e. this also lent authority to their utterances.

> It is like the third finger of the ignorant, both long and short. If we compare it with the middle finger it is short, but if we compare it with the little finger it is long. Long and short both have reality, and the teachings of existence and non-existence are similar to this.

This will suffice in explanation. I have already settled this by saying,

> The teachings of emptiness and existence are very old; neither give the Buddha's intention; but both are reasonable and do not impede the Buddha's intention.[134]

When the Buddha preached the middle <way> of no opposition[135] and then entered meditation there were five hundred *arhats* present and each one interpreted what the Buddha had said. When he emerged from meditation they asked the world-honoured one which of them had got the Buddha's meaning right. The Buddha said, 'None of these has my meaning.' So they said to the Buddha, 'If we have not got the Buddha's meaning right, have we not acquired sin?' The Buddha said, 'Although it is not my meaning, you have all followed correct reasoning, and therefore it is correct teaching, and you are blessed, not sinful.' This is found in the *Jōjitsu Treatise*, and it is very similar to the above. The *Great Treatise* also says, 'He was asked, "The higher kind of people teach *prajñāpāramitā*, but which one has the truth?" And he answered, "What the people say all has reason in it and it is all true." ' As it says in the sūtra, 'There were five hundred monks who all taught for a second time the middle way, and the Buddha said that they were all reasonable.' From this we can see that this matter was originally taught in a sūtra, and although we do not know which sūtra taught it, it is from here that the meaning of 'Emerging from Meditation' really arose.

19. *Three in the south and seven in the north.*

The words of Bodhiruci who set up the One-sounded Teaching

[134] This is a clear example of Tominaga's appraisal being critical but not thereby destructive of religion.
[135] *Naige chūgen.*

were: 'The Tathāgata taught in one rounded sound, but living beings interpreted it variously according to their dispositions.' This is harmless enough. However when we see 'For eight years he preached the Lotus' and 'Clever people entered the Dharma-world by *prajñā*', this is just a mistake made to favour the text of the *Lotus Sūtra*. Again when the two teachers Tan and On set up the two teachings of the Gradual and the Sudden, when Master Kōzuritsu set up the Three Kinds of Teaching, when Daien set up the Teaching in Four Points, Goshin the Five Kinds of Teachings, Gisha the Teaching in Six Points, Nangaku and Tendai the Four Teachings, Master Binbō the Two Teachings, Master Unbō the Four Vehicle Teaching, Genjō Sanzō the Three Kinds of Teaching and Master Hōzō the Five Teachings, they all differed in their selection of the sūtras and found it hard to deal with the differences, which is to say that they put the differences in themselves. The reason for this lay in the teaching that the *Lotus Sūtra* was preached over a number of years, which is why I say, 'The ten great virtues of past and present are recirculated in the Lotus.'[136] Tendai Daishi believed in the truth of the Lotus, made the *Lotus Sūtra* the king of the sūtras and constructed the Four Teachings referred to. This was truly a selection among the many teachings.[137] Then again National Teacher Hōzō believed in the Kegon teaching of the heights being illumined in the second seven-day <period of the Buddha's teaching> and made the Kegon the king of the sūtras. He too came out one level higher and made this the main point of the teaching. This also was truly a selection among the teachings. Since both these schools find things in the sūtras which do not fit, Tendai set up the teaching of the 'pervasive' and the 'special', while Hōzō set up the teaching of the 'raw' and the 'ripe'. Fitting the discrepancies together in this way is subtle indeed. According to Tendai's interpretation, the books are not divided, but regarded as having two kinds of milk; learning the three vehicles at once is reckoned as the Pervasive Teaching while not hearing two of the vehicles, for bodhisattvas only, is reckoned as the Special Teaching. If we

[136] This appears to be intended ironically.

[137] Kyōdo introduces the technical term *kyōhan* here, which however is not in Tominaga's text.

pursue this in terms of my exposition they are all confused. Why is it necessary to use this explanation of Pervasive and Special?

To take an example, the Jūji Chapter of the *Great Prajñā Sūtra* speaks of three vehicles under the name of Special Teaching; it does not call it the Pervasive Teaching. The story of the three beasts crossing the river arose by combining the Tokuō Chapter and the Shishiku Chapter <of the *Nirvāṇa Sūtra*> and did not originally have this meaning <about three vehicles>. The Buddha's teaching that there are three kinds of true reality: the *śrāvakas'* Dharma, the Great Vehicle <Dharma> and the Pratyekabuddha <Dharma> (in the Kanpō Chapter of the *Middle Treatise*) refers simply to the four truths, the twelve causal relations and the six ways. It does not have any other special teaching. The *Great Prajñā Sūtra* says, 'The ten stages <of bodhisattva-hood> are like the Buddha', while the *Laṅkāvatara Sūtra* says, 'The stages of far practice, of good wisdom and of the Dharma-cloud pertain to the Buddha-nature, and the others pertain to the two vehicles.' When the *Kegon Sūtra* and the *Ninnō Sūtra* assign them to the bodhisattva level these are again just the designations of different groups. Why do these have to be harmonised? If interpreted as above we see that there are contradictions. Again, in Hōzō's interpretation it says, 'The root disposition of living beings is indeterminate', and 'The Buddha only taught the Small Vehicle from beginning to end', and 'The Buddha only taught the Small Vehicle and then he turned it to the Great Vehicle', and 'First the Buddha taught the Small Vehicle, in the middle he gave the teaching of emptiness and afterwards taught non-emptiness', and 'The teaching in words does not attain the ultimate; the Buddha taught not a word from beginning to end', and 'From beginning to end the Buddha only taught the three vehicles', and 'The Dharmas of the three vehicles all arise in dependence on the one vehicle.' These belong to what is called the 'special' teaching of the *Kegon Sūtra*, which is a teaching without end.[138]

If I try to theorise about why there are so many attempts to select within the scriptures and set up a teaching, then my view is as follows. All these expositions say that the root

138 This is meant ironically.

disposition of living beings is indeterminate, and that what the Buddha taught is consistent while what people see is diverse. Saying that what the Buddha taught is consistent while what people see is diverse is natural enough in respect of trifles, when there are one or two points of difference, but it is a major matter to argue such things as that first he taught the Small Vehicle and afterwards turned it to the Great Vehicle, that in the middle of his exposition he gave the teaching of emptiness and that afterwards he taught non-emptiness. This concerns the World-honoured Nyorai's <Tathāgata's> Turning of the Wheel of Dharma and is a matter of great import in this world, indeed a matter surpassed by none. It is truly regrettable that his disciples now mistake what they saw and heard, even though they had the same seats of audience. It is even more so when they say that the root disposition of living beings is indeterminate and that for this reason there were differences when the Buddha preached the Dharma. When people prattle on without seeing any way out, their error is evident. To say that root dispositions to the three vehicles are determined and that therefore the Buddha preached three vehicles from the beginning is the hardest account of all. This would mean that if the teaching were given suitably for one person, countless living beings would fail to attain the fruits of arhatship, while if the teaching were given suitably for the many it would be no different from the Small Vehicle to start with. This brings us to the limits of the matter. People of old already debated why there were differences in the sequence of teaching, so why did they not arrive at this conclusion?

20. *Succession in the Zen Schools.*

1 – Kāśyapa, 2 – Ānanda, 3 – Śaṇavāsa, 4 – Madhyānti, 5 – Upagupta, 6 – Dhṛtaka, 7 – Micchaka, 8 – Buddhanandi, 9 – Buddhamitra, 10 – Bhikṣu Parśva, 11 – Puṇyayaśas, 12 – Aśvaghoṣa, 13 – Kapimala, 14 – Nāgārjuna, 15 – Kānadeva, 16 – Rāhalata, 17 – Saṁghanandi, 18 – Saṁghayaśas, 19 – Kumārata, 20 – Jayata, 21 – Vasubandhu, 22 – Manura, 23 – Haklenayaśas, 24 – <Bhikṣu> Siṁha: this is the order given in the *Fuhōzō Sūtra*. 1 – Kāśyapa, 2 – Ānanda, 3 – Upagupta, 4 – Śīlānanda, 5 – Utpala, 6 – Go Ku <no Indian form>, 7 – Ratnadeva, 8 – Aśvaghoṣa, 9 – Nāgārjuna: this is the order

given in the *Maya Sūtra*. 1 – Kāśyapa, 2 – Ānanda, 3 – Madhyānti, 4 – Śaṇavāsa, 5 – Upagupta: this is the order given in the *Sharihotsumon Sūtra*. The *Zen Sūtra* also gives nine people whose names are not the same. It makes Dharmatrāta the eighth and Prajñāmitra the ninth. However in monk Yū's *Sanzōki* the record of the succession in transmitting the Vinaya makes Dharmatrāta the fifty-third. These are all teachings by different groups about the transmission and do not merit belief. The T'ang monk Chi Ko compiled the *Hōrinden* and listed what are known as the twenty-eight patriarchs. The order is given as 1 – Kāśyapa, 2 – Ānanda, 3 – Śaṇavāsa, 4 – Upagupta, 5 – Dhṛtaka, 6 – Micchaka, 7 – Vasumitra, 8 – Buddhanandi, 9 – Buddhamitra, 10 – Parśva, 11 – Puṇyayaśas, 12 – Aśvaghoṣa, 13 – Kapimala, 14 – Nāgārjuna, 15 – Kānadeva, 16 – Rāhalata, 17 – Saṁghanandi, 18 – Saṁghayaśas, 19 – Kumārata, 20 – Jayata, 21 – Vasubandhu, 22 – Manura, 23 – Haklenayaśas, 24 – <Bhikṣu> Siṁha, 25 – Vāśasita, 26 – Puṇyamitra, 27 – Prajñātara, 28 – Bodhidharma. However as this was not yet to be seen in the sūtras people of old said that it was a fabrication by Chi Ko. Vāśasita and Puṇyamitra both appear in other places too. It is like, as they say, buying a hat to fit the head. Dharmatrāta and Prajṇāmitra merely recognised Bodhidharma's knowledge but did not recognise his enlightenment, thus making him out to be very foolish. This again is an argument handed down by one different group and does not deserve to be believed.

However, speaking from the standpoint of Dharma,[139] the Mind is one's own Mind and the Dharma is one's own Dharma. By our own Mind we testify to our own Dharma. Thus why do we need such a succession? It is said that we ourselves are the seven buddhas, and who will deny it? By contrast these are they who all the world over take pride in their place in the succession. I am not a follower who has seen Bodhidharma and takes pride in the succession. It was also said later, 'I have come because of the Dharma, not because of the robe.' Though referred to as a follower, this was definitely not a common follower <speaking>. Setting up a succession in the Zen schools must have been started in a later generation by Chi Ko. Later on the Confucianists were unaware of this, and being

[139] Kyōdo glosses this as 'the teaching of the Zen school'.

ashamed that they alone had none such they said, 'Gyō passed this on to Shun, Shun passed it on to U, and thus it came down to Confucius and Mencius.' This putting about of a line of transmission is laughable. Only Kan-I-Chō's refusal to answer En-Ni <is splendid> and can be compared with the 'thunderous silence' <of Yuima>. It was not at all odd.

I heard Hayashi Chūho[140] say,

> The meaning of Daruma's <i.e. Bodhidharma's> entry to China lay in this, that in India the Buddha-Dharma had already reached the counterfeit stage, things were going to rack and ruin, and there was nobody worth addressing; since China was far off the Dharma had not yet spread there, and things were still in crude condition; so having regard to the time, one should attract people to one's own way by the principle of direct pointing, and thus there would be those who would listen. It was with such resolve that he came. However when he had his first interview with the emperor Wu of the Liang <dynasty>, the latter asked about the state of morality and about imperial questions, to which Daruma replied that they were similar to those of his own India. If the emperor's question was not inappropriate then Daruma's answer was, so he bestirred himself, departed and finished his life by spending nine years looking at the wall at Shōrin <Temple>. He also said, 'The time is ripe for the arousing <of Zen>.' It was widely thought not to be.

What have the inappropriateness of his words to the emperor and Daruma's being poisoned to death for the sake of others to do with the time being ripe? This is clearly a decorative phrase of later followers. Ah, Daruma! He went to such a distant land for the sake of this Dharma-way, desiring to spread it, but his words were so lofty that no one could believe or receive it, and he died at the hand of a wicked, miserable unbeliever. I regard Daruma as the man most to be pitied in the whole earth, past and present. However, in later times this way flourished and the monks of the world could not escape from his tracks.[141] Like using mud to wash clods of earth, they ended up by making him rival Śākyamuni. This is the long and short of it. When those disciples said the time was ripe, this is all it

[140] On Hayashi Chūho see the end of this chapter and note 142 below.

[141] Kyōdo adds that they entered enlightenment like fish entering the boiling pot, but this appears to have no basis in the original text.

meant. But that is not what he originally intended. I regard Daruma as the man most to be pitied in the whole earth, past and present.

Hayashi Chūho, surnamed Shi Ryō, is a friend of my father's and is still alive.[142]

21. *The maṇḍala school.*

The maṇḍala school's support for a circle of letters[143] originally started with the *Great Prajñā Sūtra*. The Kegon account also stems from there. They both teach of forty-two letters. The *Nirvāṇa Sūtra, Monjumon Sūtra* and *Kongōchō Sūtra* also have it, but they make it fifty letters, while the *Dainichi Sūtra* makes it forty-nine letters. Sometimes the explanation is the same and sometimes it differs. This again is the terminology of different groups. The maṇḍala school say,

> What the *Prajñā* and *Kegon Sūtras* teach is the final teaching, while the *Nirvaṇā Sūtra* is the original source but only has a shallow, abbreviated meaning.

This is only to give importance to the maṇḍala school. The maṇḍala school make their circle of letters their entire speciality, and therefore it makes the circle of letters seem like their possession. The reality is that it first came from the *Great Prajñā* and that the various groups then came into existence afterwards. The view that the <Sanskrit> letter A brought all the seed-syllables into being is <the view of> one of them. Why? They all claimed that it <the letter A> was originally unproduced. When the *Shugo Sūtra* regards the <Sanskrit> letter Om as the head of all the *dhāraṇī* <i.e spells>, this too represents one group within the maṇḍala school and there is no need to seek to harmonise it.

Again, the various sequences and directions of the two maṇḍalas, the Womb and the Diamond, are also points insisted on by different groups. That the design of the Womb <maṇḍala> was copied by Zen Mu I beneath the Konzoku

[142] Hayashi also wrote one of the prefaces to *Writings of an Old Man*, for which see the relevant place in this volume.

[143] I.e. a meditational maṇḍala containing syllables representing various Buddhas, etc.

stūpa, while the design of the Diamond <maṇḍala> was revealed by Ryū Myō <i.e. Nāgārjuna> when he opened the stūpa are nothing more than emphases of one or other tradition. Later scholars are mistaken when they combine them. Consider the view that what Nāgārjuna found in the iron stūpa was the *Kongōchō Sūtra*, which can be read in Fu Kū's *Giketsu*. Later scholars are mistaken when, in surfeit of piety, they conclude that the *Dainichi Sūtra* was also stored in the stūpa. The name Vairocana appears in the *Kegon Sūtra* and was originally a title used in praise of the Buddha, but to equate it with Dainichi is a new interpretation by the maṇḍala party. Or consider the term 'secret'. It was originally a word used to exalt the Dharma. The Sarvāstivādins referred to the Vinaya as the secret tripiṭaka, and the *Lotus Sūtra* refers to the 'Tathāgata's secret supernatural powers'. In the *Nirvāṇa Sūtra*, we find, 'the secret tripiṭaka is the Tathāgata's secret words'. These are all expressions of a love of novelty. The *Dainichi Sūtra* says,

> The saying of the superlative great vehicle that characteristics are born from the flow of consciousness is the great secret of all the buddhas.

Thus while all groups have reference to 'secret', only the maṇḍala school make secretness the main point. While others treat secretness in a small way, it is a speciality of the maṇḍala party to make a big thing of it for themselves. Then consider Nāgārjuna, Nāgabodhi, Amoghavajra and Kei Ka <Ch. Hui Kuo> who had a sequence of transmission extending over five or six generations, which nevertheless covered more than a thousand years. Thus, the argument runs,

> The Dharma-teacher Hsüan Tsang saw Nāgabodhi in the Aṁra Grove in South India, at which time he was seven hundred years of age. This is when Kōbō Daishi arrived in T'ang China.

This is astounding. Is it credible? Nevertheless there have been all kinds of things in heaven and earth, so why should we regard it as astounding that the generations of transmission are few while the number of years is great? Similarly the great bodhisattvas who save the world have limitless length of life, and cease to exist along with heaven and earth themselves. So why should we wonder at an age of seven hundred years?[144]

Consider too that the discipline of the maṇḍala school lies entirely in palmistry and divination. Only the maṇḍala school knows the practices of India. China lost them at an early time and they are only passed on here. It is not strange![145] These people speak of this as Dainichi's original country. Consider also that in the *Rōkaku Sūtra* it says,

> Mantras <*shingon*> are the mother of the buddhas and the seeds of the attainment of Buddhahood. If it were not for mantras there would ultimately be no attainment of supreme enlightenment [and] The whole of the tripiṭaka arises from the *dhāraṇīs*.

In the *Daijōshōgonhōō Sūtra* it says, 'Even the buddhas seek spells, why should the lay person not practise them?' The *Rokudo Sūtra* says,

> The sūtras are like milk, the discipline is like whey, the abhidharma is like fresh curds, the *prajñā* is like mature curds, and the gate of spells[146] is like the ghee.

In the *Jūjū Treatise* it says,

> By the six perfections, and so on, is produced self-power,[147] which is slow in merit; by the *nenbutsu*, and so on, is produced other-power,[148] which is quick in merit; by the secret of the mantras <*shingon*> is produced both self-power and other-power.

These are all arguments which give self-importance to the maṇḍala school.

[144] Tominaga's heavy irony in this section is entirely lost in Kyōdo's modern translation, but maintained by Ishida.

[145] Again, there seems little doubt that this is intended ironically.

[146] This refers to the so-called *mantrayāna*.

[147] Self-power: *jiriki*, i.e. religious strength developed by one's own efforts. This refers to the bodhisattva vehicle in general, the six perfections being: generosity, morality, patience, courage, meditation and insight.

[148] Other-power: *tariki*, i.e. religious strength drawn from an external, salvific source. *Nenbutsu* (also frequently transcribed *nembutsu*) means recalling (commonly by actually calling out) a Buddha's (typically Amida Buddha's) name in faith.

22. *Heterodoxies*.

There were probably ninety-six heterodoxies.[149] The *Great Treatise* says, 'The ninety-six kinds of heterodoxy once conspired together to debate against the Buddha.' In the *Sarvāstivāda Vinaya* it says, 'The six teachers of heterodox ways each gave rise to fifteen kinds, which makes ninety-six altogether.' The *Daijū Sūtra* says, 'In the three jewels the mind is held in respect, and this surpasses all the ninety-five ways.' Then again the *Bunbetsukudoku Treatise* says, 'Among the ninety-six ways the Buddha way is regarded as the greatest.' This is the utterance of yet another group who made it ninety-six including the Buddha. The *Laṅkāvatāra Sūtra* refers to one hundred and eight heretical views.[150] They are not all given in detail. The *Vimalakīrti Sūtra* lists six teachers of heterodoxies as follows: Pūraṇa Kāśyapa, Maskarin Gośālīputra, Saṁjayin Vairaṭīputra, Ajita Keśakambala, Kakuda Kātyāyana and Nirgrantha Jñātiputra. The *Nirvāṇa Sūtra* lists six heterodoxies of asceticism as follows: fasting, frequenting a precipice, fire-walking, sitting in solitude, maintaining tranquil silence, living like a cow or a dog. The *Great Treatise* lists sixteen kinds of false subjectivity, the *Yuga Treatise* lists sixteen divergent theories of existence, the *Dainichi Sūtra* lists thirty kinds of heterodoxy, and the *Gedōshōjōnehan Treatise* lists twenty kinds of Hīnayāna heterodoxy.[151] These are all convenient summaries and do not amount to the full number of ninety-six. They are not handed down in the *Vedas*, nor did their people enter China. As to the rights and wrongs of these teachings we now get it in detail:

The *Fa Hsien Record* says,

> That there are ninety-six kinds of heterodoxy in this Middle Kingdom <of India> everybody knows. In the present generation we have their various followers. Moreover they all

149 On the use of this term for *gedō*, which literally means 'external ways', see note 9 above.

150 In this case the term used is *jaken*, which implies wrong views, at odds with the truth.

151 As the longer lists cannot be meaningfully translated with anything like the conciseness of the original they would distract inappropriately from the real argument and are omitted here. Refer to modern Japanese editions.

> beg for food but without bearing a bowl. [It further says,] 'Devadatta also has followers; they make offerings to the three buddhas of the past, but offer nothing to Śākyamuni Buddha. [It also says,] In the country of Karanu there were both heretics and orthodox together. There were three separate monasteries where they did not partake of milk or whey. These were monks of Devadatta's group.

From this we can see that heterodoxies were also handed down until later times. The heterodoxies are like the words of the Buddha in that they were handed down to later times and indeed down to the present. Kapila's <i.e. the Sāṁkhya> heterodoxy produced the *Kinshichijū Treatise* and proposed twenty-five theses. This writing still exists. Again, it is the work of a particular school, but is said to be splendid. During the Ch'in period, a brahman from the Lion country <i.e. Ceylon> came over to Kan Chū <in China> with his writing and sought to promote it. Shaku Shi Dō Yū defeated him by skilful means and so this way was discontinued. How sad! How can we now be assured of the inadequacy of this teaching? In the T'ang period, Sorashi of Persia transmitted the teaching of Mani <to China>. Futtatan's transmission of two religions[152] <at once> was a grandiloquent delusion, and this delusion made an overview of other <teachings> quite impossible.

If we now consider what the Buddhist writings have to propose on the matter, they say that taking refuge in other ways leads only to rebirth in the heavens and that their practice does not escape from the two courses of pain and pleasure. <The heterodox> say,

> Daibonten <i.e. Brahman> is the creative source of all things, so that to depart from him is to be in birth-and-death and to be in accordance with him brings release. [Also,] The formless heaven is true nirvāṇa and discipline in the concentration of the

[152] 'Two religions' stands for *nishūkyō*. Although Ishida transforms this into a different character compound by replacing the last character with that for 'sūtra' (also pronounced *kyō*), following a Chinese source (Ishida, p. 446, n.3), this appears to be, in Tominaga's text, an early use of the modern Japanese term for 'religion'. The two religions in question which were brought to China were Buddhism and Manichaeism, and as the latter claimed to be a superior blend, inclusive of other known religions, it made it difficult for a Buddhist view of heterodoxies to be maintained.

> formless brings rebirth there. [Also,] The five peaceful abodes are in the realm of Mahāśiva which is regarded as the source of creation; if recourse is taken there, release will be attained.

This is all to do with those who preach rebirth in the heavens. Then there are the eight groups of heavenly dragons and also water and fire, and so on, which all represent other ways. As the Fumon Chapter <of the *Lotus Sūtra*> says,

> To all those who need to be saved in the form of devas, dragons, *yakṣas*, *gandharvas*, *asuras*, *garuḍas*, *kinnaras*, *mahoragas*, humans, non-humans, and so on, he apperead in all those forms and proclaimed the Dharma.

In Kāśyapa's appearing as a fire-dragon, we see the same again.[153] The *Great Treatise* also refers to the practices of heterodoxies, thus,

> They smear their bodies with ashes and go naked without shame, they put human excrement on skulls and eat it, they pull out their hair and lie down on needles, they hang themselves upside down and fumigate their noses, in winter they go into cold water and in summer they toast themselves over a fire, they eat fruit and vegetables, grass-roots, cow-dung, millet and water-lettuce, they restrict themselves to just one meal for between one and two months, they inhale the wind and drink water.

There is no going beyond this in emphasising practice.

Śākyamuni emerged one level above this, and to gain the upper hand he said of birth-and-death,

> The two upper worlds give rise to great anguish at the time of death and departure and are much more severe than the lower world, just as when something falls from a high place it is smashed to smithereens. (*Great Treatise*)

Similarly, assigning Great Brahman to the Palace of Decease, making Jizaitennō a heretical Māra and expounding the way the gods guide the spirits, are all arguments for winning

153 Tominaga's point here appears to be that the adoption of diverse forms to save living beings, as proclaimed in the *Lotus Sūtra*, is on the same level as being saved by various divinities in the heterodox ways.

debate. Hence the *Great Treatise* says 'Heterodoxies serve Bonten <i.e.Brahman>; if Bonten himself were to ask it, the heterodoxies would submit.' It also says, 'Living beings always know Bonten. Bonten is expounded so as to be made their ancestor.' There it is. Again <Śākyamuni's> six years in pursuit of ascetic practice were to bring about the submission of heterodoxies, which is why the *Great Treatise* says,

> If Śākyamuni Buddha had not first practised asceticism for six years the people would not have trusted him when he reproved those not following the way. Hence he himself practised asceticism more than other people.

The *Saiikiki* also says,

> The Prince, having in mind the ulterior reason of bringing the heterodoxies of asceticism to submission, restricted his diet to sesame and rice and subdued his body for six years.

There it is. The *Inga Sūtra* says,

> The prince said of himself, 'I have now been doing ascetic practice for a full six years. If I now attain the way with an emaciated body I will have to say that self-starvation is the cause of nirvāṇa. I must take food and then complete the way.'

Hence we say that Śākyamuni's double practice of pleasure and of asceticism was in order to bring the heterodoxies to submission. Thus the exposition of what is called the middle way is also something which emerges at one level above. The *Chū-agon* says, 'There are two kinds of practice, that of the five passions and that of asceticism; departing from these two is called the middle way.' There it is.

Consider also the *Saishō* and *Keko Sūtras* of the Tao school. It is said that Lao Tzŭ crossed the western border to convert the barbarians and made the Buddha his follower, but there is no doubt that this was just a fabrication intended to go one better than the Buddhists. On the contrary Lao Tzŭ's crossing to the barbarians and spreading his teaching had the following meaning. In the story of Lao Tzŭ in the *Historical Records* it says, 'He crossed the western border, wrote scriptures and departed. There is no knowledge of his decease.' In the Jōkai story in the *Han Writings* it says, 'Lao Tzŭ went to the barbarians and created the teaching of Fu To <Buddha>.' These matters were treated in detail in the *Setsuhei*. Thinking along these lines we can see that Lao Tzŭ's was one of the heterodoxies. Was it perhaps the heresy of spontaneous arising? And he did not hesitate to make out the Buddha to be his disciple!

23. *The date of the Buddha's appearance*

The date of the Buddha's appearance is uncertain. Nīlapiṭa also tells us nothing of it, yet all the teachings about it are quite diverse. In the *Saiikiki* it says, 'From the time of the Buddha's nirvāṇa all the schools had differing doctrines', or again it says (of the time of King Tan), 'Nine hundred years have passed so far, but not yet a thousand.' Or it says (of the time of King Rei) 'More than one thousand two hundred years have passed.' Or it says (of the time of King Kei) 'More than one thousand three hundred years have passed', or it says (of the time of King Hei), 'More than one thousand five hundred years have passed.' The *Juryōshōkenroku* says,

> There are about eight kinds of teaching on the date of the Buddha's birth; first, that it was at the time of Ketsu of Ka <i.e. Hsia>, second, at the time of Bu Itsu of the late Shō <i.e. Shang> (according to Fa Hsien), third, at the time of King Shō of the western Shū <i.e. Chou> (in the *Hōhonnaiden*), fourth, at the time of King Boku, fifth, at the time of King Hei of the eastern Shū <i.e. Chou>, sixth, at the time of King Kan (according to Dō An), seventh, at the time of King Sō (according to Kan Sei), eighth, in the second year of King Tei Tei, which was Kinoe-Inu (in the *Shushōtenki* of Chō Haku Kyū).

As the present writer views this, all these theories are without basis and none can be trusted. Only the *Shushōtenki* of Chō Haku Kyū has sufficient evidence, and may have the truth.

The retired scholar Chō Haku Kyū met the Vinaya master Gu Do on Mount Ro and there received the *Shushōtenki*. In it, it says,

After the Buddha's decease Upāli compiled the Vinaya; on the fifteenth of the seventh month of that year, after the *prāvaraṇa*[154] had been observed, he put a dot at the beginning of the Vinaya, and so it continued year by year. After Upāli the masters followed on down to the monk Gabadara. When the Vinaya arrived at Kō Shū, in the seventh year of Ei Myō of Sei, on the fifteenth of the seventh month, after the *prāvaraṇa* was finished, a further dot was added, bringing the total in that year to nine hundred and seventy-five dots. About this Haku Kyū asked, 'Why was no dot added after the seventh year of Ei Myō?' and Gu Do replied, 'Up to now it was people who had attained the way who added dots, but we ordinary folk should just follow respectfully.'

Following the *Shushōtenki* Haku Kyū was able to reach back to the great beginning, altogether one thousand and twenty years, and this is the only reliable testimony. Moreover the Buddhists generally all seek to make the appearance of the Buddha come before that of Masters Confucius and Lao Tzŭ. However this <text> makes him follow by some hundreds of years and is sooner to be believed. The *Chumoinnen Sūtra* says,

> In the World of Men there is the land of Shin Tan <i.e. China>, and there I reside, revering the three sages and teaching the people.

The *Shōjōhōgyō Sūtra* says,

> Bodhisattva Kō Jō was given the name of Confucius, Bodhisattva Ka Shō was given the name of Lao Tzŭ, and Bodhisattva Gatsu Kō given the name of Gan Kai.

The *Hongi Sūtra* says moreover,

> During the ten thousand years of the Latter Dharma Bodhisattva Gatsu Kō appeared in Shin tan <i.e. China> and preached the Dharma for fifty-two years.

This does not fit. Can this be the original teaching?

[154] *Prāvaraṇa*: *jishi*, cf. note 97.

These are all Chinese distortions which were provisionally[155] so claimed. In the *Heishinroku* of the scholar Ryū we find a denial of them. They first appeared in the *Haja Treatise* of Hō Rin. Ryū quoted it to deny them. All these sūtras should be viewed as provisional claims made from Hō Rin's time onwards.

I only regard Chō Haku Kyū's *Shushōtenki* as correct. Again the figures given in the dialogues of So Yū and Ko Ta in the *Shūshoiki* are baseless fabrications out of thin air and none deserve to be trusted. Again, to say as Bu Gyō does, 'I avoid putting anything different which is not written in the *Shūshoiki*', is laughable. Only when we hear of Shitsu Ri Bō coming to preach to the Emperor Shin does there seem to be a shadow of reality. In the *Gogyōshi* of the *Historical Records* it says,

> In the twenty-sixth year of the Emperor Shin there were giants five metres tall. They wore barbarians' clothes, numbered about twelve and were seen in the Rin To district.

This is nothing but impossible bunkum. However it is followed with 'Eighteen foreign monks came to Shin', (Bu Gyō), which is also laughable. Again in the *Retsu Shi* is a saying of Confucius which runs, 'There are sages in the four quarters called Buddhas.' But the *Retsu Shi* which has been handed down is another writing spun together by a post-T'ang person with ideas of his own. Thus the *Hōonjurin* quoted the *Shūshoiki* from it, but, notice, only this part. The two words 'called Buddhas' are not there. Probably the author found them objectionable and left them out. In general this kind of thing is very common, and none can be trusted. Notice further that in the story of Katsu Kyo Hei in the *Han Writings* it says, 'He seized the golden figure used by Kyū To when worshipping heaven.' Gan Shi Ko said, 'The present Buddha image was this golden figure.' The Buddhists often quote this as evidence that Buddhism entered China before the Ming Court. However this was only an image of Vasubandhu, not of the Buddha. We can tell this from the *Hōyōki* which says,

[155] Provisionally: i.e. these claims were set up as teaching expedients though without historical foundation.

In India they worship Jizaiten. They use gold for his body and lapis lazuli for his eyes. This celestial image is designated Vasubandhu.

24. *The three teachings.*

The three teachings have been disputing for a long time. But what have they been disputing about? The Confucianists have been looking after the numerical designation <of their books>,[156] the Taoists have been cultivating their healthful life, and the Buddhists have been departing from birth-and-death. They have all been speaking up and setting forth their ways. If we try to pin it down, what the Confucianists exaggerate in is letters and what the Buddhists exaggerate in is magic.[157] The Taoists however make heaven their main point, either saying that there is a dwelling for divine recluses overseas, or trying to push ahead with their magic, so that in effect they belong with the 'other ways' of India. This pretended Way <Tao> is moreover quite wretched and is fundamentally not comparable to Confucianism or Buddhism. Its sūtras also all appeared later. The conversion of the barbarians, the thirty-six heavens, and the dwelling of the great heavenly court are all magic added to Buddhism. They have not been handed down over here and thus do not need to be debated now. The scholar Sei Sai Ryū wrote the *Heishinroku* to debate the three teachings. I have read it with the closest attention and can confirm the quality of its magic. Then there was a man who asked Ri Shi Ken about the relative quality of the three teachings, and he said, 'Buddhism is the sun, Taoism is the moon, and Confucianism is the stars'. At the time his argument was considered reasonable, but it does not touch the reality at all. I cannot explain its meaning or why it was considered reasonable. They are all small fry. How can they know the great way?

A man asked Prince Ryū Mon, 'He <the Buddha> may be a sage, but what is his teaching?' He answered, 'It is western teaching; in China it is mud.' This is to the point. Why do we have 'In China it is mud'? It is because of the value placed on

[156] I.e. settling their canon in 'four books' and 'five classics'.

[157] 'Magic': the same term as that used earlier on, especially in Chapter 8 (Supernatural abilities). Cf. also *Writings of an Old Man*, pp. 68ff. above.

magic. Someone asked me, 'He <Confucius> may be a sage, but what is his teaching?' I answered, 'It is western teaching; over here it is mud.' Why do we have 'Over here it is mud?' This is because of the value placed on letters. Here we have a case of language having conditions.[158] Because of this the way diverges. It is because countries have their customs that the way diverges. If the teaching of Confucianism is mud over here how much the more so is the teaching of Buddhism which lies to the west of the west. Since what the Buddhists exaggerate in is magic and what the Confucianists exaggerate in is letters, if we reject these we shall advance to the way.[159] Long ago Ka Shō Ten wrote the *Tasshō Treatise* to discredit the Buddha-way. Then Gan En Shi wrote another writing to attack it. Then again the monk E Rin composed the *Byakukoku Treatise* and Sō Hei criticised that. Such were the disputes between Confucianism and Buddhism. When we come to the time of Chō Sō, Ō Yō Shū wrote his *Hon Treatise*, Seki Shu Dō wrote his *Kaisetsu*, and Ko In wrote his *Sūseiben*, all to attack the Buddhists. At that time Myō Kyō Daishi Kai Sū compiled his *Bugyōhen* in answer. So again we had disputes between Confucianism and Buddhism. I have read these carefully and they are nothing more than disputes between magic and letters.

In Myō Kyō's words we have,

> Why did the Buddha's way go out beyond the world of his own state? Its emergence was not merely promoted by officials, but also by the inner law of the teaching. It was hidden and hard to see, which is why the people did not all come to believe it fully.

He also says, 'The Buddha founded his teaching in accordance with the divine way[160] and had feeling for its contents.' These references to 'being hidden and hard to see' and 'the divine way and feeling for its contents' are all merely talking about the doctrine of karmic cause and effect. This may be called magic and it is not the true meaning of the Buddha. Myō Kyō did not know this. How lamentable. Moreover Buddhism as a kind of

[158] Cf. Chapter 11 above, where this is explained at length.

[159] This argument is very close to that of *Writings of an Old Man*, hence it is not surprising that the argument about language having conditions appears there also.

[160] 'Divine way': *shintō*.

Brahmanism, administering the teaching of the people, would be just like what in Confucianism were called Confucian teachers under the ministry of education. 'The world of his own state' is the place controlled by the Kṣatriyas and hence a popular phrase for India. What does Myō Kyō mean now by 'outside'? Again it is lamentable that he ignorantly collects together these phrases.

Myō Kyō composed a compromise argument saying,

> The ten virtues and the five precepts are one and the same as the five constants: benevolence, righteousness <and so on>. The sages are different in respect of their teachings, but the same in respect of doing the good. All the teachings of the world amount to nothing other than the good. If the Buddha's Dharma were not the good, everybody would have to reject it. It is my wish that everybody should be for the public and not for arrogance. The teaching of the sages lies simply in the good. The way of these sages is nothing but righteousness. It is not essential to be a monk. It is not essential to be a Confucianist. Monks and Confucianists are secondary. The ancient sages who spoke of Buddhism, Taoism and Confucianism were one in mind while in form they were diverse. Their being one lies in their desire for men to perform the good. Their being diverse lies in their division into schools, each following its own teaching. It would not do if there were no Confucianism in the world, if there were no Lao Tzŭ, if there were no Buddha. If any one of these were lacking it would be a loss of one of the ways of goodness in the world. If one of the ways of goodness were lost, then the evil in the world would increase. I think that the three teachings help each other and make society good. This is also the natural way things are ordained. It is not something which people can grasp immediately.

His meaning seems to be that the three teachings are all ways of goodness, that if one were lacking, one good would be lost, and that this is the natural way things are ordained. Ah, what foolishness! If goodness is the main feature, why limit it to three teachings? Do not some tens of other ways, some tens of heretics, all seek the good? He says their mind is one while secondarily they are diverse, but does this not confuse people? This must be thought about. If Confucianism teaches the people the good, and the Buddha teaches the people the good, this teaching the people the good is a common principle. However it makes people exaggerate in magic and in letters.

This certainly needs thinking over!

Then again Shin Shū of the Sung said to Ō Tan,

> The purport of what the three teachings set up is the same. In general they all urge people to do good. However only scholars of advanced consciousness can see them as a single reality, and those who stagnate in one-sided attachments get further from the Way.

This too is a compromise and in short is not an adequate account. When Seki Mon E Kō held audience and gave a poem at Myō Kyō's stūpa, he said,

> I have compared my way to that of Confucius, and there is a difference of a palm and a fist opening and closing. In short they are like the hand.

He only said this believing Myō Kyō. He did not know that magic and letters in particular are as different as Ko and Etsu.

Myō Kyō also saw that the Confucianists Chō Sai and Ni Tei taught a return to man's former nature, and said of this,

> This comes from the *Fukuseisho* of Ri Kō of the T'ang Dynasty, and a return to man's former nature also appears in Yaku San's *Igen*. These Confucian teachings are at bottom no different from those of the Buddhists.

Having read this *Fukuseisho* myself, I find it says, 'If passions are not aroused man's nature is unified; given undeliberate non-conceptualising the passions do not arise, and this gives right thought.' This makes passions pertain to what is bad while the non-arising of passions is regarded as a return to man's original nature. This is the final teaching of Dhyāna. However what Chō and Tei meant was different. Chō's and Tei's meaning was that neither do the passions pertain to what is bad nor does one seek the non-arising of passions, and that a real return to man's nature entails the passions being good. This is what they called a return to man's original nature. Myō Kyō was mistaken when, dazzled by the similarities of this writing, he declared the teaching to be the same. In recent times Itō Jinsai[161] has also done this. Not only the Buddhists but also the Confucianists are led astray by letters.

Myō Kyō also said,

> When only Buddhism was flourishing, Kan Shi disapproved of the customs of the time not following the proper line and wrote a book to keep them in check. When he came to the basis of the way Kan also strongly supported it.

Hei Zan also said,

> Ryū, Chō Ro, and Shu are all wise men of recent times who think of birth-and-death as a dream or illusion, and of wealth and honour as dust and grime. They all teach sages, yet have not arrived themselves. When treating of the Buddha or Lao Tzŭ, they grant the reality but do not accept the literary form.[162] Yang repels them while Yin aids them.[163] Yet they have a quiet inward intention.

This really is a misleading way of dealing. Having learned Indian magic, they just take the Dharma like the *Lotus Sūtra* people. If it is left to those like Kan and Ryū it is no more than stealthy theft. How could one be a Confucianist? Kan's three writings presented to Dai Ten are in the collected works, but they are a Buddhist fabrication, as So Shoku has correctly argued. The real one is the one presented to Mō Kan. Myō Kyō also said,

> They vainly spell out the virtues of donation and recompense, getting themselves clothed and fed by the people. Knowing the teacher's gate they debate about virtue, but do they put it into motion?

He also said,

> In terms of the way, they pay recompense, and in terms of virtue they succeed to virtue; altough they do not marry they still support their mother and father; although they mar their

[161] Itō Jinsai (1625-1705) was clearly a person to reckon with as Tominaga hardly ever refers to people of his own time. Cf. above, pp. 13-18.

[162] They are in favour of the inner content but cannot bring themselves to say so.

[163] They teach obscurely, not clearly.

> appearance[164] they save their parents. Tai Haku's shape does not by any means diminish. Haku I and Shuku Sei certainly did not, by not getting married, live a long time.

These two sayings of Myō Kyō are very much to the point. It is not right for Confucianists to harass Buddhists <over such things>. I am not a follower of Confucianism, nor of Taoism, nor of Buddhism. I watch their words and deeds from the side and then privately debate them.

25. *Miscellaneous.*

The Preface to the *Lotus Sūtra* says,

> For the sake of all the bodhisattvas he expounded the Mahāyāna sūtras named *Muryōgi, Kyōbosatsuhō* and *Bussho-gonen*. When the Buddha finished expounding these sūtras he sat down in the lotus pose and entered the *samādhi* of innumerable meanings <*muryōgi*> with body and mind unmoved.

This passage makes him out as having already expounded. But then below it says, 'Today the Tathāgata must expound the Mahāyāna sūtra', and this passage makes him out as having not yet expounded. In one volume the beginning and end are inconsistent, so that it does not amount to a literary work. Moreover from start to finish the parts of the *Lotus Sūtra* are just words of praise to the Buddha, and do not have the real nature of a sūtra teaching. It should never have been called a sūtra from the beginning. In the *Hokkedenki* it says, 'The *Lotus Sūtra* is handed down in four versions, all with expansions and contractions. Where is the limit of the sūtras coming from the west?' It is possible that in India there was a further complete work and that what is now handed on is only the parts which remain. This is why Tendai Daishi said in explanation of this,

> The meshes of the net of the Dharma gate are the dharmas as viewed in the great and small <vehicles>, various in their measure. These are not all debated over <in the sūtra> because this teaching was given before the *Lotus Sūtra*. Therefore when we come to the *Lotus Sūtra* it does no more than reveal and

[164] By shaving their heads, as monks.

awaken the Buddha-knowledge and give predictions of future Buddhahood.

It must be said that he had read the *Lotus Sūtra* well, but he still missed the reality. Consider. According to the *Hokke-mongu, Muryōgi* is one name for the *Lotus Sūtra*. However it is a mistake to identify the *Muryōgi Sūtra* with it. What is the evidence for this? The *Muryōgi Sūtra* was written after the *Kegon Sūtra* by followers of the Lotus party, which is why their argument runs,

> First he preached the four truths for the sake of those who wished to be śrāvakas, at various places in the middle he expounded the twelve causal relations for those who sought to be pratyekabuddhas, and then next he preached the extended sūtras in twelve divisions, the *Great Prajñā*, the Kegonkaikū, the Hokkeenyūbutsue and the bodhisattvas' Rekikōshugyō.

The reality is that the Lotus party made <their sūtra> over and above the *Kegon Sūtra* as this passage shows.[165] It is not true that the present texts which lack the six characters: 'Hokkeenyū<butsue>',[166] have been abbreviated by later people and that the preface of the Lotus is to be believed.

The *Vinaya* teaches,

> The world-honoured one taught the four holy truths for the benefit of the four heavenly kings. First he preached in the sacred language <Sanskrit>, then he preached in the dialects of south India, and then he preached in the low class languages.

This shows that the Buddha was able to speak the language of various countries and that people of different hearing could all profit from it. Again in a verse of the *Vimalakīrti Sūtra* it says similarly, 'The Buddha expounded the Dharma with one sound, and living beings each understood it according to their kind', and 'Thus he gave out a true, rounded sound, so that with one exposition there were various understandings.' This merely says that the Buddha's sermon in reality came from one

[165] In this case it is Ishida who imports the term *kajō* where only *jō* stands in the text (Ishida, p. 160). The evidence lies in the sequence of the terms, Hokkeenyūbutsue coming after Kegonkaikū.

[166] Tominaga actually gives only the first four characters as all six have appeared immediately above.

mouth, while living beings in accordance with their opportunity all derived profit. The first statement emphasises the differences of expression, while the second emphasises that the sound of his voice was not diverse. Each of these statements has part of the truth, but as the *Vibhāṣā Treatise* indeed explained, it is a mistake when later scholars assign them to Mahāyāna and Hīnayāna.

Viewing things as impure is an Indian custom to which people over here will not consent. If the Buddha-mind is immaculate and thus-coming, how can it have impurities? What the *Vibhāṣā Treatise* and the *Junshōri Treatise* say about this is mistaken.

Tendai scholars suffer from the difficulty that the *Nirvāṇa Sūtra* says 'the *Prajñā Sūtra* led on to the *Nirvāṇa Sūtra*' but does not say that it led on to the *Lotus Sūtra*;[167] and that it cannot be considered that all beings attain Buddhahood in the *Lotus* period.[168] For this reason they advance 'the five flavours of the former and latter times'[169] and say that the *Nirvāṇa Sūtra*[170] was preached after the *Lotus Sūtra*. But these are all compromise teachings.

The whole of the *Lotus Sūtra* is just words of praise. It has no content of teaching, either for the *śrāvakas*, or for the *pratyekabuddhas*. All the buddhas <in the sūtra> put together give none. It also has nothing which can be assigned to the 'common', 'pervasive' or 'special' types of teaching.[171] Other sūtras have a discernible content of teaching,[172] which is

167 It will be recalled that the Tendai doctrine posits a five-stage sequence in the proclamation of sūtras. The difficulty is therefore that the *Lotus Sūtra* was considered to be the highest revelation but could not be said to have been delivered last.

168 The *Nirvāṇa Sūtra* still refers to beings who are not yet enlightened, even though, according to the theory, it appeared after the final and comprehensible teaching of universal salvation in the *Lotus Sūtra*.

169 I.e. an attempt to explain how features of doctrine overlap the various presumed stages.

170 As Kyōdo points out (p. 141) this must refer to the *Nirvāṇa Sūtra* and not to the *Prajñā Sūtra*, which stands in the received text and was repeated by Mizuta. The textual error may have arisen because of the ambiguity of *Great Sutra* (*Daikyō*).

171 The collected teaching, the pervasive or common teaching and the special teaching: *zō, tsū, betsu*. These are completed by the perfect teaching (*en*). Cf. Petzold 1979, pp. 15ff.

172 'Content of teaching': a free translation for *kyōsetsu*, appropriate for the present context.

why they could be made to belong to the 'common', 'pervasive' or 'special' type. This is the misfortune of the other sūtras![173] As it says in the *Konbei Treatise*, the Kegon teaching of Fugen, of universality <of Kannon> and of the three non-differentiations, the Mahāsāṁghika teaching of the interpenetration of defilement and purity and the Vimalakīrti teaching of all things being contained in one pore are all rounded and exquisite, so how should they be included in the common, pervasive or special? However the reason they are assigned to these is that they have a content of teaching which is said not to extend beyond the Hīnayāna. The *Lotus Sūtra* does not amount to a text, being just a hymn of praise after the teaching, and this is the good fortune of the Lotus Party. In the commentary on the Hōshi Chapter it says, 'There is no *Lotus* apart from the *Prajñā*. *Lotus* is another name for *Prajñā*.' This is a discerning view, but not quite right. The *Prajñā Sūtra* speaks of voidness and the *Lotus Sūtra* speaks of non-voidness, and so how can these be the same?

When the *Great Prajñā Sūtra* calls Sanskrit letters *raji* and the *Kegon Sūtra* makes them *taji*, these are what different schools call them, and the argument that they are translators' mistakes is wrong.

The Shinge Chapter of the *Lotus Sūtra* speaks of the conversion by enticement of a destitute son as an allegory of the impossibility of first teaching the Mahāyāna to the foolish masses. This is just a way of emphasising the *Lotus Sūtra* and suppressing others. It is not an analogy of the five periods. Tendai scholars identify the destitute son's surprise with that of the deaf-mute in the *Kegon Sūtra*. However there is nothing <in the latter> which fits the initial father and son relation and then the losing and the finding. What is the point of this? Allegories should always be followed serenely in terms of their main tenor. There is no need to come up with a make-shift one-to-one identification.[174] Moreover, if all the previous preachings of Dharma were skilful means then the storehouse of precious jewels given to the previously mentioned destitute son might also be thought to be nothing but a counterfeit! Thus we see that this way of interpreting it is a mistake. Again,

[173] I.e. because they have a recognisable content they can be assigned to stages belong the way.

[174] That is, in order to make it fit with a later doctrinal system.

referring to the twenty years is just intended to spell out the very great length of time for which they <the father and son> were separated and there is nothing <in doctrine> which corresponds to it. It is ridiculous when later expositors none the less drag things in to fit from elsewhere.

The Shutsugen Chapter of the *Kegon Sūtra* says, 'None <following> the two vehicles[175] have heard this sūtra, so how can they receive and protect it?' And in the Hokkai Chapter it says, 'Śāriputra gave no happy speech and could give no praise', and also, 'like a deaf person or like a dumb person'. These are all sayings which emphasise the teaching of their own school. They do not prepare the ground for the later downgrading of the *Āgamas*.[176] When later generations link them with this they are mistaken.

In the Hōben Chapter of the *Lotus Sūtra* it says, 'There is only one vehicle of Dharma, there are not two, and not three.' This is a provisional use of two and three to emphasise the one, and otherwise they do not refer to anything in particular. The Tendai scholars' interpretation of these in terms of the 'common' and 'pervasive', and so on, is mistaken.

The *Lotus Sūtra* says, 'Only for bodhisattvas, not for the Small Vehicle', 'only teaching other bodhisattvas in the one-vehicle way; there are no disciples of the Hearers', 'for the sake of all these sons of the Buddha I expounded this Great Vehicle sūtra', 'there is no doubt that *śrāvakas* or bodhisattvas will all become buddhas', and 'What you are practising is the bodhisattva way, and if you continue to practise it you will all become buddhas.' According to this what he had been preaching for these forty years or more was nothing but provisional, preparatory Dharma and was not the true and real way for the attainment of buddhahood. Only the Dharma preached today, that is, this Dharma originally taught to the bodhisattvas, was not made available for the <other> two vehicles. Nevertheless the two vehicles also, if they hear it and practise it and then progress to become bodhisattvas, will equally find refuge in the attainment of buddhahood. This idea derives from the kind-

175 I.e. no *śrāvakas* or *pratyekabuddhas*.

176 I.e. the point of such expressions was not, originally, to demonstrate the phased classification of sūtras, according to which the *Āgamas* came after the initial, uncomprehended Kegon teaching.

ness of the author <of the sūtra>. Hence the Tendai scholars say,

> All the *śrāvaka* disciples are reproved by the expanded sūtras, washed and sifted by the *Prajñā Sūtra*, and, made zealous by this karmic occasion, they attain buddhahood with the *Lotus Sūtra*.

Thus there are things in the above lines which do not fit. It is therefore mistaken to interpret things to fit by making up 'the flavours of entering enlightenment', 'the dull-witted attaining the fifth flavour', and so on.

In the Hiyu Chapter of the *Lotus Sūtra* it says, 'I followed a Buddha of ancient times, heard a Dharma like this, and saw how all the bodhisattvas received their predictions and became buddhas.'[177] In the Chōju Chapter of the *Nirvāna Sūtra* it says,

> When I first attained right awakening there were many bodhisattvas who enquired about its meaning. [Also:] When I was first on Vulture Peak, with Maitreya, propounding the world-related teaching, Śāriputra and five hundred hearers did not understand, so how much the less the supreme principle of leaving the world.

In the *Great Treatise* it says, 'From the night of Enlightenment to the night of the Nirvāṇa I have always preached *prajñā*.' These are all statements which are awkward for those setting out periods <of teaching>. The *Nirvāṇa Sūtra* expositor says,

> There is no spiritual mountain of the Kegon's 'seven places and eight meetings' and therefore the sūtra <expounded there> has not yet been transmitted.

This too is based on belief in periods <of teaching>. Other cases like this are the view that the T'ang translation of the *Shuryōgon Sūtra* was not expounded in one phase, but was assembled in sections according to type, that the *Daii Sūtra* does not belong anywhere, and that the *Zuiō Sūtra* is indeterminate as between Mahāyāna and Hīnayāna. In the

[177] The original text starts a new paragraph here, after the quotation from the *Lotus Sūtra*, but the quotation by itself means nothing in Tominaga's argument and hence, as in other editions, no break is made.

Hōdōdarani Sūtra is found the prediction <of Buddhahood> for *śrāvakas* at Śrāvastī, and therefore the Tendai scholars regard the expanded sūtras as having appeared afterwards. Again, because the *Nirvāṇa Sūtra* refers to the 'lotus storehouse world sea', they regard the *Kegon Sūtra* as coming after the *Nirvāṇa Sūtra* and because Kālodāyin received his prediction <of buddhahood> in the *Lotus Sūtra* and attained extinction in the *Nirvāṇa Sūtra* they regard the 'whey' teaching as coming afterwards. These statements are all struggling with difficulties for the above reason. In the *Vimalakīrti Sūtra* again it says, 'In this Mahāyāna there are texts of the vanquished kind', but this too does not fit. The scholars say, 'There are no fixed periods of teaching in the expanded sūtras', and thus we see that the human mind cannot always be cheated.

The layman Vimalakīrti was the pioneer of the *upāsakas*. He acquired the way excellently and set up his own school. Through not renouncing, yet teaching the same meaning as the renouncers, he became the mentor in his school. Saying that he came from the Myō-ki <world> as in the *Vimalakīrti Sūtra* or that he was formerly Konzoku Nyorai (as in the *Shiyuizanmai Sūtra* and the *Hotsujaku Sūtra*) are all points made by those who later made this way their main concern. The *Great Treatise* also says, 'Vimalakīrti and Kanzeon are regarded as the leading bodhisattvas.' Presumably they were the pioneer bodhisattvas. Consider also that it says in the *Vimalakīrti Sūtra*, 'Three times was the wheel of Dharma turned in the great thousand.' <Thus> this sūtra must have been written after the *Jinmitsu Sūtra*.

Shi Shi Gai <i.e. Harivarman> composed the *Jōjitsu Treatise*. Originally he belonged to the Caityavādins, but then he changed his track to the Mahāsāṁghikas. He made a comparative study of the Mahāyāna and the Hīnayāna, selected their good points and recorded them. This also establishes a position for one school. The Tendai scholars miss the point when they write him off as Hīnayāna because he has sayings from <various parts of> the Tripiṭaka.

The *Laṅkāvatāra Sūtra* speaks of sudden and gradual. En of Zui set up two teachings on the basis of this. However his argument that this was originally based on stages of attainment misses the point.

Gen Ju assigned the *Lotus Sūtra* to the last stage of teaching. It should be observed that in his *Gokyōshō* there are two places where he quotes the *Lotus Sūtra* to show that it belongs to the last stage. Because of this Shō Ryō, taking it up, said, 'The *Lotus Sūtra* is the sudden of the gradual', which was in fact Gen Ju's meaning. In recent times Master Hō Tan argued against Shō Ryō with a view to harmonising the *Lotus Sūtra* and the *Kegon Sūtra*, but this missed the point.

The Tendai <school> say, in disparagement of the Kegon <school>, 'They teach neither that *śrāvakas* attain buddhahood nor the length of eternally attained buddhahood.'[178] The Kegon <school> say, in disparagement of the Lotus <school>, 'The *Kegon Sūtra* is the sudden of the sudden while the *Lotus Sūtra* is the sudden of the gradual.[179] In the *Kegon Sūtra* there is the request to bodhisattvas[180] which is not found in other sūtras.' The Tendai <school> say in answer, 'The *Lotus Sūtra* also has the request to the bodhisattvas.' The Kegon <school> say in answer, 'In the Seshumyōgon Chapter it says that an inconceivable kalpa has past since the Buddha attained the way.' In short, when they all quarrel over these illusory arguments, what has it to do with the way?

When Mei Chō Raku of the Han performed his comparative test by fire, the fact that only the Taoist sūtras burned was a victory of magic. What has this to do with the way? Similarly, what the *Retsu Shi* calls an apparition is a magical person, and does not indicate the Buddha. It is ridiculous that monks go on talking about this.

Supernormal powers are a little different from magic, but they end up as magic. In the *Fuhōzō Sūtra* it says,

> Saṁghayaśas emitted light from his five fingers, but Aśvaghoṣa suspected it was magic. Usually the law of magic is that when

[178] Literally 'the length of life of the long-lasting attainment <of Buddhahood>, the main teaching of Chapter XVI (Chinese numeration) of the *Lotus Sūtra*.

[179] Since a gradual approach to Buddhahood had come to be seen as inferior to a sudden attainment of enlightenment (i.e. Buddhahood), 'sudden' came to be used as a designation for the quintessential teaching. Thus 'the sudden of the gradual' is good but the 'sudden of the sudden' is one better, indeed hard to answer. Cf. p. 78, note 27.

[180] This mysterious phrase is probably related to Brahman's request to the Buddha to preach.

> you recognise it as such it disappears. However this light glowed more and more brightly.[181]

It may be that Buddhism thereby seeks the way <through supernormal power> while the heterodoxies seek profit, but they are the same in that they delude people. This is like the case of letters in China where a distinction is made between ethics and ornamental style. The *Vimalakīrti Sūtra* speaks of 'taking sport in supernormal powers'. The Indians taking sport in supernatural powers is like the Chinese taking sport in the performing arts.

In the Musa Chapter of the *Prajñā Sūtra* it says,

> All the devas say, 'We have seen the second turning of the wheel of Dharma in the land of mankind'. Countless hundreds of thousands of devas attained non-regression.

The *Great Treatise*, in explanation of this, says,

> Question: The first proclamation of Dharma led people to attain the way, and this is called turning the wheel of Dharma, so why is there now talk of a second turning of the wheel of Dharma? If it is called turning the wheel of Dharma whenever the Buddha preaches, they are all wheels of Dharma, so why limit it to two? Answer? The first proclamation of Dharma is called the reality-determining first wheel of Dharma. After the first turning right up to the exhaustion of Dharma it is <also> called the turning. The devas saw that there were numerous people in the assembly who drew benefit from it, and therefore in praise they spoke of it as the second turning of the wheel of Dharma. At the first turning of the wheel of Dharma eight ten-thousands of devas attained non-regression from Dharma and one person, Anyakyōjinnyo, attained the Way. Now countless devas have attained non-regression from Dharma and for this reason it is referred to as the second wheel of Dharma. The present turning of the wheel of Dharma is similar to the first turning.

Now, consider. The questioner's point is that the Buddha's preachings are all one, with no distinction between end and beginning, so why should there now be a limit of two? The point of the answer is that there never was any difference in the

[181] I.e. thus proving that it was no mere illusionist magic but genuine supernormal powers with a greater power to convince people.

Buddha's teaching between now and the beginning; it was just that on the second occasion the benefit was particularly great and hence there was merely an outbreak of praise; there was no difference in the proclamation. This was the original purport of the treatise. However when later generations set up their periods they quoted this to testify that the first turning of the wheel was in the deer park and that the Prajñā <phase of teaching> was the second, thereby completely missing the basic point. When it is related to the five periods and the Kegon <teaching> is said to be the first turning, this too misses the point completely.

When all the bodhisattvas receive the Buddha's prediction <of their Buddhahood> this is called in the Mahāyāna *juki* <i.e. receiving prediction> and in the Hīnayāna it is called the proximate cause and the proximate result. Prediction is also magic, and the Mahāyāna goes beyond <the Hīnayāna> in it.[182]

Santa is an abbreviation for *samāhita*. Various explanations of this by people of old are all mistaken.[183]

In the *Gobunritsu* it says, 'In the sea there are eight wonders.' There are also wonders in the teaching in twelve divisions. They are what we would now call marvels. In the sixty-fourth book of the *Butsuhongyō Sūtra* there is the book of *adbhuta* <marvels>. What in the Zui <period> were called wonders we would now call tall stories.

In counting breaths up to ten the Indian principle is to count breathing out and breathing in together and the Chinese principle is to count them separately.

In the Myōji Chapter of the *Nirvāṇa Sūtra* the ten abodes come after the ten faiths, and the Shakugi Chapter is the same. In the Kyōge Chapter of the *Ninnō Sūtra* the third stage is the stage of cutting off views and in the Juji Chapter the fourth stage is the stage of cutting off views. In the *Great Treatise* there are eight thousand cases of 'non-regressions' but then again they call it 'pure as to the eye of Dharma'. If in one sūtra

[182] Or 'excels in it', but Tominaga's point is that this is one of the ways in which the Great Vehicle sought to outdo existing forms of Buddhism.

[183] It is a question here of different kinds of meditation which people attempted to squeeze out of the diverse terminology. Tominaga's point is that since the one is an abbreviated form of another these attempts fall flat.

or treatise there are so many contradictions, how many more there are between schools!

Originally there were three Buddhas. In the *Kegon Sūtra* there are ten Buddhas. Originally there were six powers. In the *Kegon Sūtra* there are ten powers. Originally there were three knowledges, eight deliverances, four kinds of eloquence and six states of existence. The *Kegon Sūtra* put the number up to ten for all of them, which must be said to be strange. It is similar with the *Kinshichijū Treatise* which sets up twenty-five truths, a clear advance on the Buddha's four truths. They may be numerous but what are they based on?

The *Great Nirvāṇa Sūtra* says, '*Hanne* means non and *han* means birth, so the principle of non-birth is called great *nehan* <nirvāṇa>.' Its basic meaning is that what was originally called death is also called attaining the way. Similarly Soshi calls rising up to heaven attaining the way. It is in reality similar. Not being born is to have a pure and peaceful mind. There is not one speck of grime to be reborn. It is like the non-birth of the *arhat* which has the same meaning. However the expositors of the time explained it in terms of birth-and-death and therefore there are various terms such as residue, non-residue, and five insights, but the reality is that these were not part of the original truth. It is the same with the six kinds of insight. The *Great Prajñā Sūtra* and the *Vibhāṣā Treatise* add to the five kinds an 'appearance-insight' while the *Kusha Treatise* adds a 'formless insight'. Again there is no one fixed doctrine. However, as there is variation with regard to the rebirth of bodhisattvas there are also teachings such as rebirth for promising to aid and train, and rebirth for a vow. The reality is that these do not fit it in.[184]

In the *Misshakurikishi Sūtra* of the *Daihōshaku Sūtra* it says,

[184] Tominaga seems to be arguing that teachings on the re-birth of bodhisattvas for compassionate purposes do not fit in with the original ideas of nirvāṇa. There may indeed be Mahāyāna answers to such an objection, generally stated, but Tominaga's point is that developed ideas of this kind are certainly not the same as the historically earlier teaching on nirvāṇa.

On the seventh day after first attaining the way, he turned the wheel of Dharma in the deer park and gave extensive benefit to throngs in the three vehicles.[185]

In the *Mishasokuritsu* and the *Fuyō Sūtra* it says, 'On the twenty-seventh day he preached for Trapuṣa.' In the *Sarvāstivāda Vinaya*, *Vibhāṣā Treatise* and *Shutsuyō Sūtra* it says, 'On the seventy-seventh day he brought across five people.' In the *Inga Sūtra* it says, 'On the thirty-seventh day he brought across five people.' The *Lotus Sūtra* is the same. In the *Sarvāstivāda Treatise* it says, 'On the sixty-seventh day he brought across five people.' The *Shibunritsu* is the same as this. The *Great Treatise* says the fifty-seventh day and in the *Jūniyu Sūtra* it says two years. These are all designations made by different schools, so why should they necessarily be made consistent? In the *Fuyō Sūtra*, the *Kōsan Sūtra* and the *Fugenbosatsushōmyōkudoku Sūtra* it says he left home at nineteen and attained the way at thirty. In the *Hōzō Sūtra* he left home at twenty-five and attained the way at thirty. In the *Jūniyu Sūtra* and the *Saiikiki* he left home at twenty-nine and attained the way at thirty-five. In the *Bonmō Sūtra* he left home at seven years old, and in the *Kūgyōzanmai Sūtra* he attained the way at twenty-seven. Nobody can resist these differences, so again why should they necessarily be made consistent?

Similar are the teachings about the Buddha's birth, said by some to be in February, by some in March and by some in April. This arises from the difference of New Year's Day in the three dynasties. Now it cannot be investigated <any more>. Similar are the teachings about the Buddha's nirvāṇa, which some say was in March and others say was in September, and again some say was on the fifteenth and others say was on the eighth. Thus various teachings exist. Note that in the *Shibunritsu* it says, 'Hair should be shaven once every half month, but allowing the extreme length of two fingers' thickness it may be cut once every two months.' Two months

[185] That is, to large numbers of *śrāvakas, pratyekabuddhas* and bodhisattvas.

means fifteen days each of white days and black days,[186] making a two-month period of thirty days in all. This is the Indian custom of regarding fifteen days as one month and thirty days as two months so that a twelve-month year is regarded as twenty-four months. If we think on these lines the fifteenth is the middle of a thirty-day month and the eighth is the middle of a fifteen-day month. This is where talk of the fifteenth or the eighth comes from. Those who say the eighth are right. Again, if we think about it in this way and regard six months as one year, then the seventh month will be the January of the second year, while its March will be the ninth month of the twelve month year. This is where talk of March or of September comes from. However this has not yet been clarified in detail. Again if we think about it in this way it is the same with the teachings about Śākyamuni's ascetic practice being six years or being twelve years, or again the *Memyōden* saying that Me Myō <Aśvaghoṣa> lived three hundred years after the Buddha while the *Maya Sūtra* says it was six hundred years, or the *Ryūjuden* saying that Ryū Ju <Nāgārjuna> lived seven hundred years after, as compared with saying it was three hundred years after. It is evident that the later traditions had these differences only because of the Indians regarding six months as a year and one year as two years. As to the rest, there is an inexhaustible complexity of teachings about the divisions of time which are ultimately all very obscure. In general this kind of thing is not worth debating and it is not essential to search it all out.

In the *Fukuden Sūtra* of the *Chū-agon* the classification of those who study and those who have finished is differentiated by ranks such as the lower aspirants, attainers and so on. The *Vibhāṣā Treatise*, the *Kusha Treatise* and so on all mix this up. Thus it is not surprising that there are different statements by the various schools. However it is just the same with the Hīnayāna and their statements. Many scholars have got this far and suffered perplexity.'

As an old monk of eighty years he was finished with birth and finished with life. This is the truth of it. They say his diamond body was free of disease (*Great Treatise*). Or they say

186 The white days are the days of the moon's waxing and the black days are the days of its waning.

that the *Tathāgata* by skilful means displayed nirvāṇa (*Nirvāṇa Sūtra*). Or again, they say that for this aeon he is always present on Vulture Peak (*Lotus Sūtra*). Or again, they say that the Buddha's life lasts for seven hundred aeons (*Ryōgon Sūtra*). Or again, they say that Śākyamuni is in the peaceful palace of heaven from beginning to end. These teachings are all nothing but the magicising variations of different groups.

In the Zokurui Chapter of the *Lotus Sūtra* it speaks of 'the remaining deep Dharma of the Tathāgata'. The Tendai <school> interpret this in terms of six skilful means. Gen Ju interprets it in terms of the Kegon 'special teaching'. Here each just fits it to his own teaching, but really it is wrong. The authors are setting themselves on a pedestal, but such vague talk refers to nothing. Similarly when the *Great Treatise* speaks of things like 'the first gate of entering the Buddha-Dharma', these are just ways of making oneself lofty or deep. It is also mistaken when the maṇḍala school quote it and accommodate it to their 'bright way of the first Dharma'.

The *Jōbonnōnaion Sūtra* says, 'When the Buddha was about to bear <his father's> coffin himself, the earth quaked.' In the *Fuyō Sūtra* it says, 'The Buddha's body rose up into the air and thus he avoided having reverence paid to him by his father, the king.' In the *Zōichi-agon* it says, 'When his foster mother Daiaidō <Mahāpajāpatī> died, the Buddha himself carried one leg of the bier and Ānanda carried one leg.' In the *Urabon Sūtra* it says,

> When the disciples of the Buddha train in filial piety, they should constantly remember their fathers and mothers in steady thought up to the fathers and mothers of seven generations.

In the *Mishasokuritsu* it says, 'If parents do not approve, leaving the household <life> is not permitted.' Or again it says, 'Reduce the amount of clothing and food and nourish one's parents.' Or else they say, 'Even if there is no Buddha in the world one should serve one's parents well. To serve one's parents well is to serve the Buddha' (*Daijū Sūtra*). Or else they say,

> On one's left shoulder bear one's father and on one's right shoulder bear one's mother; broadly walking the great earth is no recompense for obligation. (*Bumoonjū Sūtra*)

Thus Śākyamuni's teaching certainly takes filial piety seriously. However there really were mad inversions in later times such as the affair of the Ōbaku monk Dai Gi To.[187] It was for such fellows that hell was invented. In general, in the Buddha-Dharma of China there is much estrangement of parents. This originally arose out of frustrating the Confucianists and in India it is not evident at all. (The affair of the Ōbaku monk Dai Gi To comes in the *Shōjūsan*.)

In the *Shibunritsu* it says, 'The Buddha caused the monks to pay reverence in accordance with age, but not to pay reverence to the normal white garment.' The *Nirvāṇa Sūtra* says, 'The monks do not pay reverence to layfolk.' This refers to layfolk in a vague way. So to with 'the usual white garment'. The *Bonmō Sūtra* says on this, 'The rule of the monks does not allow of paying worship to kings, parents or the six kinds of relative. They do not pay reverence to departed spirits.'[188] This is very severe, and extending it to not paying reverence to parents is extreme. However, in the *Bonmō Sūtra* it also says, 'Accord filial piety to parents, to teacher monks and to the three jewels.' We see from this that although the *Bonmō Sūtra* is severe it does not dispense with filial piety towards parents.

In Amida's Buddha-land all the people have bodies of light. They are always bright and never grow dark. As they do not depend on the brightness of sun and moon, how shall they distinguish noon and night-time? However the sūtra text itself refers to day and night, the six hours, clear dawn, and so on. These are the author's muddles.[189] All the birds in the buddha-land would dislike being born <as birds> in respect of recompense for wrong-doing and therefore it is later explained that 'these are apparitions produced by the Buddha'.[190] This shows the author's careful attention <to detail>.[191]

The Dharma-master Dō Shō saw that in Fa Hsien's translation of the *Nirvāṇa Sūtra* it said, 'Apart from the

187 He took no notice of his mother's dying of starvation.

188 Literally 'demons and gods'; *kijin*.

189 Literally 'ruptures and leaks'.

190 I.e. if they were real birds they would suffer unhappiness at having been reborn in a lowly state and this would spoil the mood in the Pure Land. Hence imitation birds are produced. (Perhaps this is the explanation for the large number of plastic flowers in Japan.)

191 Although Tominaga does not otherwise have much to say on Amida Buddhism, he is rather rude about it here.

icchantikas everybody has the buddha-nature.' He said, *icchantikas* are included in the class of living beings, so why do they alone not have the buddha-nature'? When it came to the *Great Nirvāṇa Sūtra* it said in the Shōgyō Chapter 'The *icchantikas* as men, although they act against the good, nevertheless have the buddha-nature.' With regard to this all the masters had to give in with shame. It seems to me that the *icchantikas* were regarded as *icchantikas* because they did not originally have the buddha-nature. However should not even an extremely bad man be able to convert his mind? Converting the mind depends on oneself. It does not depend on others. This is where the seed of buddha-nature really lies. Why should we say he has no buddha-nature? As to the type of language here, it is a transformation. Again, to inanimates is assigned the Dharma-nature and to animates is assigned the buddha-nature. (The *Great Treatise* no longer contains this saying.) This is the basis of 'buddha-nature without exception', apart from plants and trees. The ideas of 'no world outside the mind' and 'no discrimination between refinement and rubbish' makes the Buddha equal to the Dharma and expands the meaning. As to the type of language here, it is an expansion.

Teachings may be diverse, but their main point comes back to doing the good.[192] If these teachings are sincerely and well kept and each is fervent in doing the good, what need is there to select and criticise? Buddhism is all right. Confucianism is all right. If they are sincerely endeavouring to do the good, then they are one school. How much more so with those who make their own the same religion of the Buddha while differentiating it into sects. I know none who, though vainly quarreling over whether the sects have differences, are not doing the good. Letters are all right. Magic is all right. If the intention sincerely lies in doing the good, then why should they not be all right? I know none who, though vainly indulging in magic or in letters, is not concerned with doing the good.

End of second <scroll> of *Emerging from Meditation*.

[192] This is not printed as a separate paragraph in the original text but here Mizuta and Ishida are followed in regarding it as such. It may be regarded as Tominaga's general conclusion, which is consistent with the tenor of *Writings of an Old Man*. After the mass of critical detail the positive note which is sounded here should not go unregarded.

Note on editions used

The editions of *Emerging from Meditation* (*Shutsujōkōgo*) have been authoritatively surveyed by Umetani Fumio (Mizuta and Arisaka 1973, 685-91). Exemplars remain from four main printings and there are also some sub-editions. The manuscript used for the cutting of the blocks for the first printing (the block copy or *hanshita*) is presumed to have been written by Tominaga himself. The first printing was done in 1745, and exemplars are preserved in the following libraries:

National Diet Library (Kokuritsu Kokkai Toshokan). N.B. The *Shutsujōkōgo* is held in the Kameda Collection.

Ōsaka Foreign Language University Library (Gaikokugo Daigaku Fuzoku Toshokan). N.B. The *Shutsujōkōgo* is held in the Ishihama Collection.

Ryūkoku University Library (Ryūkoku Daigaku Toshokan).

Exemplars of later printings, which display minor variations, are preserved in various university and municipal libraries around Japan.

The first complete modern edition based on the earliest printing was that of Yoshikawa Entarō in 1944. A more recent edition was prepared by several hands and edited by Kyōdo Jikō in the series *Gendai bukkyō meicho zenshū* (No. 1) (Nakamura, Masutani and Kitagawa 1971). The volume is subtitled *Bukkyō no shomondai*. Another modern edition prepared by Mizuta Norihisa appeared shortly afterwards in the series *Nihon shisō taikei* (No. 43) (Mizuta and Arisaka 1973). Both of these editions print the original text of 1745 preserved in blocks held at the National Diet Library in Tōkyō. Kyōdo's volume also contains a modern translation and annotations. Mizuta's edition contains a Japanese reordering (*Kakikudashibun*) of Tominaga's *kanbun* (Chinese) text. A modern Japanese translation was also prepared by Ishida Mizumaro for the series *Nihon no meicho* (No. 18) (Kato 1972). This was prepared before the appearance of Kyōdo's version, although it was published shortly afterwards.

Each of the above modern editions was extremely helpful in various ways. At the same time it should be noted that the modern 'translations', unlike the syntactical reordering mentioned above, frequently include explanatory phrasing which bears no direct relation to the original text, which is relatively concise and sometimes quite pithy. The English version presented here is based on the latter.

*

Writings of an Old Man (*Okina no fumi*) was first published in 1746 and exemplars of this printing are held in two libraries, namely:

National Diet Library (Kokuritsu Kokkai Toshokan), in the Kameda Collection.

Ōsaka Furitsu Toshokan (Ōsaka Municipal Library).

The work was lost from sight for many years until an exemplar was rediscovered by a bookshop proprietor 'in an old temple' in Kyōto some time in the Taishō Period (1912-1926). This was acquired by Kamedo Jirō and is now located in the Kameda Collection mentioned above. At the time of discovery it was believed to be the only exemplar still in existence, but in 1930 another came to light at an Ōsaka market. The source for this and the statement immediately above is a contemporary newspaper cutting, dated 26 June 1930, preserved on the inside flap of the Ōsaka exemplar. On 4 March 1935 this exemplar came into the possession of the Ōsaka Municipal Library. Meanwhile a facsimile edition had been published (1924) with a four-page postscript by Naitō Konan.

Modern annotated editions of *Writings of an Old Man* were published in two well-known series on Japanese thought, in 1966 and 1971 respectively. The first was volume 97 in the series *Nihon koten bungaku taikei* (Ienaga *et al.* 1966). The title of the specific volume was *Kinsei shisōka bunshū* and the editor for *Writings of an Old Man* was Ishihama Juntarō. This may be regarded as the standard modern edition and it was used as the main working edition during the preparation of the English version presented here. To Ishihama's name were added in the contents page those of Mizuta Norihisa and Ōniwa Osamu. The same Mizuta Norihisa was responsible for *Writings of an Old Man* in volume 18 of the other series. *Nihon no shisō*, the general editor being Nakamura Yukihiko (Nakamura 1971). This latter edition is provided with a modern sentence-by-sentence paraphrase. Eight months later, in 1972, there appeared another annotated modern version in volume 18 of the series *Nihon no meicho*, under the general editorship of Katō Shūichi (Katō 1972). The editor responsible for *Writings of an Old Man* was Narabayashi Tadao.

As this is the same volume as that which carries Ishida Mizumaro's modern version of *Emerging from Meditation* it is one of the few publications to contain both of Tominaga's main writings. At the same time the original text is not included. As in the case of *Emerging from Meditation* the modern paraphrases all contain many glosses and should be regarded as popularisations for the modern reader rather than as translations in an exact sense. Nevertheless they were extremely helpful. Katō Shūichi's English version (Katō 1967) was likewise extremely useful in the early stages. The reader interested in such details may compare for himself the points at which it seemed necessary or desirable to translate differently. Katō has been followed in adding the word 'Comment' as necessary, which does not appear in the original text, and in omitting the words 'To the right is chapter I' (etc.) Katō's translation did not include the three prefaces.

As originally published *Writings of an Old Man* contained thirty-one double pages of text including Tominaga's own preface, while the other prefaces take up six double pages of text and were numbered separately. The title, *Okina no fumi*, preceded Tominaga's own preface which was not actually designated as such. On the other hand this introductory paragraph of his was signed and dated. On balance it should be regarded as an integral part of the work, unlike the other prefaces written by the author's friends. The paragraphing within the text, and the distinction between 'text' and 'comment', were expressed very clearly in the format of the original pages and have therefore been followed carefully in the translation given here. What might be described as a pirate edition was published in 1779 under the title *Okinamichi no shiori* (i.e. 'Guide to the Old Man's Way'), as mentioned earlier in the discussion of Tominaga's early reception and influence. The only extant exemplar is in the Ōsaka Municipal Library (Ōsaka Furitsu Toshokan). The newly devised title is written in five Chinese characters, avoiding the phonetic *hiragana*. As traditional Japanese publications are usually concluded with the words 'End (of) ...' the new title is found at the end of the work also. On the page folds typical of older Japanese books the running title (*Okina no fumi*) is reduced to *Okina* (i.e. 'Old Man'). In the prefaces, including Tominaga's own preface, the new title is incorporated at the beginning and the date at the end is omitted in each case. The second preface, in *kanbun*, is omitted entirely. The omission was concealed by leaving out the page numbers for the prefaces as well and replacing them with the running *jo* (i.e. 'Preface') on the folds. As in the original edition Tominaga's own preface is numbered as page one of the main text. The main text is entirely unchanged.

Conventions

Japanese names are given in their Japanese order, surname first.

Both texts translated here are peppered with proper names which may be read either in a Japanese way or in a Chinese way. Tominaga himself would have thought of them in terms of their Japanese pronunciation, and therefore this is followed here even for names of people or writings which existed in China. An exception is made for well-known names which occur in the sections dealing explicitly with China in *Writings of an Old Man*, for there the main intention is to reflect on the specificity of the Confucian tradition. An exception is also made for a few other very well-known names such as those of the Chinese Buddhists Fa Hsien and Hsüan Tsang.

The appearance of Indian (Sanskrit) names or other terms usually implies that these appeared in the original texts in transliterated form. Indian forms (such as Nāgārjuna for Ryūju) have been provided in a few cases where they are very widely known or for the sake of consistency in a particular context. However wholesale re-Sanskritisation has not been undertaken, for this would have been alien to the flavour of Tominaga's works. It would also have been contrary to the principles expressed in *Writings of an Old Man*!

Since Tominaga adopted a pragmatic approach to sūtra and treatise names, using many abbreviations, it would be inappropriate to burden the modern reader with the full titles of works simply for pedantry's sake. The modern Japanese versions of *Emerging from Meditation* are therefore not followed in their practice of putting the reconstituted complete titles in additional brackets. In English this would greatly disturb the flow of the text. However, where Tominaga has used inconsistent abbreviations which would be baffling to modern readers, these have been unified. 'Sūtra' stands for

-kyō, and 'Treatise' stands for *-ron*. In most cases where the Japanese reading of a name is simply a transliteration, via Chinese, of an Indian original, the better known Sanskrit form is given. In some cases a conventionalised English title has been used: for example *Great Treatise* stands for *Daichidoron*, which Tominaga often abbreviates to *Dairon* or *Chido*. A full list of the works quoted with their abbreviations and conventionalised English titles if any is incorporated in the index.

A few quotations from Buddhist writings in *Emerging from Meditation* are apparently intended to be in indirect speech, but this is often difficult to decide and Kyōdo and Mizuta do not always agree. In general this translation errs on the cautious side in that quotation marks are not used in the more doubtful cases (in effect following Mizuta more frequently). In any case the use of quotation marks does not imply that Tominaga was necessarily quoting reliably: one must reckon with abbreviation and with some inaccurate quotation from memory.

In Tominaga's original writing there appear a few notes in half-size print, mainly consisting of the names of works quoted. These have been included in the text of the translation in rounded brackets. Square brackets are used for the standard phrase [It also says,] which, in the original text, simply links two related questions. Angle brackets indicate small additions necessary for the flow or clarity of the text but without a direct counterpart in the original. These have been kept to an absolute minimum as the translation is not intended to be a paraphrase.

Bibliography

Ackroyd, Joyce (trans.), *Told Round a Brushwood Fire, The Autobiography of Arai Hakuseki*, Tokyo 1979.

Anesaki, Masaharu, *Bukkyō seiten shiron*, Tōkyō 1899.

Bellah, Robert N., *Tokugawa Religion*, New York 1957.

Berling, Judith A., *The Syncretic Religion of Lin Chao-En*, New York 1980.

Beasley, W.G. and Pulleyblank, E.G., *Historians of China and Japan*, London 1961.

Bowers, John Z., *When The Twain Shall Meet, The Rise of Western Medicine in Japan*, Baltimore and London 1980.

Boxer, C.R., *The Christian Century in Japan 1549-1650*, Berkeley and London 1951.

Boxer, C.R., *The Dutch Seaborne Empire 1600-1800*, London 1965.

Boxer, C.R., *Portuguese India in the Mid-seventeenth Century*, Delhi 1980.

Bruin, J.R., Gaastra, F.S., and Schiffer, I. (eds.), *Dutch Asiatic Shipping in the 17th and 18th Centuries*, 3 vols. (vols. 2 and 3 available at time of writing), The Hague 1979.

Dore, R.P., *Education in Tokugawa Japan*, London and New York 1969.

Dunn, C.J., *Everyday Life in Traditional Japan*, London and New York 1969.

Fischer, J. and Yokota I., *Das Sūtra Vimalakīrti*, Tōkyō 1944.

Fischer, Peter, *Studien zur Entwicklung des Mappō-Gedankens und zum Mappō-Tōmyōki*, Hamburg 1976.

Forke, Alfred, *Geschichte der alten chinesischen Philosophie*, Hamberg 1964.

Forke, Alfred, *Geschichte der mittelalterlichen chinesischen Philosophie*, Hamberg 1964.

Forke, Alfred, *Geschichte der neueren chinesischen Philosophie*, Hamburg 1964.

Giles, Herbert A., *A Chinese Biographical Dictionary*, no place indicated, modern facsimile from 1898.

Glamann, Kristof, *Dutch Asiatic Trade 1620-1740*, Copenhagen and s'Gravenhage 1958, 1981.

Glamann, Kristof, 'European trade 1500-1750', in Cipolla, Carlo M. (ed.), *The Fontana Economic History of Europe*, vol. 2, Glasgow 1974, 427-526.

Glamann, Kristof, 'The changing pattern of trade', in Rich, E.E. and Wilson, C.H. (eds.), *The Cambridge Economic History of Europe*, vol. 5, London 1977, 185-289, 645-51.

Goodman, G.K., *The Dutch Impact on Japan (1640-1853)* (T'oung Pao Monograph V), Leiden 1967.

Grapard, Allen G., 'Voltaire and East Asia – a few reflections on the nature of humanism', in *Cahiers d'Extrême-Asie* 1 (1985), 59-70.

Han, Yu-shan, *Elements of Chinese Historiography*, Hollywood 1955.

Hauser, William B., *Economic Institutional Change in Tokugawa Japan, Ōsaka and the Kinai Cotton Trade*, London 1974.

Horner, I.B. (trans.), *The Middle Length Sayings (Majjhima-Nikāya)*, vol. 1, London 1954.

Hurvitz, L., Chih-I (538-597), *An Introduction to the Life and Ideas of a Chinese Monk* (Mélanges Chinois et Bouddhiques XII, 1960-62), Brussels 1962.

Ienaga, S. *et al.*, *Kinsei Shisōka Bunshū* (Nihon koten bungaku taikei 97), Tōkyō 1966.

Ishida, Mizumaro (see Katō 1972).

Ishihama, Juntarō, *Tominaga Nakamoto*, Ōsaka 1940.

Jaini, Padmanabh S., *The Jaina Path of Purification*, Berkeley 1979.

Kaempfer, Engelbert, *The History of Japan,* 3 vols. (trans. J.G. Scheuchzer), Glasgow 1906.

Katō, B., Soothill, W.E., and Schiffer, W., *Myōho-Renge Kyō, The Sūtra of the Lotus Flower of the Wonderful Law*, Tokyo 1971.

Katō, B., Soothill, W.E., and Schiffer, W. (ed.), *Tominaga Nakamoto, Ishida Baigan* (Nihon no meicho 18), Tōkyō 1972.

Katō, Shuichi, 'The life and thought of Tominaga Nakamoto, 1715-46, A Tokugawa Iconoclast', *Monumenta Nipponica* XXII, 1-2, (Jan. 1967), 1-35.

Keene, D., *The Japanese Discovery of Europe, Honda Toshiaki and other Discoverers 1720-1798*, London 1952.

Kuiper, J, Feenstra, *Japan en de Buitenwereld in de achttiende Eeuw*, s'Gravenhage 1921.

Kyōdo, Jiko, 'Tominaga Nakamoto, Shutsujō Kōgo', in Nakamura (H.) *et al.* 1971, 1-507.

Lamotte, Étienne, *L'Enseignement de Vimalakīrti (Vimalakīrtnirdésa)*, Louvain 1962.

Leemhuis, Fionella, 'Contatti fra Olanda e Giappone', *Il Giappone* IX (1969), 121-42.

Leemhuis, Fionella, 'Gli Olandesi a Deshima', *Il Giappone* XI (1971), 64-84.

Leemhuis, Fionella, 'I primi lasciapassare commerciali rilasciati agli Olandesi degli Shōgun', *Il Giappone* XV (1975), 26-38.

Legge, James, *The Chinese Classics*, vol. 1, Oxford 1893 (second edition).

Legge, James, *The Works of Mencius*, Oxford 1895, reprint New York 1970.

Lidin, Olof G., Ogyū Sorai, *Distinguishing the Way (Bendō)*, Tōkyō 1970.

Lidin, Olof G., Ogyū Sorai, *A Tokugawa Confucian Philosopher* (Scandinavian Institute of Asian Studies Monograph Series 19), Lund 1973.

McEwan, J.R., *The Political Writings of Ogyū Sorai* (University of Cambridge Oriental Publications 9), London 1962.

Mizuta, N., and Arisaka T., *Tominaga Nakamoto, Yamagata Bantō* (Nihon Shiso Taikei 43), Tōkyō 1973.

Nakamura, Hajime, *Kinseinihon no Hihanteki Seishin*, Tōkyō 1965.

Nakamura, Hajime, *Parallel Developments, A Comparative History of Ideas*, Tōkyō and New York 1975.

Nakamura, Hajime, *Bukkyōgo Daijiten*, Tōkyō 1981.

Nakamura, Hajime, *Ansätze modernen Denkens in den Religionen Japans*, Leiden 1982.

Nakamura, H., Masutani, F., and Kitagawa, J.M., *Gendai Bukkyō Meicho Zenshū (1) Bukkyō no Shomondai*, Tōkyō 1971.

Nakamura, Yukihiko, *Andō Shōeki, Tominaga Nakamoto, Miura Baien, Ishida Baigan, Ninomiya Sontoku, Kaiho Seiryō*, (Nihon no Shisō 18), Tōkyō 1971.

Nosco, Peter (ed.), *Confucianism and Tokugawa Culture*, Princeton 1984.

Oda, Tokunō, *Bukkyō Daijiten*, Tōkyō 1972.

Orsi, Maria Teresa, 'Il Rangaku Kotohajime di Kikuchi Kan', *Il Giappone* XIV (1974), 73-102.

van Opstall *et al.*, *Handeldrijven op Japan 1609 tot 1808*, no place indicated, 1983.

Petzold, Bruno, *Tendai Buddhism*, Yokohama 1979 (posthumous).

Pye, Michael, 'Aufklärung and religion in Europe and Japan', *Religious Studies* 9 (1973), 201-7.

Pye, Michael, *Skilful Means, A Concept in Mahāyāna Buddhism*, London 1978.

Pye, Michael, 'Religion and reason in the Japanese experience', *King's Theological Review*, Spring 1982, 14-17.

Pye, Michael, 'The significance of the Japanese intellectual tradition for the history of religions', in Slater, D., and Wiebe D. (eds.), *Traditions in Context and Change* (Proceedings of the XIV Congress of the International Association for the History of Religion), Ontario 1893.

Pye, Michael, 'Tominaga Nakamoto (1715-1746) and religious pluralism', in Daniels, G. (ed.), *Europe Interprets Japan*, Tenterden (England) 1984, 191-7.

Robert, Jean-Noël, 'Résumé de Conférence', *Annuaire (Ecole Pratique des Hautes Etudes, V. Section – Sciences Religieuses)* Tome LXXXIX 1980-81, 209-14.

Rosthorn, A., *Die Anfänge der chinesischen Geschichtsschreibung*, Wien 1920.

Rothermund, Dietmar, *Europa und Asien im Zeitalter des Merkantilismus* (Erträge der Forschung, Band 80), Darmstadt 1978.

Rubinger, Richard, *Private Academies of Tokugawa Japan*, Princeton 1982.

Sadler, A.L., *The Maker of Modern Japan, The Life of Tokugawa Ieyasu*, London 1937, reprint Tokyo 1978.

Sargent, G.W. (trans.), Ihara Saikaku, *The Japanese Family Storehouse or the Millionaires Gospel Modernised*, Cambridge 1959.

Schubring, Walther, *Die Lehre der Jainas, nach den alten Quellen dargestellt*, Berlin und Leipzig 1935.

Sheldon, C.D., *The Rise of the Merchant Class in Japan, 1600-1868* (Monographs of the Association for Asian Studies, V), New York 1958.

Smith, Thomas C., *The Agrarian Origins of Modern Japan*, Stanford 1959.

Tamburello, Adolfo, 'La componente internazionale nel Giappone Tokugawa', *Il Giappone* IX (1975), 5-23.

Thomas, Edward J., *The History of Buddhist Thought*, London 1951.

Thurman, R.A. (trans.), *The Holy Teaching of Vimalakirti*, Pennsylvania and London 1976.

Tsukahira, Toshio G., *Feudal Control in Tokugawa Japan, the Sankin Kōtai System* (Harvard East Asian Monographs 20), Cambridge, Mass. 1970.

Tsukamoto, Zenryu (*et al.*), *Mochizuki Bukkyō Daijiten* (enlarged edition), Tōkyō 1958.

Tsunoda, R., de Bary, Wm. Th., and Keene, D., *Sources of Japan Tradition*, New York and London 1958.

Ui, Hakuju, *Bukkyō Jiten*, Tōkyō 1965.

Vos, F., see van Opstall *et al.* 1983.

Wakimoto, Tsuneya, *Kindai no bukkyosha* (Nihon no bukkyō 14), Tokyo 1967.

Wataru, Miki, *Village in Ottoman Egypt and Tokugawa Japan – A Comparative Study* (Institute for the Study of Languages and Cultures of Asia and Africa, Tōkyō Gaikokugo Daigaku), Tokyo 1977.

Woo, Kang, *Histoire de la Bibliographie Chinoise*, Paris 1938.

Index of writings

NB. Cf. Conventions on pp. 188–9

Index of characters for names of writings

This index is limited to the names of writings referred to in *Emerging from Meditation*, which may appear in abbreviated form, and the names of a few other Japanese or Chinese writings. The latter may appear in this work in their Chinese pronunciation. Due to the profusion of other proper names it was not possible to include a comprehensive character index. This may be remedied in a more specialised publication. In the meantime reference should be made to the modern Japanese editions.

Abidon	阿毘曇
Agon	阿含
Bakuzōkyō	縛象経
Basharon	婆沙論
Bendō	弁道
Benmei	弁名
Bidonron	毘曇論
Binimokyō	毘尼母経
Bonmōkyō	梵網経
Bosatsuzō	菩薩蔵
Bugyōhen	輔教編
Bukkyōshirin	仏教史林
Bumoonjūkyō	父母恩重経
Bunbetsukudokuron	分別功徳論
Bunsan	文纂
Bushūron	部執論
Busshogonenkyō	仏所護念経
Busshōron	仏性論
Butchiron	仏地論

Index of other names